Bert Bielefeld (Ed.)

Project
Management
Architecture

THE ROBERT GORDON UNIVERSITY

Bert Bielefeld (Ed.)

Project
Management
Architecture

BIRKHÄUSER
BASEL

Contents

Construction Scheduling _141

Appendix _367

Foreword

Once design and planning work have been completed, an architect's key task is project management for the building programme: planning the sequence of work, putting contracts out to tender, deadline and cost planning, site management, and finally handover to the client.

As a rule, a course of study covers such important practical aspects in one subject area only, and so they tend to be handled peripherally. But these aspects of an architect's work are very important to the client. However, students or newly qualified professionals will usually have little insight into an architect's everyday work: at best their first experience of it will come from practical matters in planning practices or on building sites. This compendium defines the field for this large remit very clearly, with reference to the five Basics most relevant to this subject matter, thus giving readers a tool that will help them to manage their building projects effectively and offer a wide range of support for planning implementation.

Basics Project Planning uses readily comprehensible introductions and explanations to structure architects' project work. Every planning and working phase is presented in context, accompanied by the most important information, down to the final working steps, thus providing a first, general account of the basic tasks and circumstances, so that students and newly qualified professionals will be able to build up comprehensive insight into their later field of work, and find their way around particular planning practices and project structures.

Building costs are an essential subject for clients, and they make a direct impact in terms of a project's success or failure. *Basics Budgeting* explains how building costs are put together, calculated and updated. The book offers practical insights, structures the cost planning processes during the planning and building phase and explains how to assess and evaluate the influence of costs and the risks they may present.

The actual co-ordination of planning and building processes is a complex and responsible job, particularly for large building projects. Usually this will involve gaining an overview of a large number of participants and their work. To assist with this, *Basics Deadline Planning* provides instruments for controlling and structuring the process as a whole. This forms an essential basis for good co-operation, for example in relation to agreeing contract deadlines for the contractors involved, and it is also an active instrument during the planning and building process, showing how responses to imponderables and hitches must be made.

Basics Tendering uses clients' requirements to explain the various ways in which building work can be put out to tender and explains basic tendering principles. One major and practical aspect here is organising tendering for a building project. The ways in which tenders are awarded, fixing award units, time planning and not least different tendering styles all have to be taken into detailed account, and so a range of possibilities is assessed, from the merely functional down to detailed description of the work to be done. Readers can find out what the components of a tender are, why they are there and how they are to be put together individually.

Basics Site Management fills in gaps in the knowledge of students and newly qualified professionals who still have little building site experience, and lays out the working fields involved in site management in a structured way with the aid of easily comprehensible explanations. It explains what makes a good site manager: tools include closely thought through building site organisation, smoothly functioning deadline planning, consistent cost control, and finally constant monitoring of the quality of the finished work, down to a professional handover to the client.

Bert Bielefeld, editor

Hartmut Klein

Project planning

Introduction

A project starts with the intention to translate a three-dimensional idea, a need for space or a property investment, into built reality. This "project" suggests both the desire for a convincing and high-quality concept and also the intention to stay with the concept until it is realized and completed. Project planning aims to bring an intention once expressed to its conclusion, and to turn the idea into built reality.

Client/architect

Every project has to be initiated by a client; this applies to building, too. The client commissions someone – an architect – to draw up a design for preparing, planning, supervising, and executing a building project. The core task for the classical architect is project planning from investigating basics via the design to planning the work, tendering, site management, and building completion. For both client and architect, building costs, keeping to deadlines, and the quality of the completed work are highly relevant.

Idea and realization

The first impetus for planning a project can come to an architect in a variety of ways. In many cases a building client or investor will go directly to an architect he or she knows, and explain ideas and requirements for a project in a more or less concrete form. Building projects are often awarded via competitions or specialist reports, with several architects' designs competing to be chosen by the client on the basis of a previously formulated tender.

But the reverse is also conceivable: the architect approaches potential clients and puts him-/herself forward for a possible commission within an acquisition process. This involves careful research in order to find suitable clients needing buildings, or likely to need them in the near future.

Planning steps/
decision levels

In order to progress from the project idea to the completion and use of the real building, the project has to be planned and worked out step by step, in increasingly complex detail. The original abstract idea is gradually fully formulated, concretized and implemented in phases.

The project takes shape, is put on paper, the first sketches are drawn up. The number of people involved increases, sketches become scale plans, plans become the basis for applications. After permissions have been issued by the authorities, tenders have to be invited from building firms and tradespeople, and commissions awarded to contractors. The start of building is the first step towards actually realizing the project.

The aim of putting up a building becomes reality once the various trades have been successfully coordinated on the building site.

Various steps have to be taken if a building project is to be planned and implemented sensibly and with foresight. These will differ according to the particular project and its structure and size. But the course of events is similar in each case, and can be generalized, even when responsibilities can be allotted in various ways. Thus in German-speaking countries the architect is the responsible key figure from the design phase to handing over the building, whereas in North America and many other European countries, responsibility is handed over to other partners after the design phase.

The client has to make decisions on various levels according to the different project phases.　　Decision levels

1. <u>Deciding on the project</u>: In order to decide to embark on a project at all, various parameters (e.g. plot of land, function, financial and schedule framework) have to be examined for their fundamental acceptability. Decisions about carrying out planning are made by bringing in the necessary parties involved in the planning.
2. <u>Deciding on the concept</u>: If the architect's initial ideas (supported by parameters like functional connections, statements about volume and area, and rough costings) are already available, the client must decide whether he or she wants to have this first concept developed further to match his or her intentions.
3. <u>Deciding to submit the building application</u>: Once the concept including the above-mentioned parameters has been worked out further, the client has to decide whether to submit the existing design for permission from the building authorities, as only limited modifications can be made once this step has been taken.
4. <u>Deciding on implementation qualities</u>: Once planning permission has been obtained, the realization phase is prepared. In this context, the client has to decide between a number of possible qualities and material surfaces for the building work. This decision is usually based on material tests, samples, descriptions, and statements about cost development.
5. <u>Deciding about awarding building contracts</u>: Realization documents are prepared on the basis of previous decisions and contractors' implementation submissions collected. Now the client has to decide which contractor should be awarded the work. He or she is supported here by the architect's assessments and recommendations.

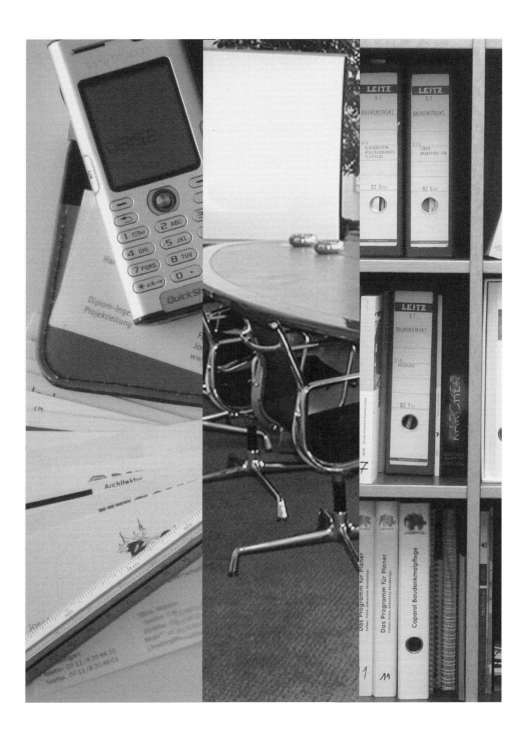

Project participants

The two most important parties to the project are undoubtedly the commissioning client and the planning architect. But there are a number of other "parties to the project" who have to be included in the planning process according to the size and ambition of the planned building. > Fig. 1

THE CLIENT

The client is the person or entity on whose authority a building is planned or erected. Legally the client can be a natural person or a juridical person under civil or public law.

Client and user may well be the same person, depending on the project at hand. In this case the architect has to seek agreement or clarification of the building project from only one person. But in public building projects in particular, and sometimes with private developers as well, the architect often has two persons as opposite numbers whose aims may well not be identical. There can also be further decision levels,

Client/user

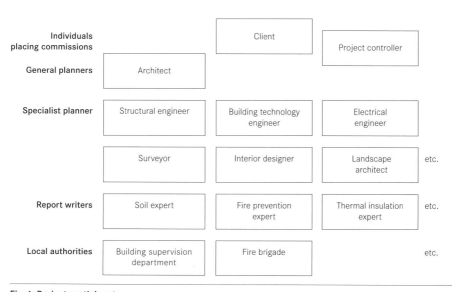

Fig. 1: Project participants

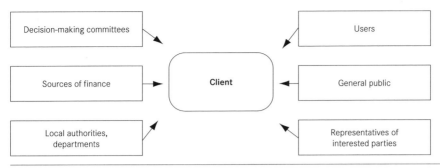

Fig. 2: Possible participants on the client's side

such as external financial providers or supervisory committees on the client's side who can influence the planning and building process. The subsequent users depend on the project. They may be the teachers in a school, firefighters in a fire station, or doctors and nurses in a hospital. The client will generally involve them in planning at an early stage, but sometimes they can define requirements lying outside the client's scope. It is important to do justice to both sets of ideas and requirements if the planning is to be a success. > Fig. 2

THE ARCHITECT

In the construction field it is usually the architect or an expert planning company working in the building trade who will provide the required planning services.

Contacts/
representatives/
agents

The architect is the appropriate contact for all building questions. He or she advises the client on all matters appertaining to implementation, and works as his or her agent and representative with everyone involved in the building process: the authorities, other specialist planners or the firms and tradespeople carrying out the work.

Analysis, idea and
solution

The architect examines the client's wishes critically in terms of their feasibility, gives advice and supplies ideas about the financial viability of the project, a realistic schedule estimate and possible design variants, thus working out possible approaches to solutions step by step with the client. Part of the architect's work is to develop convincing ideas and convey them successfully. A high level of successful teamwork is required when a large number of people are working on a project. Architects require a high degree of social competence and people skills to lead and

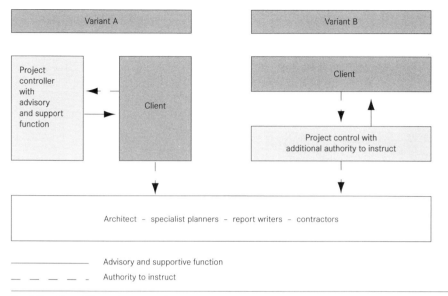

Fig. 3: Function of the project controller

guide all those involved. The various requirements within the individual planning phases are described in the planning process chapter.

THE PROJECT CONTROLLER

The number of people involved in a project as experts also increases with the size of the project. If the project size and time involved are so great as to exceed a client's capacities and expertise, it makes sense to involve a project controller.

The project controller takes over the technical, financial and legal client functions that can be delegated. In other words, he or she is also a client's advisor but does not usually have the authority to represent the client legally. > Fig. 3

The project controller's work does not usually relate to the architect's direct planning services (i.e. preliminary planning, design planning, etc.), but to management of the overall project, starting with financial analysis, providing resources and handling the contract, including facility management.

Project management

For large projects in particular, the project controller can offer the architect valuable support in terms of project management, as well as in coordinating and controlling the personnel involved.

SPECIALIST PLANNERS

The architect will provide almost all planning services for a relatively small building project such as a detached house. But here as well, two other project partners are essential if the process is to be implemented correctly.

A chartered surveyor is generally commissioned to draw up an official site plan that will be required by the building authorities as part of the permission process, or will be needed later for the building survey.

Then the statically relevant parts of the building – floor slab, walls, ceilings and roof – will be dimensioned by an appropriately qualified structural engineer.

For smaller building projects like a detached house the architect would usually also undertake the planning for electrical installations, heating, sanitation, and designing the outdoor areas; or work it out jointly with the firms and tradespeople commissioned to carry out the work.

When planning larger-scale building projects like public buildings (sports hall, town hall, fire station, etc.), large office complexes or prestigious company buildings, all the services will be provided by specialist engineers.

The engineer's contribution to providing services includes planning heating technology and sanitation, in other words water supply and sewage disposal. He or she will also take on planning for ventilation, cooling or air conditioning, and gas installations.

The electrical engineer does not just plan to supply the building with electricity and light, he or she is also jointly responsible for devising lightning protection, for fire and smoke alarms, and for signing escape routes.

Work that is usually carried out by the architect can be handed over to specialists in some ambitious and prestigious buildings.

An interior designer is employed to design particular areas or plan individual fittings.

Garden and landscape architects design and plan the exterior areas in agreement with the architect. Here, the landscape architect's brief can extend from creating ambitious private gardens to planning functional public squares or green spaces, sports grounds, or even noise protection facilities.

Landscape architect

In the case of large, complex properties the architect can recommend that the client should employ a facade planner because of the diverse requirements of facades.

Facade planner

Lighting designers or lighting planners can be commissioned to arrange particular and general lighting. They will simulate and plan the technical and creative effect by day and by night.

Lighting designer

■

EXPERTS

Unlike specialist planners, experts do not provide specific planning. They act in an advisory capacity, prepare reports describing conditions or establishing causes, and suggesting solutions for problems arising. Experts can be brought in to deal with almost any area. The following are the most important fields of activity in building:

A soil expert or geologist may be needed, according to local conditions and subsoil, to provide information on possible foundation construction or existing groundwater, by means of trial digging and test drilling, or from existing maps.

Soil experts

■ **Tip:** It is worth setting up a meaningful project structure at an early stage. All participants needed in specialist planning roles must be brought in at the right time. Important elements of project organization include setting up an address list containing data for all participants, agreeing on regular discussion dates (jour fixe), drawing up written minutes with information about completing work with deadlines and agreements about data exchange arrangement between parties (DXF, DWG, PDF, etc.).

Building historians   If a building that is being refurbished has historical value, consulting a building historian can be beneficial. He or she will compile a history of the building and can offer assessments of structures worth preserving. This will at least establish the restoration horizon, i.e. the period of time within which the refurbishment should be performed.

Traffic planners   If the building project impinges on the local traffic situation or requires changes to the existing infrastructure and transport access, a traffic planner can be brought in.

Fire prevention experts   It is essential, especially in a building project that makes heavy demands on planning, to consult fire prevention experts. They can provide crucial planning information that conforms with the law and is likely to qualify for the required permissions by drawing up fire protection reports or concepts and checking that they are correctly implemented.

Heat and sound insulation experts   It makes sense to commission heat and sound insulation experts for many types of building. They will deal with heat, damp and sound insulation requirements for new build, but can also assess faults and damage in existing buildings.

Acousticians   Acoustics are another aspect of building physics assessments. This aspect deals less with insulation for impact, airborne and footfall sound than with calculating the best acoustics for demanding spaces, such as lecture theaters or concert halls. Here, acousticians are essential contacts for architects at the planning stage.

Pollution experts   Advice from pollution experts may be needed for existing buildings in particular, i.e. for conversion, refurbishment and redevelopment. They can examine and assess the construction materials already present in buildings. Current findings show that materials that can impair the well-being of occupants and users have regularly been used. Particular problems can be caused by effects on health during refurbishment and when removing harmful materials (e.g. asbestos).

Pollution experts' findings and suggestions are particularly important for correct tendering and the safe handling of hazardous materials.

Health and safety coordinators   EU building regulations insist that health and safety coordinators are employed once a building site exceeds a given size. This service can be performed by the client or the architect if they have the requisite qualifications, or by a separate person. This means that the building project will be monitored in terms of safety at the planning and realization stages, so that the client's and the contractor's employees and non-participating third parties are protected from danger as far as possible.

DEPARTMENTS AND AUTHORITIES

So far, the experts mentioned are only those involved in the planning stage of the project. The institutions and authorities whose permission is required at various stages must also be mentioned, as the project cannot be realized without them. For example, it makes sense even at the early stages of the project to mark out the general conditions for realizing the project using existing development plans provided by the municipal or local authorities.

It is essentially the architect who will deal with the building authorities in the course of the project. They are responsible within the building control process (planning permission) for ensuring conformity with building and other relevant regulations. Building control department

Other departments may become involved in the process according to the scale and demands of the permissions sought. These may include the land registry and surveying department, the land holdings office, the town planning department, the monument preservation authorities, the environmental department, the civil engineering department, the city parks authority, and many others. For public building projects, plans usually have to be submitted to the local fire brigade or to a fire and disaster prevention office, who will provide information and define requirements for fire and rescue. > Chapter Planning process, Gaining permission

CONTRACTORS

Contractors are of course important partners in a building project, as well as the planners and relevant authorities. The tradespeople and building firms are the people who implement planning on site, using realization plans and service descriptions. Two different models are essentially available to a commissioning client:

The client can award service provision for individual trade services to firms able to provide the service concerned. (A trade service means work that is generally provided by one craft branch.) Single service

Alternatively, the client can award the entire contract to a single contractor, also known as a general contractor, who will carry out the work him-/herself on the basis of the plans provided, or employ subcontractors. > Chapter Planning process, Tendering, Construction General contractor

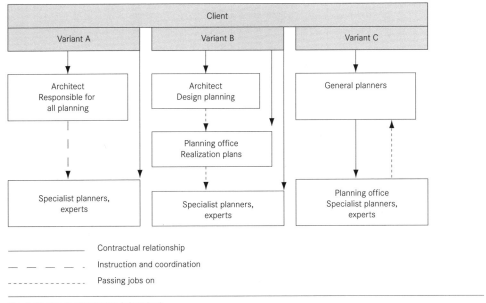

	Client		
Variant A	Variant B		Variant C

Architect
Responsible for
all planning

Architect
Design planning

General planners

Planning office
Realization plans

Specialist planners,
experts

Specialist planners,
experts

Planning office
Specialist planners,
experts

———————— Contractual relationship

— — — — - Instruction and coordination

- - - - - - - - - Passing jobs on

Fig. 4: Contract structures (planning)

CONTRACT STRUCTURES

A client has various possibilities available for fixing the commissioning of planning and realization services contractually. > Fig. 4.

Planning contracts
— The client concludes a separate contract with each planner and expert. Here the architect coordinates those involved in the planning.
— The client enters into a contract with an architect to provide design services. Subsequent planning services relating to tendering and site management are transferred to specialist planning practices, which can also provide the required expertise and appropriate specialist planning.
— The client concludes a contract with a general planner who will then commission all the other planners and experts needed for the project as subcontractors. Thus, the client has only one contact and contract partner for the entire planning process. Here the subcontractor undertakes, on behalf of another contractor (main contractor), to provide part of the service that main contractor has to supply for his or her client.

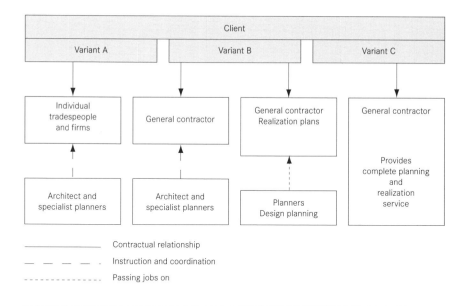

Client		
Variant A	Variant B	Variant C

Individual tradespeople and firms	General contractor	General contractor Realization plans	General contractor
Architect and specialist planners	Architect and specialist planners	Planners Design planning	Provides complete planning and realization service

——————————— Contractual relationship

— — — — . Instruction and coordination

- - - - - - - - - - - Passing jobs on

Fig. 5: Contract structures (realization)

Variants for commissioning realization services: > Fig. 5   Realization contracts

— After general and detailed planning, the client concludes individual contracts with all the trades required. Here the architect will coordinate the individual trades.
— After general and detailed planning, the client concludes a contract with a main contractor who will provide all the services, or employ subcontractors.
— After submitting the design, the client concludes a contract with a general contractor who provides the engineering services that are still required (final planning, structural planning, expert planning, expert opinions, etc.) as well as the building services, or employs subcontractors.
— The client concludes a contract with a general contractor who takes over all the planning, including the design and subsequent realization, and employs all the other participants (architects, planners, experts, firms carrying out work, etc.) as subcontractors.

The ways of grouping the commissions described above can vary from country to country. The boundary between commissioning planning and implementation services can be drawn in different places. But for most combinations the sequence of planning steps will be similar, as the planning phases required have essentially to be carried out independently of the nature of the contract partner.

TEAM BUILDING

Cooperation All those involved go through an intensive process in various phases from the first contact between client and architect until the keys are handed over when a building project is finished. It is important from the outset that a basis for cooperation is found so as to deal with critical situations that may arise during the project. Since the client has a justifiable interest in the project's being implemented within the agreed financial parameters and timescale, this does not mean a superficially harmonious cooperation, but involves all participants working constructively together to carry out the work at hand to their mutual satisfaction. Building can never be a covert activity, and so the planners and authorities involved, as well as the client and financier, represent a general interest that can be addressed by all concerned in a spirit of social cooperation. > Fig. 6

Planning team Planning and realization can last for a period of several years. This depends on the size of the project, which can be dealt with in several building phases if the parameters require. So the planning team and also the underlying concept, the basic idea, should be viable in the face of all

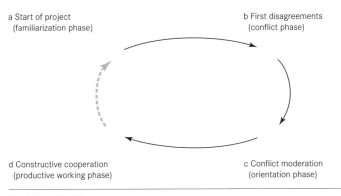

a Start of project
(familiarization phase)

b First disagreements
(conflict phase)

d Constructive cooperation
(productive working phase)

c Conflict moderation
(orientation phase)

Fig. 6: Team building

kinds of situations and challenges. A project can be planned in considerable detail and with great foresight, but as it proceeds new insights and changes will occur that need joint answers. As the project progresses, more and more planners become involved, the responsible authorities and departments have to be included, and increasing numbers of firms and tradespeople will be drawn into the work as services are put out to tender and commissioned.

The roles that crop up in every project (client, architect, specialist Team ability planner, tradesperson, etc.) are usually played by changing partners and individuals. This makes the architect particularly significant as coordinator in the team-building process. The project team – like every other working group – goes through various social action phases.

The initial phase is often marked by expectant politeness, the team members tend to be excited, curious and waiting to get to know each another better. But the project at hand requires everyone involved to produce work that affects the others. This can lead to both professional and personal conflicts. If there are confrontations and tension, people should never lose their objectivity, and here the architect can be in demand as a mediator as well as a coordinator. It is necessary in this "orientation phase" to reach the mutual understanding that everyone is working towards the same goal, and this can be achieved only by working together and maintaining respectful forms of interaction and behavior. But confrontations over matters of expertise must definitely not be excluded.

Once the best working basis has been found, the team members should ideally approach each other in a spirit of trust, frankness, inventiveness and solidarity. This will make the project team able to work effectively, powerfully and purposefully towards realizing the project aim. So directing the planning team with this end clearly in sight is an essential part of the architect's work along with effective project management, and without it the planning team may lose sight of its goals.

General conditions and aims

Planners have to deal with three basic targets at every project planning phase. These are crucially important to the client, but also to the architect. First come the cost framework defined by the client, and the time the building is due to be completed. The client will also express wishes in terms of <u>built quality</u>, which depends directly on the other two parameters, <u>costing</u> and <u>scheduling</u>.

COSTS

Building costs are enormously important to clients, and so they will expect reliable professional advice from the architect from the outset.

The client derives cost security implications from the aims the building project is required to meet. Commercial, public and private building clients will differ in the way they formulate their aims.

Cost security

A <u>commercial client</u> will address economic aims when determining a costing framework. Here the desired cost-effectiveness for their capital, or that of third parties, is most important. Both the continuing yield and retention of value for the future are important for this investment.

A <u>private client</u> is investing in his or her own future, as they want to use the property themselves. The important thing here is the future potential of the planned building project. Both the client's financial resources and stable value should be considered when implementing the planned project.

A <u>public client</u>'s building intentions derive from the duty to provide the infrastructure for the services they have to deliver. Here the work will be differentiated according to administrative size and structure. For example, building commissions from regions or local communities can relate to securing emergency services, fire and disaster protection, health services (hospitals) and education (schools). Smaller communities are responsible for providing kindergartens, adult education facilities, community centers, and other educational provision. A public client's decision will tend to be based on estimated need as well as social or idealistic aims. The cost-effectiveness of the measure will be defined by the longest possible period of use. But the resources available for such

```
┌─────────────────────────────────┐
│                                 │
│         Volume or area          │
│                                 │
└─────────────────────────────────┘

                 ×

┌─────────────────────────────────┐
│       Cost specification        │
│      EUR/m³ oder EUR/m²          │
│                                 │
│         Price indexing          │
└─────────────────────────────────┘

                 =

┌─────────────────────────────────┐
│                                 │
│         Estimated costs         │
│                                 │
└─────────────────────────────────┘
```

Fig. 7: Establishing costs – cost specification

measures are restricted even for public clients, and subject to approval by the appropriate political committees.

Cost framework
A client can provide the architect with a cost estimate as a framework for implementing the project. This can be agreed as a binding upper limit or as an approximate target. The architect calculates feasibility on this basis, and provides the client with information about possible standards, floor area and volume on the basis of the budget. Here, imponderables and uncertainties in the nature and scope of the costs should be indicated.

Another possibility is for the client to supply the architect with information about function, spatial program and the desired quality of the built product. The architect will then estimate the expected costs on the basis of these requirements.

In practice, the two procedures are often mixed. As clients are usually accustomed to being certain about costs from other areas and business fields, keeping within the costing framework becomes increasingly significant even at an early stage.

Cost specification
The architect will use a variety of instruments for estimating costs independently of the actual planning phase, ascertaining all costs as the product of a quantity factor and a cost specification. The cost specification reflects the ratio of costs to a reference unit like area or volume. For

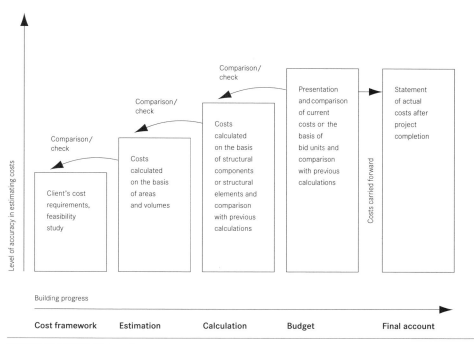

Fig. 8: Ways of estimating costs

example, a typical cost specification would be EUR 1000/m² gross floor area. > Fig. 7

It is essential that the current cost development levels are available to the client as an aid to decision-making when planning stages require it. The first step is the decision to make a start on the project, to decide whether the idea actually is viable. And after the first sketches and drafts have been drawn up, the probable costs are estimated on the basis of very rough reference points. These <u>cost estimation</u> reference points can include the required useful floor space, the gross floor area or the gross volume of the property. If planning has moved on further and the design has been fixed, costs have to be calculated before a decision can be taken about submitting a building proposal.

Steps in ascertaining costs

A more precise <u>cost calculation</u> can be drawn up on the basis of detailed information about the supporting structure and individual structural components, based on rough or more precise structural elements.

Rough elements might include exterior and interior walls, ceilings or roofs, and more precise elements the individual layers within the rough elements (ceiling rendering, reinforced concrete ceiling, screed, floor covering, etc.). The overall costs to be determined at this stage ensure a higher degree of certainty about costs than previous costings.

When services are being allotted to contractors and traders the next step is to present the current state of costs. This has to be reconciled with the previously established budget for the individual awards, in order to compare real market prices with the <u>cost planning</u> and then intervene to impose controls where necessary.

When the building project is complete the architect compiles the overall construction costs. This <u>cost determination</u> records the actual building costs accrued.

Cost control It is important to check new findings and detailing in the cost planning against previous stages and the client's cost stipulations regularly, so that any discrepancies can be recognized at an early stage. The further a project progresses, the more difficult it is for the architect to intervene in cost development and bring discrepancies under control. In the building phase it is necessary to make mixed cost control calculations based on calculated costs, on services that have already been commissioned, and sometimes on services that have already been rendered and paid for, as different pieces of work may not run in phase. > Chapter Planning process, Construction

Cost tracking Architects can build up their clients' trust by supplying an uninterrupted flow of information and by tracking costs conscientiously in accordance with the original budget estimates, thus showing their clients
● that they are able to handle capital entrusted to them.

● **Important:** The client has the right to demand a current statement of costs throughout the duration of the project. As the architect is interested in keeping to the cost stipulations formulated at the outset, he or she must always be in a position to list costs comprehensibly and present them so that they can be compared with previous cost information.

DEADLINES

Like cost stipulations, deadline stipulations are important in many respects for the cost of the project. Notice may already have been given on existing rental contracts because long notice is needed, or the moving-in date may already have been fixed because of financial constraints (production starting, seasonal business, etc.). The architect has to address the stipulations critically in terms of their feasibility and plan the sequence of deadlines for the project in agreement with the client. Here it is not just the building phase that has to be taken into account, but also the preliminary planning.

The stipulated deadline will usually be based on the <u>final deadline</u> for realization. It is also possible to lay down a deadline for the <u>start of building</u>, if for example this is linked with the funding payments. Another variant on a time stipulation is the <u>shortest possible realization period</u>. Here the beginning and end of the process do not have to be laid down rigidly. A <u>short realization period</u> should reduce the restrictions and obstacles caused to the project by the building phase as far as possible.

A <u>project schedule</u> is drawn up to represent the overall time needed to complete the project. This considers both the planning and the realization phase. It can help to compile a separate <u>production schedule</u> (work schedule) for the building phase for the sake of clarity. But here the fact that building depends on planning and commissioning contractors must always be taken into consideration. > Fig. 9

At the beginning of the project, it will take a certain amount of time for the project to be clarified by the client and the architect. A complex process of agreement will then be developed involving the specialist planners and the responsible authorities. The architect has to establish a basis for work and circulate it to all concerned so that the planners can start work. Conversely, the architect is dependent on the planners' progress and their submission of completed documentation as the project proceeds. > Fig. 10

Today, schedules are worked out using dedicated computer programs. The simplest way of presenting the schedule can be a list naming the procedure and the start and end dates. But this is not particularly clear given the large number of processes involved in building projects.

A network plan shows the various processes in terms of their mutual dependency and the connections between them. This approach works well for illustrating the interlinking connections, but does not show time sequences.

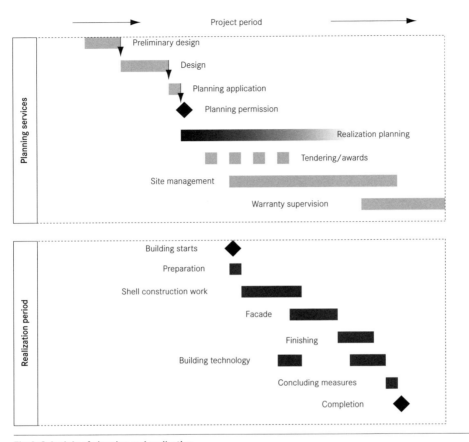

Fig. 9: Schedule of planning and realization

Bar chart   The most usual presentation mode is the bar chart or Gantt diagram. The Y axis lists the individual events or processes and the X axis shows time. The duration of each process is represented by bars above the time axis. Overlaps and related items can be established without difficulty, especially with modern scheduling programs. Vital connections can be shown by linking the end of process A → beginning of process B, etc.

Milestones   Milestones are important phases or direct deadline stipulations within the overall project schedule (building starts, completion, etc.). For example, building permission is an important scheduling milestone. Adequate time must be allowed for the examination of documents by the

Bar chart

	February	March	April	May
Foundations	▓▓▓			
Ground floor walls		▓▓▓		
Ground floor ceiling			▓▓▓	

Network plan

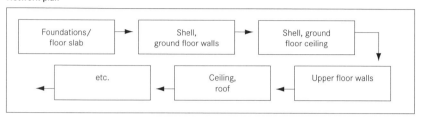

Deadline list

	Company	Start	Duration	End
Foundations	Company A	05.02.	22 WD	04.03.
Ground floor walls	Company B	01.03.	24 WD	30.03.
Ground floor ceiling	Company B	23.03.	26 WD	20.04.

Fig. 10: Ways of representing schedule plans

authorities, as necessary changes defined in the permission documents can affect the start of building. Implementing milestones and presenting events and processes in color make the bar chart clearer and more intelligible to all concerned.

A target-performance comparison can be used to check the schedule against actual building progress to establish whether the project is running according to plan. The aim of scheduling is to identify at an early stage if the final deadline is at risk and to counter this where appropriate. It is only by constantly checking and monitoring processes that it is possible to get things back in hand in time.

Target-performance comparison

QUALITY

Technical standards

In principle, quality can be defined in two different ways. Generally speaking, the current standards, directives, regulations and laws are an unalterable basis for planning and realization. These <u>codes of practice</u> are universally acknowledged among experts. Fundamentally they apply to every building project as a technical standard and do not have to be required or stated explicitly in contracts. However, correctly and comprehensively applying all valid standards and directives is an important sign of quality in a building project, and one that cannot be taken for granted at the realization stage.

Standard of individual finish

The client lays down the standard of individual finish for a building personally. He or she defines the building's visual appearance, describing all the structural components in terms of material quality, form and color, within the bounds of what is technically possible. Here the client's financial latitude will be one of the factors in determining the final standard, as there can be considerable cost differences for different standards of finish. The color scheme and the shape of the building usually make less impact on the budget than the choice of materials. For example, large areas of glass in the facade or the interior cost more than closed masonry or reinforced concrete surfaces. Using oak rather than plastic for windows is visually more prestigious, but more expensive; as it is to install high-quality parquet that needs special laying as opposed to a

Fig. 11: International
standardization
organizations

Fig. 12: Establishing finishing standards individually using samples

textile floor covering. These examples can be continued throughout the list of structural components. It is important for the architect to discuss the standard of finish with the client at an early stage, to help him or her to decide by presenting samples and to make it clear what the cost implications will be.

The recognized codes of practice, directives and standards cannot Quality descriptions be further defined in terms of quality. Individual standards of finish need to be clearly defined in writing, however: at the start of the project a non-binding standard of finish is fixed, e.g. "high standard" or "average standard," which leaves a great deal of scope for interpretation. Such statements are consistently refined in the course of the planning process.

First, the finish for the loadbearing structure and the essential building components has to be fixed. As the project proceeds, detailed decisions have to be taken about every component. The architect helps the client to decide by providing samples and finish variants with costings. Once the decisions have been taken, they are recorded by using a general qualitative building description or by compiling a detailed room book, in which rooms used for the same purpose can be considered together. The data sheet gives the name of the room, its number and floor, and information about walls, ceilings, floors, doors, windows, radiators, and sanitary and electrical fittings.

This quality description forms the basis for cost calculation and points to be fixed in the service specifications that will need be drawn up later. If the client expresses wishes about additions or changes in the course of the building process, the architect is required to point out the effect this will have on cost, with reference to the defined standard of finish.

The existing technical standards and the individually fixed standard Monitoring quality of finish are monitored by the site manager during the building process. Here, quality control means checking materials when they are delivered and installed, monitoring the quality of craftsmanship, establishing that details are being executed as prescribed, and ensuring conformity with all current standards and laws. Consideration for legally defined dimensional tolerances is also part of this monitoring process.

The quality of a new building is reflected not just in a convincing design, but also in the correct application of technical standards and successfully implementing the client's individual requirements.

DECIDING ON A PROJECT

At the start of a project, a building client has to clear up a number of fundamental issues. First of all, the financial viability of the project has to be checked. If the location for the new building has not been fixed, a suitable plot of land must be found. The client will also fix the completion date and cost framework for the building project. In the past, these questions were essentially settled by the client him-/herself before the actual planning phase started. As the general conditions building clients are working under are becoming ever more complex, the architect can now be a helpful contact even at this early stage.

At the beginning of a project the work to be covered must be clarified, the client's ideas and intentions identified and checked for feasibility. This involves both the client's financial possibilities and also a realistic estimate of the time the project will take. So, for example, the architect has to test the client's ideas against specimen projects to see whether his or her ideas can be implemented at all, and to discuss a realistic approach with him or her where appropriate.

Scheduling and costing

The architect can advise the client about choosing a plot or assessing one that is already available. He or she will give hints and appraisals with reference to position, character, surroundings and other conditions relating to location for the planned building project. Involvement in acquiring a site or advice on possible finance is not usually one of the essential services provided by an architect.

Consultation about the site

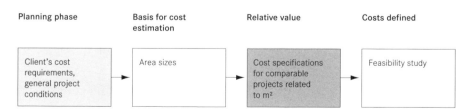

Planning phase	Basis for cost estimation	Relative value	Costs defined
Client's cost requirements, general project conditions	Area sizes	Cost specifications for comparable projects related to m²	Feasibility study

Fig. 13: Costs according to client's requirements

Authorities and specialist planners

An inexperienced client should then be informed about the necessary involvement of authorities and specialist planners. He or she has to know which additional planners are required to implement the building project and which additional reports, analyses and investigations have to be acquired or carried out before work can start, as in most cases he or she will have to conclude contracts with those concerned. > Chapter Project participants, Contract structures

Degree of planning involvement for participants

Not every client is familiar with the individual stages and development steps in the course of a building project. Architects are able to aid their clients in making decisions, especially when choosing the necessary specialist planners such as structural engineers and building technicians, and advise them about the specialists' competence and the scope and cost of specialist planning services; of course the architects' own services must be defined as well. Agreements of this kind should be made as early as possible, so that different views about the services commissioned and required do not emerge at a later stage.

Bidding for commissions and acquisition

At this early stage of a project, architects should support their clients'projects to the utmost and make it possible to realize the new building, as they are on the threshold between acquisition and commission. This exploratory phase is often seen as bidding for a commission without remuneration. Here it should be made clear to the potential client that the basic matters defined at the outset such as costing, timescale, choice of location, and selection of the people involved are crucial to the successful and conflict-free implementation of the building project.

○ **Hint:** The appropriate fee tables or recommendations will show essential and additional services. Additional services could include models for demonstrating designs, detailed inventories, or drawing up room and function programs. Architects will do well to agree on the scope of the work phases to be commissioned, as well as on the service requirements associated with them and where appropriate any additional or special services that may need to be commissioned.

■ **Tip:** It is recommended that a written file memo should be created before every meeting with the client and distributed to all participants. This makes it possible to build on previously agreed decisions and subsequently confirms agreements hitherto made only verbally.

This first phase typically includes a high degree of consultation, so that the two most important partners in the project get to know each other and create a basis for successful and trusting cooperation.

Once a positive decision has been made about a project a written basis for a contract should be drawn up for the cooperation between client and architect, stating the scope of the work to be done and the fee the architect is to be paid.

Architect's contract/fee

○

CONCEPT PHASE

After the basis of the project has been defined and cooperation between the planners and the scope of their brief fixed contractually, the architect can start to address the actual conceptual building project at hand.

The key data defined in writing now have to be translated into sketch form for the first time, in order to convey an idea of possible approaches to the project. > Fig. 14

Sketches

The way in which the design is presented is very largely left to the architect. He or she will usually make some early sketches by hand, or prepare simple CAD drawings to convey his or her ideas to the client. CAD systems in particular make it possible to create variants on views and ground plans with relatively little effort, to present the client with a selection of possible alternatives.

Presenting the design

○ **Hint:** Architects are faced with a number of liability risks in the course of the planning process. Engineers and architects are threatened with liability not just at every realization phase, but also when the contract is concluded. They are liable not only for faulty planning, for mistakes in awarding tenders and for other infringements of contractual duties, but not infrequently for defects caused by the contractors as well. Most countries insist that professional risks indemnity insurance be taken out to cover these risks as far as possible.

Fig. 14: Sketches

Fig. 15: Working model

Preliminary design Ground plans, sections and views should be presented to scale, which will usually be 1:200 in the early stages.

The architect should always be mindful of making matters comprehensible for the client when presenting the preliminary design. He or she has had a great deal of practice in reading ground plans or section drawings. But someone who is not used to addressing plans on different scales will often see them as just an abstract representation, and may well need help in getting bearings and understanding the access situation and room disposition. The creative idea behind the plans, the three-dimensional effect or the urban connections with the surrounding area and the functional links between the differently used rooms and space usually need detailed exposition by the architect if he or she wishes to convince the client about the creative thinking invested. It is his or her job to work with the client on translating the latter's functional and financial stipulations into architecture. The client's suggestions and reservations can be extremely productive and stimulating for the architect's own work. So far it is not just the client who has been moving on unfamiliar terrain: the architect will also come across matters that are new when working on a variety of projects.

A preliminary design that meets the requirements and that can convey a distinctive architectural approach or a creative idea will then crystallize out from exchanges with the client, the eventual user and the other specialist planners.

●

Correct presentation to scale is also required at a relatively early stage, as it is on this basis that the client examines the way the required room planning is being implemented and decides about further work on the concept. A first project-related cost estimate will now also be drawn up as an additional basis for decisions. This involves establishing quantities via rough units (areas, volumes), and multiplying them by characteristic cost specifications for comparative objects. A cost specification represents the cost per quantity unit (e.g. EUR 1000/m^2 gross floor area).

Cost estimation

> ● **Example:** An architectural practice that works only in housing construction will not usually need to readdress the current standards and directives for housing construction and the wishes expressed by housing associations. But for other building work, such as educational buildings (kindergartens, schools, colleges), sport (swimming pools, sports halls, etc.), buildings for cultural purposes (assembly areas, concert halls, stadiums), office or industrial complexes the architect will have to address particular project parameters such as special regulations for public buildings, workflow, etc.).

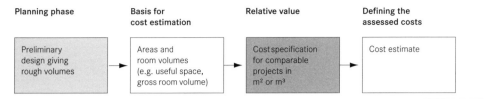

Planning phase	Basis for cost estimation	Relative value	Defining the assessed costs
Preliminary design giving rough volumes	Areas and room volumes (e.g. useful space, gross room volume)	Cost specification for comparable projects in m² or m³	Cost estimate

Fig. 16: Cost estimation during the preliminary design phase

Cost specification levels are estimated on the basis of realized building projects of a similar character. As there are still a lot of imponderables at this early stage, the architect should make it clear to the client that the information will not be available in more precise form until a later stage, and that it presently represents the area in which the costings are currently moving. > Chapter General conditions and aims, Costs

DESIGN PHASE

After the client has decided to set a project in train, work starts on putting the concept into practice. Looking back at the jointly prepared results from the first concept phase should provide the following information as a basis:

— Preliminary conceptual sketches (ground plans, views, sections, perspectives, etc.)
— Function schemes
— Space allocations
— Distribution of quantities and areas

■ **Tip:** As determining costs depends to large extent on volume and quality of finish, costs as presented are subject to a high uncertainty factor at this early stage. Cost risks can be considerably contained by a comparative costing in terms of gross volume, gross floor area, and useful space.

● **Example:** A building can have the same volume on a square or a long rectangular ground plan. But the comparatively expensive facade area will differ distinctly in ratio to the gross volume. The building with a square ground plan needs a considerably smaller facade area, which greatly reduces cost. Difference of this kind should be borne in mind when using cost specifications.

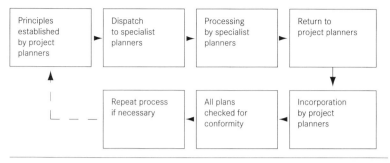

Fig. 17: Involving the specialist planners

The design principle now needs further development on the basis of these requirements, concrete constructions should be fixed, the necessary technical fittings integrated, and the standards of finish agreed.

One concrete example: the position of a sports hall on the plot as been determined as part of the "conceptualization process." The required dimensions of the building are derived from the space needed for the playing area and the necessary ancillary rooms. The links between the individual spaces within the hall as a whole were established at the concept stage. The architect has already presented the first ideas about the external appearance of the building using sketches or views.

So far the type of loadbearing structure to span the hall, what heating or ventilation systems should be installed, where and in which outside walls apertures are required to provide light, and how many, and not least what materials will be used to build floor, wall and ceiling, have not yet been established.

Thus there is a need for more discussions with the client and also with the specialist planners. The term "system and integration planning" is now used for this project phase.

System and integration planning

Various systems (loadbearing structure, heating, etc.) have to be discussed and coordinated; they cannot be considered separately because of the many interfaces needed. For example, if the necessary spaces needed for ventilation, lighting and installations are not considered in the case of a closed beam over the playing area, it is difficult to provide the necessary height for the hall economically. If the building technician is

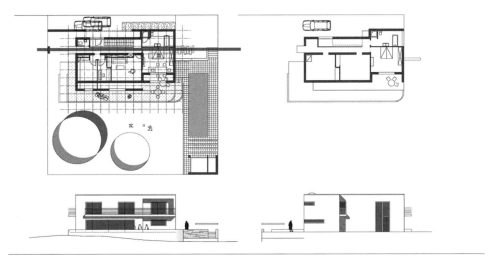

Fig. 18: Draft plan

planning the best possible heating equipment but forgets the planned large area of south-facing glazing, conditions could well be intolerable in the summer months. Hence the architect has to find the best possible solutions for the various systems, working with the specialist planners, and must define the mutual dependencies of the individual specialist plans in order to come up with the best overall solution.

Draft plans   Developing the preliminary design requires plans to be drawn up on a larger scale. All the ground plans, views and required sections are usually drawn on a scale of 1:100 in the next design phase. The aim is not to dimension all the sections of the building completely, but just to reproduce the essential external dimensions of the building, the relevant room

○   dimensions, and where needed the aperture dimensions.

> ○ **Hint:** More precise information on plan presentation and dimensioning can be found in *Basics Technical Drawing* by Bert Bielefeld and Isabella Skiba, Birkhäuser Publishers 2007.

At this stage, a plan is not intended for working purposes, but is simply aimed at the client, the specialist planners, and the building authorities. It does not usually make sense to work in detail here, as the plan will change considerably in discussions with the client, the specialist planers and the authorities, and excessive detail would create an undue amount of work.

Draft ground plans show room uses and room areas. The surrounding buildings and the existing topography should also be represented, according to locality.

Plan presentation

The free presentation acceptable in the concept phase now has to give way to a largely uniform approach to drawing plans, as the completed draft plans also form the basis for the subsequent application for planning permission, and have to meet the authorities' requirements. Different countries have also issued their own presentation directives, though much is laid down in international standards.

The draft plan must provide the client with details about the form the building will take, and the architect also exchanges plans with the specialists involved. It therefore makes sense to clarify the interfaces between the planners and the data transfer type (e.g. DXF, DWG or PDF formats with a fixed level structure), so that information can be exchanged as efficiently as possible and without unnecessary conversions.

Exchanging plans

The basic quality of finish and the standards for fittings have to be fixed with the client as part of the draft planning process. A detailed description of the planned building should be drawn up as a basis for later work by all those involved in the planning. It will be revised in subsequent planning steps recording all the qualities of finish that have been decided. This means that the architect can refer back to the originally defined standards if changes are requested later, and thus justify additional costs.

Quality of finish

More precise bases for planning and details on chosen systems (load-bearing structure, building technology, etc.) now make it possible to assess the costs more thoroughly. At this stage in the planning, building costs should no longer be assessed in terms of interfaces and building volume > Chapter General conditions and aims, Costs but structured in detail around individual cost groups such as walls, ceilings, roof, heating system, exterior areas, etc. This gives the client a serious basis for deciding whether the building project should go ahead as planned, which means that the plans can be submitted to the building authorities in their present state as an application for planning permission. > Fig. 19

Cost calculation

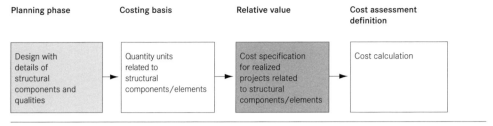

Planning phase	Costing basis	Relative value	Cost assessment definition
Design with details of structural components and qualities	Quantity units related to structural components/elements	Cost specification for realized projects related to structural components/elements	Cost calculation

Fig. 19: Cost calculation during the design phase

If the costs are identified in such detail that they can be allotted to contractors (trades) at a later stage, this will make it possible to produce a targeted cost comparison in terms of previous cost estimates when awarding service contracts, thus meeting a key requirement for transparent cost monitoring.

When working out the design, the architect must produce plans capable of gaining planning permission. As these plans will form the basis for permission and for drawing up working plans, prior negotiations with the authorities may be needed to ensure that they are viable for such submission. Here a major part is played by current legal regulations and standards, which can vary considerably from region to region. Their validity is also affected by the function to be accommodated (housing, work, places for assembly, etc.). The main requirements to be met relate to fire prevention, protection at work, places for assembly, housing construction standards, etc.

These provisions are there to protect the user, the environment and society as a whole. The architect has to advise the client about legal requirements and observing the rules as part of this design phase.

GAINING PERMISSION

Application for planning permission

The responsible authority now has to decide whether the planned project will qualify for planning permission. The essential information is already available in the scaled plans that have been drawn up. All that may need to be added are dimension chains, room names, and information about areas and volumes. The surveyor who will have been involved from an early stage completes a site plan, unless this has already been prepared by the architect or the building authorities. The architect is responsible for compiling or revising all existing plans in an orderly manner, providing a uniform plan heading and signature line for the client. Some authorities require this signature on the plans. It is also an important component of the architect's contractual relationship with his or her client. The subsequent working plans will be drawn up on the basis of these first plans. If the client wants changes to be made at later stages, the architect will be able to refer to the jointly agreed design or permission plans where needed. Desired changes often result in additional costs or delays in the building phase, which can be documented comprehensibly on the planning basis that has already been established.

Another set of forms has to be submitted along with the planning documents, giving the authorities structured information about the client and the key people involved at the planning stage such as the architect and structural engineer. The building project is also described in words, the building type defined (housing, school, etc.), as well as the type of use, estimated building costs, net floor area, enclosed space, and the essential building materials to be used.

Forms and documents

The structural engineer records his or her qualifications and the statical information relevant to the building. According to the country, proof that energy-saving regulations have been met may be required, and according to the nature and size of the project, a sound insulation and fire prevention certificate, a certificate of the required number of parking spaces, and the site ground use ratio. To secure access, an additional drainage application is usually required, showing connections to local sewerage systems and public utility supplies.

The authorities now check the plans submitted with reference to the building regulations, but not for possible structural or functional defects. Even incorrect information from the authorities about the proper implementation of all the valid regulations does not protect the architect from possible liability claims. Architects are therefore well advised to make themselves entirely familiar with all the relevant laws and locally applicable building regulations.

If doubts arise about whether a client's wishes are likely to obtain permission, the architect should point this out to the client at an early stage and will recommend that experienced legal advisers be brought in where necessary. Architects should not allow themselves to be drawn into giving explicit legal advice in controversial cases, although they do have a general duty to advise and instruct their employers.

Duty to advise and inform

It is usually the architect's duty to submit the entire package of documents. Requirements about the form of the necessary documents vary

Submitting documents

nationally and regionally. It therefore makes sense to contact the authorities at an early stage to clarify the formal requirements.

Once the examination has been completed, written planning permission will be sent directly to the client. As a rule, this is accompanied by detailed information from the individual departments about the standards that have to be met. If there are still discrepancies in the documents, such as failure to identify the site manager responsible, or omission of the structural engineer's certificate of competence, these details can be submitted subsequently.

Information and conditions

The planning permission will also contain information and conditions for the realization phase, e.g. with reference to:

— Emergency escape routes
— Appropriate provision for the handicapped
— Statutory labor protection requirements
— Fire prevention
— Tree protection
— Immission protection
— etc.

All these requirements must be observed and implemented at the realization phase, as must the requirement that the project must be inspected by the building authorities in an on-site visit before the building is used. Here, the authorities will check the building with the architect and the client on site after completion on the basis of the application for planning permission and the conditions and comments made by the authorities.

■ **Tip:** It is also now established practice to submit a sufficient number of copies of each document. An authority will inevitable take time to examine documents, especially if they have to pass through different departments (fire brigade, transport office, trading standards department, etc.). If sufficient copies of applications for permission and planning documents are submitted, they can be distributed to all the departments involved at the same time, which will speed up their return considerably.

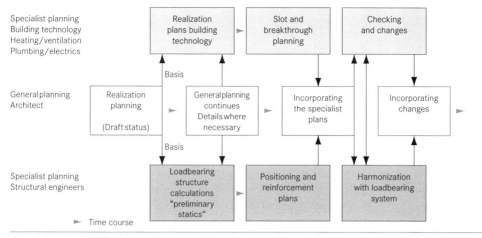

Fig. 20: Coordinating planning

WORKING PLANS AND QUALITY OF FINISH

The previous working phases on the project were aimed at clarifying and fixing the client's ideas. The detailed plans produced in this way have been checked with reference to the building authorities for their viability in the permission process and the feasibility of the building project.

The realization phase is central to further processing of the existing plans. The participating specialist planners are now key figures in the process. In concrete terms, the architect must inform all the specialist planners about the current state of the plans, and pass on the building authorities' conditions to them. The structural engineers can compile a preliminary statics report showing the main dimensions of the loadbearing structural components on the basis of the draft plans, if this has not already been done at the preliminary planning stage. The building and electrical engineers need information relating to fire protection (fire alarms, fire compartments), requirements for drainage and connection to the local supply systems like water, sewerage, gas, electricity, and data cables.

Bringing in the specialist planners

It makes sense to hold regular planning meetings at intervals to be agreed jointly. A pattern that seems to work is a fixed date on the architect's or the client's premises, on a weekly cycle. The architect keeps minutes or notes of the meetings, containing the decisions that have been taken. The contents of minutes can be structured as follows:

Planning meetings

— Project title
— Minutes numbered consecutively
— Date and location of the meeting
— Participants (starting with a list of participants, in which each participant records his or her name and contact details such as telephone number and e-mail address)
— Distribution list (all the participants present and people who have to be informed additionally)
— Content of minutes. Here the following tabular structure seems to work:
  Column 1: Agenda points numbered consecutively
  Column 2: Heading with agenda point followed by content
  Column 3: Responsibility (who has to deal with what)
  Column 4: Deadlines for dealing with this part of the project
— The final, obligatory point of discussion should be the date of the next meeting, location and the attendees required. Items for discussion that are already established should be identified, so that the participants can come to the next meeting prepared.
— The minutes will be signed by the person who has compiled them and any documents attached listed (schedules, planning documents, etc.).

There are of course various views about how minutes should be organized. The aim is to record the content of the discussions briefly and succinctly, thus creating a basis for further meetings and following up the decisions taken.

It also makes sense at this stage for the client to be involved in the meetings and for all the minutes and other essential correspondence between the planners to be passed on to the client. The client has to make a large number of decisions about realization details. The planners will provide the necessary documentation for this, and will have to advise him or her about the consequences in terms of cost, schedules, and the quality of finish.

Constructive cooperation and good coordination between the individual specialist planners is an important prerequisite for the building site to run smoothly. Meetings of this kind will continue into the building phases, when site meetings will take place, as well as planning meetings.

It therefore makes sense to agree on a planning sequence as part of the scheduling process. The structural engineer, the electrical engineer and the building technology engineer take the architect's plans as the basis for their own planning. Their planning work is then built into the architect's working plans. Thus each is partly dependent on the other, and also needs a certain amount of time to deliver his or her own part of the work appropriately.

The architect fixes the dimensions and details for the loadbearing structural components in cooperation with the structural engineer. Construction variants are examined in terms of their financial viability. The building services engineer plans the heating system, the necessary cooling and ventilation systems, the plumbing required, and possible alternative energy sources. The electrical engineer defines the electricity supply standard, the necessary data cabling, and the lighting concept. If other specialist planners are involved, such as an acoustician, a landscape architect or an interior designer, they will also ask the client for information about the work they are required to do. And not least, the architect him-/herself has to make a number of decisions about materials, colors and shapes for all structural components.

Specialist planner's work

The way the different disciplines interlock and the necessity for agreement at the earliest possible stage will be illustrated taking additional floor height as an example.

Agreement between specialist planners

Even at the design stage the client will have identified the height for the rooms. The story or construction height has been defined on the basis of local conditions and the maximum possible building height, as part of the permission-seeking process. Now the client would like to fit a cabled power and data supply via floor ducts, with supply sockets in the floor. At the same time, the heating engineer responsible is planning to install underfloor heating. This will mean that it is scarcely possible to realize the room height as originally planned, as building the necessary ducts and floor heating into the space under the floor will increase its height significantly.

○ **Hint:** Keeping the planning and site meetings separate is strongly recommended. Good results are not achieved if there are disputes about planning details in the presence of the people doing the work that the planners could have agreed some time ago.

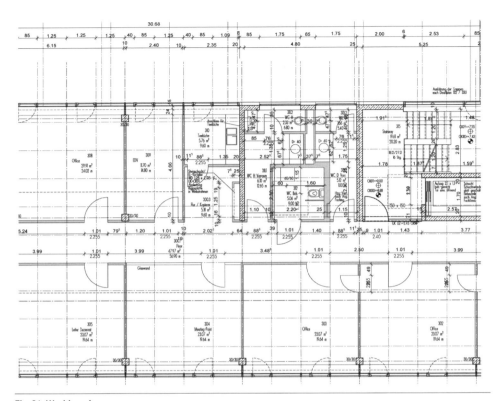

Fig. 21: Working plan

Information flow This example shows that different requirements can be formulated that may well not be met within the planned dimension parameters. Solutions can usually be found for problems of this kind by including the planners, to ensure discussion between them and a seamless flow of information. The earlier and the more thoroughly the planning takes place, the less the subsequent planning and building sequence is likely to be disrupted. Increased costs and extended building periods often arise as a result of superficial and imprecise planning. > Fig. 21

Working plans Project plans will now usually be drawn in detail on a scale of 1:50 or smaller. These so-called "working plans" for all the trades are complemented by the necessary details on an appropriate scale.

Data exchange As most drawing today uses CAD systems, data will usually be exchanged in digital form. Standards have been established for the date exchange formats currently on the market. Correct vector data are needed for further processing by a planning partner (e.g. DWG or DXF file formats). These data do reflect the precise dimensions of a building, but they are often presented in very different forms, as the different specialists work with very different CAD systems (architecture, statics, building services, surveying). It may thus be advantageous to send printed plans, called pixel files (TIFF, JPG, PDF), as well as exchanging vector data.

The approach and style for building realization given below should be used in dealing with plan content. Clear structuring into ground plans, views and all the necessary sections is essential. Logical presentation of the details and consecutive numbering for all planning documents require that the sets of plans be structured for the trades doing the work as well.

Plan contents

■ ●

TENDERING

After dealing with the permission process and drawing up working plans, the architect then has to compile the documents for inviting bids to carry out the building work. Information previously drawn on the plans now has to be clearly structured in written form.

Tendering documents

If a tradesperson is to submit a bid that is realistic in market terms, he or she needs full information about the work required. This information is supplied in the form of tendering documents, which contain general information about the building project, contractual conditions, technical requirements, a description of the specific work required, and explanatory plans.

■ **Tip:** It is not necessary to present sections of a building that can be covered by drawings multiply and separately in detail for each trade. A detailed section through an attic or the edge of a roof, for example, can contain information needed by the shell constructor, the carpenter, the roofer, and the plumber. The shell builder will discover the thickness and edging needed for the attic upstand. The carpenter recognizes the position and dimensions of the purlins, the roofer the form of the roof projection, and the plumber the desired finish for the flashing, sheet metal or guttering required.

● **Example:** Some trades, such as facade constructors, will need a complete detail series for the various detailed points. A sound basis for tendering and the subsequent execution of this work can be provided by using a clear structure with reference to top, bottom and side facade connections, logically numbered.

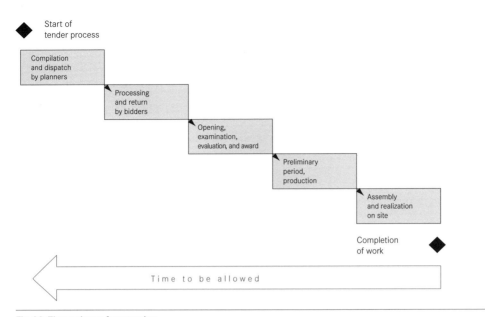

Fig. 22: Time scheme for a tender

Start of
tender process

Compilation
and dispatch
by planners

Processing
and return
by bidders

Opening,
examination,
evaluation, and award

Preliminary
period,
production

Assembly
and realization
on site

Completion
of work

Time to be allowed

Qualities/
costs/deadlines

Qualities and standards of finish are defined within descriptions of the work required. The planner must take the available budget into account when describing the work. When the various commissions are awarded, the client will have a chance for a first check of actual market prices as compared with the costs established by the architect.

When planning and drawing up the tender documents the client's schedule requirements are significant in two respects. First, the architect has to have the tendering documents available at the right time for the work to be awarded to contractors within the correct timescale, and that work can be started according to schedule. > Chapter Planning process, Tendering Second, the tender documents contain deadlines for the contractors for carrying out the work as part of the contract.

■ **Tip:** Detailed information about bids and awards can be found in *Basics Tendering*, page 213 ff.

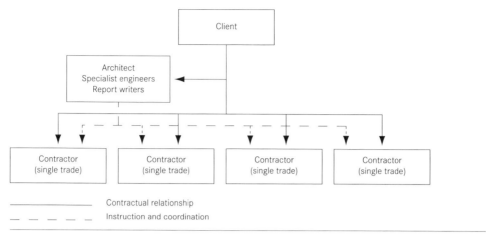

Fig. 23: Award by trade lot

As part of the deadline monitoring process, the architect has to draw up and dispatch tendering documents so that the trades and contractors can be available at the right time for the building phase to run as planned. Sufficient time should be left for formulating the descriptions of the work required. The client's requirements must be taken into account, and possible overlaps with work by other specialist planners identified. Ambitious work may require agreement with specialist firms and advisers. Insight gained in this way can also affect the final planning stage or the way in which additional details are worked out.

Tender scheduling

When drawing up tender documents, the planner will take note of the time sequence at the building site. For building tenders of this kind the individual service packages or bidding units can be brought together in terms of time to reduce the amount of organization and editing needed. Or as an alternative to tendering by individual bidding units, the work required can be put out to tender in toto and awarded to a single contractor. > Chapter Project participants, Contractors

If the tender accompanies the building process the work can be carried out in phases. But planning and tendering for an award of all the work for the project must be carried out before building starts, which means more time must be allowed for planning before building starts. > Fig. 22

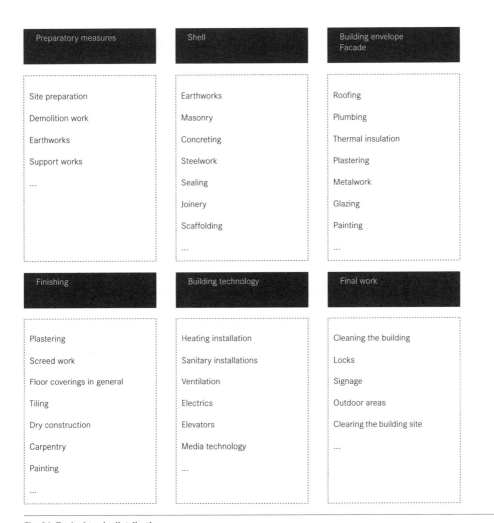

Preparatory measures	Shell	Building envelope Facade
Site preparation	Earthworks	Roofing
Demolition work	Masonry	Plumbing
Earthworks	Concreting	Thermal insulation
Support works	Steelwork	Plastering
...	Sealing	Metalwork
	Joinery	Glazing
	Scaffolding	Painting
	...	...

Finishing	Building technology	Final work
Plastering	Heating installation	Cleaning the building
Screed work	Sanitary installations	Locks
Floor coverings in general	Ventilation	Signage
Tiling	Electrics	Outdoor areas
Dry construction	Elevators	Clearing the building site
Carpentry	Media technology	...
Painting	...	
...		

Fig. 24: Typical trade distribution

Tendering by trades (trade lots)

A trade defines the scope of a piece of work that can generally be performed by specialist craft or technical firms. The classical way of awarding building work is by offering individual tenders according to trade – a bid unit is the term defining the work to be done within a contract. According to the situation and the requirements, several trades may be combined in one bid unit (package award), or subdivided into smaller bid units (part lots).

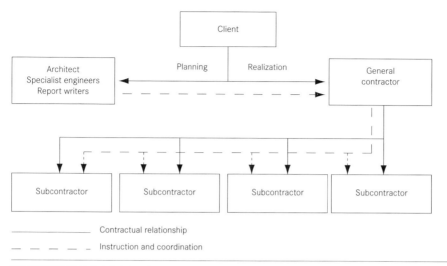

Fig. 25: General contractor award

If the work required is very extensive (e.g. building a motorway), or if there are other grounds like risk distribution or including several firms for reasons of capacity (several building phases, working in parallel), then a trade service can be broken down into part lots. This is the term used when a trade service is split down into several sections requiring similar or identical craft services. > Fig. 25

Tendering by part lots

All the trade lots may be awarded to a single contractor (general contractor). The advantage here is that the person awarding the contract has only one contact, and only one contract partner, for carrying out the work. The general contractor is responsible for coordinating individual pieces of work. As a rule, a fixed price and a completion date are agreed with a general contractor. > Chapter Project participants, Contract structures

General contractor awards

Tendering for building work can be carried out in two fundamentally different ways. > Fig. 26

Tender types

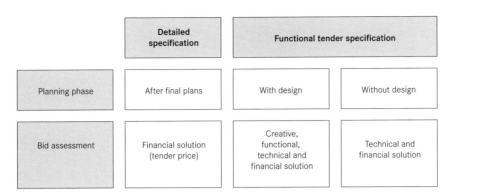

	Detailed specification	Functional tender specification	
Planning phase	After final plans	With design	Without design
Bid assessment	Financial solution (tender price)	Creative, functional, technical and financial solution	Technical and financial solution

Fig. 26: Characteristics of tender specification types

Detailed tender (bill of quantities)

Detailed tendering by individual trades requires complete, thoroughly structured working and detailed plans. Individual tenders are then put out on this basis, according to defined award units. Both the required result and the procedure for carrying out the work are laid down in detail. The contractor finds a detailed specification giving quantities, materials and building techniques in the tender. The planner must describe the work required completely and unambiguously, so that each bidder is working on the same basis when calculating a bid. A tender specification is structured into the following components:

— Title
— Subtitle
— Job item > Fig. 27

Structure level: title — The actual tender specification is broken down into titles dividing subsections of the work meaningfully. This grouping of subjobs by trade or room structures the tender specification, and it becomes easier to calculate and check prices (example: the roof as a bid unit can be divided into title substructure, title roof covering and title drainage).

Structure level: subtitle — Subtitles enable further title divisions. It can make sense in the case of large building projects in particular or complex trades to subdivide in this way, and thus establish distinctions within the job (for example by building phases or structural components).

58

Detailed tender specification
Trade: painting – interior

Title: 03 Painting – walls

Item no.	Short text		
	Long text	Unit price	Total price
	Quantity – unit	(up)	(gp)
03	Walls		
03.10	Wall paint		
	Check surface for suitability, support and adhesion qualities clean surfaces, prime absorbent surfaces. Intermediate and final coat Gloss undercoat: dull matt Color shade: old white		
	Make: .... (Information from bidder)		
	350 m²		

Fig. 27: Example of a tender item

The smallest subunit in a tender specification is the job item, which describes the work to be done. Here a distinction is made between short and long text.

Structure level: job items

Short text is the name for a job item heading. Under each heading is a long text describing the work to be done comprehensively and in a way that can be generally understood. Standard text models can be used, but they can also be formulated as wished. Figures are also provided for the required "quantity" and the "quantity unit," e.g. 25 m^3.

Long text / short text

In order to provide correct information about the scope of the work, relating to each job item, the architect must establish the necessary quantities and dimensions (m, m^2, m^3, 25 of each, etc.), using the existing working plans.

Functional tender specification (tender program)

A functional invitation to tender is formulated more generally and simply, and describes the desired result of the entire building project. It fixes a completion date, but leaves organizing the building work to the contractor as far as possible. As essentially only the desired aims are described, and some of the planning work devolves to the contractor, it is possible to award the work being tendered for at an earlier stage in the planning process. But the client and the architect have much less influence on implementation and the treatment of detail than in a detailed invitation to tender, which can have a deleterious effect on design quality. If this tender type is chosen, a decision has to be made between a tender specification with or without design.

A tender specification without design identifies the requirements made of the building on the basis of a construction or room program. The aim here is that an ideas competition should be held as the contractor draws up the tender documents. If a design is submitted, the structural and room program requirements are supplemented by concrete ideas about design and arrangement. But the functional nature of the tender is preserved, as the way in which the planning is implemented technically is left largely to the contractor. In a functional tender specification, the bidding contractor takes on the quantity risk, as he or she has to establish materials, building processes and quantities him-/herself and factor them into a bid prize. This is not the case with a detailed tender specification.

Structuring a tender

In principle a tender is structured in the same way whether it is in detail or program form. It will look like this: > Fig. 28

— Textual elements
    — General information about the project
    — Contractual conditions
    — Technical requirements
    — Information about building site conditions
    — Tender specification (detailed or functional)
— Drawn elements
    — Site plan/site mobilization plan
    — Ground plans/views/sections
    — Detailed plans if needed
— Other elements
    — Pictorial documentation
    — Samples
    — References/examples of finish
    — Reports/studies

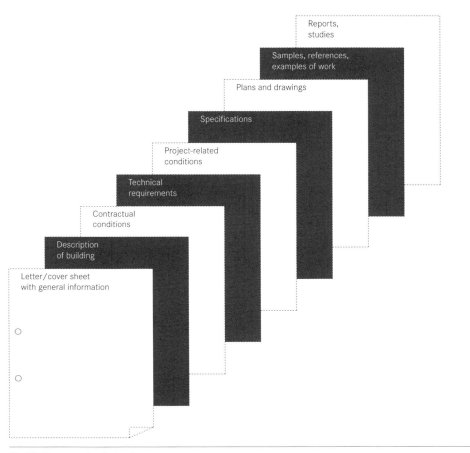

Fig. 28: Components of a tender

The cover sheet lists general information and award modalities (submission deadline, realization deadlines, nature of award process, etc.). The client and the key individuals involved in planning are named. A short, general description of the project should also be placed at the beginning.

General information about the project

Once a commission has been agreed, the bidder's submission becomes the basis for the contract, working from the tender. Arrangements fixing the contractual modalities are therefore built into the tender documents. A distinction is made between general and special contractual conditions.

Contractual conditions

General contractual conditions are based on national and international standards, and include the following information:

— Nature and scope of the work
— Remuneration
— Deadlines for realization
— Notice
— Liability
— Building acceptance
— Warranties
— Invoicing
— Payments

Special contractual conditions are project related. They complement the general contract conditions and contain the following information:

— Submitting invoices
— Payment modalities
— Arrangements for subcontractors' services
— Discounts

Technical requirements

General and special technical requirements are seen to include standards in the sense of the recognized codes of practice and project-related, additional or higher demands made on the quality of the completed work.

Building site conditions

A description of the situation on the building site is important information, complementing the site mobilization plan, for the contractor when calculating his or her bid. It makes sense to include the following information:

— Location/address
— Possible road access
— Storage facilities
— Scaffolding/cranes
— Site-supplied water and power
— Sanitary facilities

Tender specification

The tender specification is at the heart of the tender documents. > see above

Drawing elements

The drawings and sketches enclosed are intended to help the bidder to fully understand the work required. It is perfectly acceptable to submit the planning documents in a reduced form. But representation to scale is urgently required to make it easier to calculate and check quantities using the plans.

Any samples, photographs, etc. accompanying the tender documents are intended to complement the service descriptions outlined in the textual section and the plans.

Other descriptive elements

Whatever kind of tender process is chosen by the client and the architect, the greater knowledge of the individual craftspeople is always needed. In this phase the architect wears his or her experienced "building services provider's" hat, rather than working as a creative designer. The tender is the interface and connection between planning and realization. Implementing high-quality design can only succeed if the tender phase is executed conscientiously.

THE AWARD PROCEDURE

After the architect has assembled the necessary documents in order to be able to attract tenders for carrying out the building process, he or she then has to find suitable firms and craftspeople who are in a position to realize the building project in line with the client's and the architect's ideas.

Suitable firms are those who have the necessary specialist knowledge and prove reliable enough to carry out the work required, have sufficient capacity in terms of personnel and machines available at the time the work is to be carried out, and can realize the project within the estimated cost framework.

These contractors, craftspeople or building firms can be found in various ways. For smaller, private building projects the architect can suggest to the client craftspeople with whom he or she has often worked before and had good experiences with them, so that a satisfactory result can be expected.

For larger projects, and especially for public construction works (national, regional, local authority), the architect is obliged to request bids for the work required on the basis of various procedural models. > Fig. 29

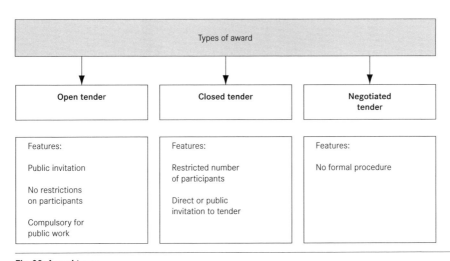

Fig. 29: Award types

For public building projects, tenders have to be issued and bids Open tender sought on a public basis. The bidders are informed about the tender procedure by announcement in the press, and can acquire the application documents from the client or the architect, against a fee. In open procedures of this kind, the lowest bid should be taken in unlimited competition. The basic principle of this kind of award is that there is a public invitation to submit a bid, and no restriction on the number of participants.

A restricted procedure may be used only if there is good reason, in Closed tender exceptional circumstances. Here, a limited number of contractors are directly invited to submit a bid. Before issuing the tender documents it is important to ascertain that the selected firms are prepared in principle to submit a bid, otherwise there is a risk that no bids will be submitted before the opening date. Unlike a public tendering process, it is no longer permissible to investigate a bidder's professional competence after the bids have been opened. Merely by selecting the potential bidders to be approached the architect is bindingly confirming their expertise and financial and technical capabilities to the client, as well as their reliability.

The chosen bidders are sent the documents directly, without a fee, in contrast to the public tendering process. Opening the bids is identical in each case.

Negotiated or private award procedure must be specifically justified Negotiated tender for public building projects. The required competition is restricted even further in such cases, as here the client negotiates with one bidder only.
> Fig. 30

○

○ **Hint:** Of course a private client is not obliged to choose one of the processes described, and will thus probably tend not to keep to an open process or a negotiated procedure when awarding building contracts. But it still highly advisable to request several bids, in order to achieve a price in conformity with the market. Bid prices can vary considerably. A bidder will usually be more inclined to submit a more reasonable bid if aware that others are also bidding.

Fig. 30: Tender award sequence

Opening date/
submission

In public award procedures a binding submission date is named, by which all bids must have been submitted. Bids are opened at the appointed time, in the presence of bidders. Bids that are submitted later cannot be accepted because transparency and equality of opportunity are essential.

Computational and
technical examination

Once the bids have been opened the architect must examine and assess them in detail. A formal examination establishes whether they are correctly signed and that nothing has been crossed out or added within the bid documents. This is essential if the bids are to be compared with each other. Otherwise a bidder could gain an unfair advantage vis-à-vis a competitor who has met the requirements correctly. The computational examination is concerned not just with comparing the bid prices; the key factor here is comparing the individual prices and the calculations made, as the unit prices will become the basis for the contract.

> ○ **Hint:** The unit price is the bidder's statement of cost for one quantity unit within a service item. This forms the basis for invoicing the work actually delivered at a later stage. The total price is arrived at by multiplying the unit price by the stated quantity or the quantity actually billed. The net bid sum is the sum of all the total prices.

Invitation to tender for painting
Limited tender

Price comparison list

Spec. item	Short text	Quantity/unit	Bidder A	Bidder B	Bidder C
1.10	Cleaning	50 m²	€3.50 €175.00	€4.00 €200.00	€4.20 €225.00
1.20	Preliminary coat	50 m²	€2.50 €125.00	€2.40 €120.00	€2.90 €145.00
1.30	Undercoat	100 m²	€4.50 €450.00	€5.00 €500.00	€6.20 €620.00
1.40	Topcoat	100 m²	€0.50 €50.00	€0.80 €80.00	€1.20 €120.00
⋮	⋮	⋮	⋮	⋮	⋮
Total	Title 1	net	€850.50	€915.00	€1,280.20
	Title 2	net	€1,320.00	€1,280.50	€1,450.90
	Title 3	net	€720.00	€835.00	€830.50
⋮	⋮		⋮	⋮	⋮
Total		net	€4,850.50	€5,210.50	€6,160.30
		gross	€5,771.50	€6,200.50	€7,330.76
		Discount	–	–	–
		Deduction	–	5%	–
		Overall total	€5,771.50	€5,890.48	€7,330.76

Fig. 31: Price comparison

A price comparison list is drawn up in order to present the bids man- Price comparison ageably. > Fig. 31 Here all the bid prices are inputted into a computer pro- gram for comparison. In principle, this could be done using a spreadsheet program like Excel, but tendering-award-invoicing programs are custom- ary, which make it easier to compile a price comparison list. The mini- mum and maximum prices are already clearly marked here, and differ- ences can be eliminated using percentages, and so deviations in unit prices between the bids can be identified. This is the first indication of the nature of the bidder's calculation and possible misunderstandings of the texts in the tender documents.

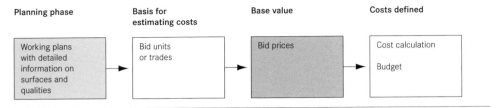

Planning phase	Basis for estimating costs	Base value	Costs defined
Working plans with detailed information on surfaces and qualities	Bid units or trades	Bid prices	Cost calculation Budget

Fig. 32: Fixing the budget

Award proposal   After finishing the examination, the architect submits a commissioning proposal to the client, which makes it possible to expect that the required work can be delivered within budget. > Fig. 32

Cost control   Once all the bids from the individual trades or bid units are available, it becomes possible to compare the calculated and the approved budget. This provides the client with reliable evidence about whether the architect has calculated the costs correctly or not. It is vital to compile the budget on the basis of bid units while cost calculations are still at the planning stage, so that costs can be readily understood. Then if tendering ensues on the basis of single trades or trade lots, it is possible to intervene and impose control on subsequent tenders if costs are exceeded.

Award meeting   Before the client commissions a contractor, it may be advisable to hold an award meeting. In public building projects, later negotiation of bid prices is prohibited, but for a private client it can be an instrument for establishing favorable prices. An award meeting can be useful as part of a public tender procedure in clearing up questions about realization effectiveness and possible alternative offers.

Building contract   The actual building contract between client and contractor or craftsperson is not primarily a matter for the architect, although he or she does have to advise the client about contractual items such as deadlines, contract penalties, payment modalities, discounts, warranty periods, safety retentions or similar matters.

Time required   Reference has been made above to the time needed to draw up tender documents correctly. > Chapter Planning process, Tendering Sufficient time must also be planned into scheduling of the bidding procedure.

For a public building project, legal deadlines have to be met as part of the award process. After the tender specification for work required has been published and contractors have applied for the documents, the bidders need sufficient time to compile their offers. After these have been returned, the planner also needs a certain amount of time to assess the offers, so that they can be examined conscientiously. If the award procedure for a public contract is to be conducted by political committees, times for meetings should be taken into account, as well as deadlines for drawing up the documents needed for those meetings. Thus the period of time between drawing up the tender specification and commissioning a contractor can extend to several months, according to the type of client. Some trades needing to prepare workshop drawings and to order and process materials need a long lead time before doing the work on the building site; this should also be considered in the scheduling context.

CONSTRUCTION

All the planning activities described so far are needed to arrive at the actual core of the project: implementing the plans on the building site. ■

In public projects, the actual start of building is a good enough reason for the client to celebrate, as it is now that the public and the neighborhood will actually acknowledge in earnest that things really are under way. A private client will be more likely to throw a "topping-out party" after the joiner has fitted the roof truss, and then the later opening of the building. A public client will often launch the project, given that it is an important one, for the general public by turning the first sod, by arranging a "digger bite," or if the project is sufficiently large, by laying a foundation stone.

Start of building

■ **Tip:** More detail on realizing a building can be found in *Basics Site Management,* page 291 ff.

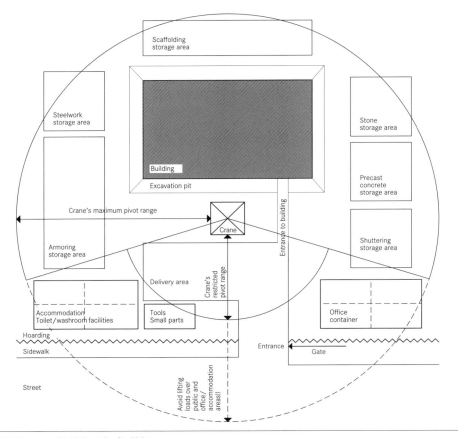

Inside the figure:

- Scaffolding storage area
- Steelwork storage area
- Stone storage area
- Building
- Excavation pit
- Precast concrete storage area
- Crane's maximum pivot range
- Crane
- Entrance to building
- Armoring storage area
- Shuttering storage area
- Delivery area
- Crane's restricted pivot range
- Accommodation Toilet/washroom facilities
- Tools Small parts
- Office container
- Hoarding
- Sidewalk
- Entrance
- Gate
- Street
- Avoid lifting loads over public and office/accommodation areas!!

Fig. 33: Diagram of building site facilities

Diagram of building site facilities

The first measure to be taken is setting up and securing the building site. A scale site plan should be drawn up, providing information about the size of the area to be built on, the position of the site fence, the access gates, deliveries, storage facilities, working areas, scaffolding areas, crane positions and swing radius, locations for rest and rubbish containers, and the excavation pit. Connection points for building power and water must be established and also drawn in where appropriate. As a building site will make considerable impact on the surrounding area during the construction period it is essential to reach an agreement with the local authorities, and contact with the immediate neighborhood is

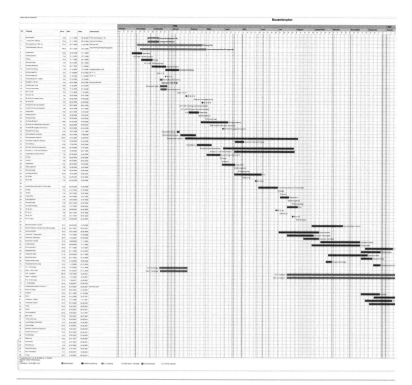

Fig. 34: Example of a construction schedule

recommended. The authorities should be informed in good time about when building is actually due to start.

One of the most important elements of the site manager's job is to draw up a schedule, usually in the form of a bar chart. > Chapter General conditions and aims, Deadlines This coordinates the main building processes and trades, bearing the completion date in mind. It is important here that the individual trade jobs are brought together and effectively matched. If the first version of a working schedule is reviewed after the project is finished, it is likely that a number of deviations from the planned flow will

Scheduling

be found. An enormous number of things affect the schedule, including periods of bad weather, awarding problems, delivery bottlenecks for materials, and possibly even insolvencies during the building period and delays caused by contractors. As the schedule is based on a logical sequence of jobs, delays by a single trade can often affect subsequent trades and the whole building process considerably. The site manager has to keep an eye on all components so that countermeasures can be taken in good time, and provide information about postponing the completion date.

Intervening in the schedule

If a schedule is to be properly maintained, it should allow for any necessary interventions into the building process. The client's stated completion date is unlikely to be met if there are building delays shortly before the end of the building period, so early interventions should be made where needed.

Interventions can take the form of raising worker capacity or increasing the length of time worked. Dividing the work into sections can also be helpful, so that trades working later in the sequence are not held up. It is also possible for part of the work to be done at a later date, at least if this does not affect intermediate deadlines or later work. As a last resort, the quality of finish can be modified in order to speed up the building process.

General site supervision

The presence of the site manager on site depends to a large extent on the size and complexity of the project. The architect will usually look after small domestic projects him-/herself, without a separate on-site office. But building projects on a larger scale need an on-site office and site supervision by one or more managers who are present all the time.

The site manager needs all the current plans and the building contract including the specifications for the jobs that have already been awarded for his or her dealings with the contractors. It is absolutely essential for the site managers to familiarize themselves with the plans in detail, so that the work can be supervised and directed according to requirements.

On-site meetings

For larger projects, the site office is also used as a place for meetings that take place regularly. The specialist planners and the firms working on the site should be invited, as needed and according to the way the work is progressing. The meetings should be minuted on the basis of jour-fixe minuting standards. > Chapter Planning process, Working plans and quality of finish

It also makes sense for all new participants in the building process to exchange address data at an early stage, though care should be taken that the information is always passed on via the site manager responsible. ○

The site manager is obliged to keep a construction diary as a record Construction diary of the work done on site. As the construction diary is often used subsequently to provide evidence, the following entries are of considerable importance:

— Date
— Weather conditions (temperature, time of day, etc.)
— Firms working at the site
— Number of workers per firm
— Nature of work done
— Orders, statements and acceptances
— Handing over plans, samples, etc.
— Material deliveries
— Special events (visits, hold-ups, accidents, etc.)

As has already been suggested, the presence of the site manager Presence depends largely on the project in hand. For example, keeping a construction diary does not depend on the site manager being present every day. It has only to be brought up to date if the site manager is or has to be present on site. On-site supervision has to be concomitant with keeping to the permission requirements, the working plans and the job specifications, observing the recognized codes of practice. ●

There is no doubt that the site manager must be present at important and critical phases of the work, for example if sealing and insulation work is being done, reinforcement materials introduced, concrete of the

○ **Hint:** Even the architect, if he or she is not one and the same person as the site manager, should not give instructions directly to workers without including the site managers. A building process is so complex that individuals involved cannot have a complete grasp of all the interlinked procedures and events. To avoid disagreements between the parties involved, all information must be conveyed via the site manager, who is responsible for overall coordination.

● **Example:** If the responsible site manager is present on a prestigious building site twice a week, and can keep to deadlines and guarantee the quality of the work done, the client will have no grounds for objections. But errors of coordination can creep in even if he or she is permanently present, or building supervision could leave something to be desired. An architect conducting site management also owes "success" to his or her activities in this field.

required quality being delivered, for loadbearing constructions with appropriate anchorage, for excavations, if heat insulation is being fitted, when constructing sound insulation, etc.

But there is no need for site management to be present for simple, routine work. An experienced site manager can limit his or her presence on site appropriately.

Health and safety officer

The site manager is obliged to attend to traffic safety and hazard prevention on the building site. He or she is supported in this by the health and safety coordinator, who makes regular patrols to check that accident prevention rules are being followed, and to point out potential danger to the site manager if they are not. > Chapter Project participants, Experts

Specialist site management

The site manager has on a limited role, essential dealing with coordination, in terms of specialist firms working on the site, who are supervised by specialist engineers. He or she should on no account take on specialist management for trades operating beyond his or her competence.

Coordination

The site manager is the key link in coordinating work with the specialist trades. Two examples illustrate the importance of the "site management" control center. Only the site manager responsible can coordinate the interlined processes between placing dry partition walls and boarding one side of them, installing electrical equipment or additional plumbing and subsequent closure and painting of the walls, and then the final fitting of the electrical switches, as the individual trades have no cause to consider the work done by other specialists afterwards. Another classic case where more coordination is needed is parallel planning of underfloor heating with cable ducts under the screed. All the trades involved have to know about the timing for the work sequences, allowing time for the screed to dry and setting up heating protocols. This information has to pass via the responsible site manager, who then devises a sensible and feasible sequence of events, together with the specialist planners.

Acceptances

In the course of the building project, both the architect's work and that of the firms employed is appraised. By accepting the work, the client is stating that he or she acknowledges the service rendered. This process can have considerable legal consequences. As a rule the building is accepted after completion of the shell or at the final completion stage. Compliance with the permission documents or with the current building laws is tested at this point. Acceptance of connection with official supply grids is carried out with the suppliers responsible for water, sewerage, power, gas, etc. The heating system is accepted by the local master chimney sweep. Special technical facilities, for example conveyor systems or elevators need to be accepted separately by technical monitoring services.

Formerly, the client had a "compliance claim" vis-à-vis the contractor or trades, and risk of loss used to lie with the contractor as well. "Risk of loss" means the risk that the work has to be done again without remuneration because of an event or damage that takes place before acceptance.

Compliance claim and warranty stage

An appraisal of planning work can also be demanded, depending on different local legislation, and in a way that differs from building acceptance. Here the completed work is assessed for compliance with the plans as originally passed after completion and before the building is handed over and used.

Appraisal

The warranty stage begins at the point of acceptance. This will be dealt with in more detail in the next chapter. During the warranty or limitation period any deficiencies faults that occur must be made good, so long as this does not involve disproportionate effort or expense. The warranty period starts again once the deficiencies have been made good.

Trades will not usually wait until the work is complete and accepted before invoicing the client. Hence "payments on account" or "part payments" are usual, according to building progress and the work done. Payments are usually made on the basis of the working plans. If a particular piece of work is not recorded there, or deviates from it, a joint inspection will take place on site with the worker so that the invoice submitted can be checked correctly.

Inspection

The contractor will formally address the actual invoice to the client, but will send it to the architect, who is responsible for checking it professionally and computationally. He or she may have to correct the invoice, and forward it to the client with a certificate that it has been checked. The architect must always remember when checking that he or she is the client's agent, and that thus it is not his or her duty to examine the invoice to the advantage of the contractor, in other words to the client's disadvantage. Ultimately the certificate on the invoice is just a recommendation that the client should pay the invoice.

Checking invoices

As invoices are now increasingly coming in from the trades, the client is obliged to make large sums of money available, as well as for the fee payments already due for planning the building project. He or she is thus increasingly interested in being aware of the current cost situation. The budget estimated for the project is usually limited, dependent on

Statement of costs

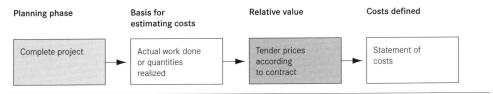

Planning phase	Basis for estimating costs	Relative value	Costs defined
Complete project	Actual work done or quantities realized	Tender prices according to contract	Statement of costs

Fig. 35: Costs established after completion

credits, subsidies or permission from committees, and thus cannot be exceeded at will. Comparing the commission sums as related to offer sums and building contract with the actual sums invoiced after the various trades have completed their work is thus crucially important to the client. Furthermore, if costs are constantly monitored, it is possible to intervene effectively if costs are in fact exceeded. Thus the cost situation will come closer to the actual costs after the building is completed as building progresses. After completion the final costs can be summed up in a statement of costs. > Fig. 35

Handover   After acceptance, as described above, by authorities and of the trades' services rendered, the property is handed over to the client. This does not have to be accompanied by a tour of inspection of the building. But the client does have the right to request that all the required planning documents are handed over. This documentation includes a full set of working plans, as well as installation plans for services, technical operation information, reinforcement plans, acceptance protocols and certificates. The documents will be more or less numerous according to the building, but they must be compiled in such a way that they can be used correctly. All the information for subsequent maintenance work, refurbishment or change of use must be available. Here the specialist planners are also required to make the necessary information available to the client.

The architect's duties are not absolutely completed with handover. There may be some work remaining to be done, and deficiencies complained about in the work done by the contractors have to be monitored and handled.

Opening   Generally it is hoped that completion of a building is something that should be celebrated appropriately. The architect hands the building over to the client officially by presenting him or her with a symbolic key. In the

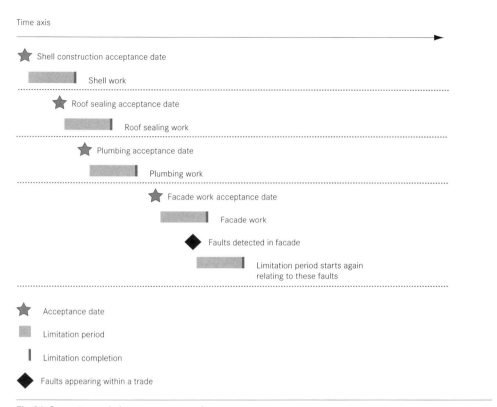

Time axis

Shell construction acceptance date

Shell work

Roof sealing acceptance date

Roof sealing work

Plumbing acceptance date

Plumbing work

Facade work acceptance date

Facade work

Faults detected in facade

Limitation period starts again
relating to these faults

Acceptance date

Limitation period

Limitation completion

Faults appearing within a trade

Fig. 36: Guarantee period sequence – example

case of pubic projects, this occasion can be used to attract attention and enhance esteem.

But apart from this, the commitment shown and services rendered by everyone involved in the building process can be acknowledged. The architect should also pay tribute to the client. The architect owes his or her fee not least to the client's readiness to invest, whether privately or publicly.

THE WARRANTY PERIOD
The architect can continue to perform valuable services for the client after the building is completed. A detailed and systematic documentation of the building, independent of the document handover described above, contains a structured record and analysis of all the data used in

the planning. This does not mean coming up with new planning work of drawing up new plans, such as presentation plans, but merely brings together all the documents dealt with in the course of the project planning process.

Warranty periods   A crucial part of the work required after the building has been handed over consists of monitoring the warranty periods for work done by the individual trades. The services rendered were almost all completed at different periods, and thus also accepted at different times. The warranty period starts with acceptance. Different periods can be agreed according to the basis of the contract. Hence it is vital to put all the warranty periods needed for monitoring very carefully. Shortly before the warranty period is over the architect must make a tour of inspection to check the building for any deficiencies, and examine the structural components thoroughly. However, it is not necessary to use special examination methods or equipment.

Eliminating defects   If the examination reveals defects, they should be notified to the client. An appropriate time can be allowed in order to correct them.

Final examination   It can also be helpful for the architect to conduct a final examination of the project with reference to cost guidelines, related to square meters, cubic meters or individual trades. It can also be useful for planning future projects to examine the costs incurred and the time needed for the practice to complete the work.

The work needed during the warranty period can take a disproportionately large amount of time in relation to the fee due. But this time and effort can be limited effectively, not least with aid of good planning and the right selection of competent building firms and workers, as well as through conscientiously discharged site management.

In conclusion

When planning the project, the architect takes responsibility for realizing it successfully. The project manager responsible must have his or her eye on the initial aims throughout every phase of the project. Planning requirements in terms of cost, schedule and quality are the coordinates at which work must always be directed.

The architect is the client's expert contact person in all fields of building. He or she will advise the client about building planning questions, and the relevant technical, economic, creative, civic, and ecological aspects. He or she functions as the recognized and qualified coordinator between everyone involved in the building project, such as specialist planners, contractors, workmen, local authorities and departments.

The architect introduces the planning steps in logical sequence and arrives at the decisions needed at every planning phase with the client.

In the realization phase he or she checks the sequence of events to ensure that all the aims formulated at the planning stage are achieved.

At a time of increasing specialization in every field, realizing a building project requires a wide range of knowledge and ability from the planner. Being an architect is an attractive profession not just because of the creative design possibilities, but largely also because there are so many different challenges. As the previous chapters explain, financial and strategic skills are extremely important. And architects must also address all the relevant legal matters in the course of their work. The ability to work in a team and to be able to deal with all kinds of people requires a high level of social competence. The architect will come into contact with a large number of professional partners in the course of the project, whether it is the partners involved or the trades who will work on implementing the building project. Each building project means coming to terms with the implications of new and interesting fields of work. And not least a planner needs a marked ability to articulate his or her designs and ideas responsibly to society, which he/she is contributing to designing.

Realizing a project from the idea to handing the building over embraces almost all of an architect's field of activity. Every new planning stage brings new challenges. Successful completion and an effective opening confirm and underline the planner's achievement.

Bert Bielefeld – Roland Schneider

Budgeting

Introduction

The relevance of
construction costs

Estimated and actual costs are a key topic for client and architect in many building projects. This is not least because the client has to invest a considerable sum in a building project, a sum that in many cases is far larger than other expenditure. It is therefore essential for the client that contractors work within budgets. This applies particularly when money is being invested in properties to provide a return on investment, where subsequent income (such as rents or sales) is set against the necessary expenditure (building costs, financing costs, depreciation, maintenance costs). The yield or profit (income minus expenditure) from property investments is a key criterion in deciding in favour of the project, and in its success. Even slight building price rises during the construction phase can drag the project into loss – with consequences that can last for many decades.

An additional factor is that construction projects – unlike industrial production – are usually highly individual in character, or can even be like prototypes. This means that processes and structures can be carried over unmodified from one project to another only to a limited extent, so imponderables and surprises may occur that affect timing or finance in a way that was wholly or partly unforeseen at the beginning of the project. Additionally, a lot of time can elapse between deciding in favour of a project and completing the building, so that estimates made at the beginning of the project about shifts in market prices, for example, may sometimes not hold good over a period of time.

Life cycle costs

Even if this time span can entail considerable financial fluctuation, it is very short if measured against the life cycle of a building, but will still make a substantial impact. Financial decisions, e.g. about options for construction or domestic services, have an effect throughout the entire use or life cycle of the building, and lead to differing running costs. If the costs generated (heating, water and power supplies, repairs, maintenance etc.) while the building is being used are added up, they will be substantially greater than the initial investment. But investment in a building project has to be raised within a very short period of a very few months or years, while running costs extend continuously over decades. Higher initial investment in technical equipment, such as more efficient heating systems, for example, can achieve significant savings within the lifetime of the building. > fig. 2

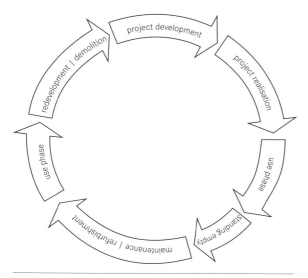

Fig. 1: Life cycle costs

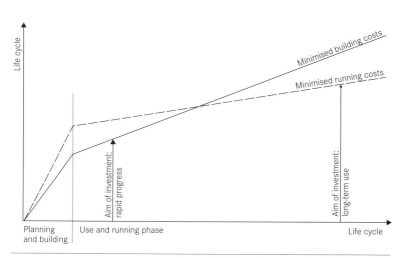

Fig. 2: Links between investment and use costs

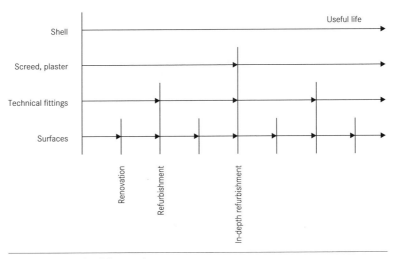

Fig. 3: Life cycle of building sections

Alongside the investment costs while a new building is under construction and the on-going maintenance costs, new investment is needed at various intervals (maintenance and replacement costs) in the life cycle of buildings in order to raise the structure to a more up-to-date technical standard or to repair significant damage. Here a distinction is made according to the part of the building concerned between various cycles that may well turn out differently from project to project. The shell of the building is generally the longest lasting section, and the end of its useful life usually coincides with demolition and rebuilding. Sections with a robust finish such as the outer shell, plaster and screed are also pretty durable and have to be replaced only after some decades. Technical fittings (e.g. ventilation plants, plumbing, electrical installations, data systems technology) and surfaces subject to wear and tear (e.g. paintwork, floor coverings) last for a considerably shorter time and some of these are subject to very short investment cycles according to their function, construction method and maintenance level. > fig. 3

This is why it is important to consider subsequent ease of replacement and the life cycles this implies at the planning stage. If technical features with short life cycles such as data cables or ventilation ducts are installed underneath longer-lasting items (e.g. screed or plaster), these will have to be removed and replaced as well during the procedure, along with all coverings and surfaces. This would mean that future investment would be significantly more costly than would be the case if reversible and accessibly installed installations in a shaft were used, for example.

Generally speaking, clients will keep a careful eye on holding construction costs in check and – in the case of a longer-term interest in the use of the building – on their impact on the use phase as well. So architects and planners must accept that an interest in information and success are a central planning outcome and build the necessary working steps into the process. Keeping to budget and to the planned completion date are among the few physical known quantities that clients can and will use to judge the quality and professionalism of the architects and planners involved. Clients' expectations

Basic budgeting principles

Some basic principles have to be set down at the outset if budgeting is to be understood. As well as defining the technical terms involved, it is above all necessary to ensure that the areas of influence and fluctuation range of building costs are grasped, as this is the basic essential for assessing the validity of costing. Handling imponderables and cost risks transparently is a key feature of responsible care for the client during the planning and construction process.

CONCEPTS AND STRUCTURES

Costs within the life cycle

If the entire life cycle of a building is considered, further use and disposal costs have to be taken into account alongside the actual construction costs. ISO 15686-5 defines life cycle costs (LCC) in the narrow sense as the sum of construction costs, running costs, cleaning and maintenance costs, and demolition or end of life costs. More broadly speaking, whole life costs (WLC) also include external costs not relating to construction, such as income, financing costs etc. > fig. 4

Fixing the budget

A budget is fixed for almost all projects when the decision to put them in train is taken, regardless of whether it is a new building or an existing project, or whether a private or a public client is involved. The budget is not the same as the sum of money that provides the planning base for the work of architects and specialist planners. As a rule the budget contains additional cost factors for the client, e.g. plot acquisition, financing costs, additional internal costs, legal advice and solicitors' costs etc. Project related cost factors are relevant to the planning team
○ as a costing specification.

○ **Hint:** A distinction has to be made between a costing specification as a fixed budget emanating from the client and the cost guarantee submitted by an architect. Here the architect is guaranteeing to keep within these costs and is thus liable for any additional costs that may be incurred – even if he or she is not responsible for generating them.

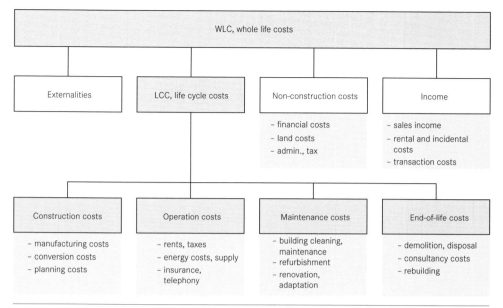

Fig. 4: Life cycle costs allocated according to ISO 15686-5

All subsequent costings in the planning and building process have to address this. A distinction has to be made between the maximum and the minimum principle when dealing with a costing specification.

Under the <u>minimum principle</u>, it is assumed that the client has fixed quality requirements and that these are to be realised at the lowest possible building costs. This applies, for example, when there are already fixed rental contracts in place, including building descriptions relating to later users, or if a hotel chain is building another hotel following a tried and tested, financially optimised scheme.

Minimum / maximum principle

The <u>maximum principle</u> works on the principle that that there is a fixed limit to costs, and that the greatest possible building volume and quality is be realised on this basis. This is the case for publicly funded housing, for example, where the maximum living space is to be realised within a fixed amount of funding. > fig. 5

<u>Budgeting</u> is the generic term for all activities carried out during the planning and building process. Generally this includes listing costings,

Budgeting

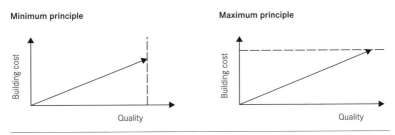

Minimum principle   Maximum principle

Fig. 5: Minimum and maximum principles

monitoring and checking results and events within the process, and also controlling activities such as feeding price increases into the budget.

Costings are prepared in stages in the course of the planning and building process, especially when the client has to make key decisions. For example, if it is necessary to decide whether a variant preliminary design should be pursued further or a planning proposal should be submitted to the authorities for approval, then the current cost position should be determined as a basis for the decision.

Two essential factors are involved in cost control. First, it means matching the current costings to the cost specifications and the previous costing stages, in order to be able to identify and evaluate any deviations from the process that may have occurred. Then the costs within the process have to be reviewed continuously, so that the client can be informed in good time about substantial cost-related consequences. This puts the client in a position from which it is possible to order direct measures such as quality adjustments or area reduction where necessary. Such interventions in the process are called cost control.

Cost classification   Another key factor is the way in which costs are presented and structured. Here a distinction is made between two fundamental ways of looking at things:

Cost classification based on structural components uses building systematics to structure the building costs that have been determined. Cost generating elements are listed according to the amount of detail required in terms of structural components (ceiling, wall, roof etc.) or by

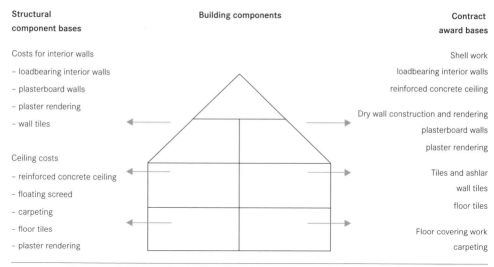

Structural component bases	Building components	Contract award bases
Costs for interior walls		Shell work
– loadbearing interior walls		loadbearing interior walls
– plasterboard walls		reinforced concrete ceiling
– plaster rendering		
– wall tiles		Dry wall construction and rendering
		plasterboard walls
		plaster rendering
Ceiling costs		
– reinforced concrete ceiling		Tiles and ashlar
– floating screed		wall tiles
– carpeting		floor tiles
– floor tiles		Floor covering work
– plaster rendering		carpeting

Fig. 6: Structural component-based and contract award-based

single structural elements (floor covering, screed, ceiling rendering etc.). Here the costs are fed into so-called cost groups. > chapter on costing parameters

Cost classification based on award after tender is based on the subsequent structure of award units within the tendering and contract process. In this case, skills-related cost structures (shell, roof covering, screed, rendering, paintwork, electrical work etc.) are taken as the basis. > chapter on working with a trade-oriented costing in the contract award phase

COSTING PARAMETERS

Building costs are calculated mainly by following a scheme of multiplying volumes/quantities within a costing parameter and then adding in individually identified costing parameters where appropriate. Here a distinction has to be made between various cost parameter types.

— Cubic capacity/plot area-related costing parameters
— Cost parameters for building components/raw elements (ceiling, roof, wall)
— Cost parameters for building components/light elements (ceiling rendering, reinforced concrete ceiling, screed, floor covering)
— Unit prices/tender prices (request for tenders or previously concluded projects)
— Construction estimate from contractors (personnel costs, material costs, site overheads)

Fig. 7: Specimen structural component based costing following German DIN 276

100 Plot	110 Plot value
	120 Additional plot costs
	130 Clearing
200 Preparation and access	210 Preparation
	220 Public access
	230 Private access
	240 Balancing charges
	250 Transitional charges
300 Building – building construction	310 Excavation
	320 Foundations
	330 Exterior walls
	340 Interior walls
	350 Ceilings
	360 Roofs
	370 Structural fittings
	390 Other building construction measures
400 Building – technical facilities	410 Sewerage, water and gas fittings
	420 Hot water facilities
	430 Ventilation facilities
	440 Electrical installations
	450 Telecom and IT facilities
	460 Conveyor systems
	470 Facilities for specified use
	480 Building automation
	490 Other technical equipment measures
500 Exterior work	510 Plot areas
	520 Reinforced areas
	530 Exterior buildings
	540 Technical facilities in external buildings
	550 Fixtures in external buildings
	560 Bodies of water
	570 Planted and seeded areas
	590 Other exterior facilities
600 Furnishings and artworks	610 Furnishings
	620 Artworks

700 Additional construction costs	710 Client requirements
	720 Preparation for property planning
	730 Architects' and engineers' fees
	740 Expert reports and consultation
	750 Artistic work
	760 Financing costs
	770 General additional construction costs
	790 Other additional construction costs

<u>Volume- or area-related costings</u> estimate the overall costs for a building by using parameters that are easily calculated from a design. In order to do this, the allotted overall sum required for a building and corresponding values such as

Volume- or area-related costings

— gross cubic capacity (GCC) as the building volume
— gross floor area (GFA) as the sum of all the storey areas including construction areas or
— usable area (UA)

has to be established. Dividing these into each other gives rough values per square or cubic metre for future projects. Values of this kind often come in very useful in the early stages of a project, when no precise data, plans or quality requirements are available.

One major problem when using volume- or area-related parameters arises because these do not relate to the actual <u>cost factors</u>. > fig. 8

Cost generators
○

○ **Hint:** A part of a building is known as a cost factor if it contributes to building costs in manufacture. 1 m² of reinforced concrete ceiling or 1 m² of masonry wall are direct cost factors, for example, but 1 m³ of building volume or 1 m² of usable area generate costs only indirectly, because they all share proportionately in different cost factors. This inevitably involves conversion problems.

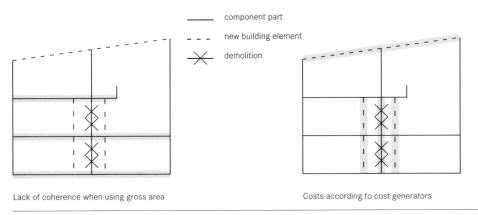

Lack of coherence when using gross area   Costs according to cost generators

Fig. 8: Lack of precision in volume-/area-related building cost determination

Component- and building elements

Parameters based on cost factors (building components, technical facilities etc.) for a building are correspondingly more accurate. Component-related parameters (also called component elements) sum up the costs for a complete section of the building (ceiling price per m², roof price per m²), and so are very simple to calculate after a superficial general survey of all parts of the building. Building-element related parameters (also called fine-element) allot a set quantity and a specific costing parameter to each individual structural element (m² of floor covering, m² of screed, m² of reinforced concrete ceiling, m² of ceiling rendering, m² of ceiling paintwork). This makes it possible to establish building costs much more precisely than with component elements.

● **Example:** The price for a component ceiling element does not reveal anything at all about the individual elements of the ceiling at first. But there are clear price differences relating to ceiling construction (timber beams, reinforced concrete) or floor coverings (natural stone parquet, PVC covering etc.). This means that existing prices must always be supported by additional information and should not be applied to a particular project without embarking upon more elaborate calculations.

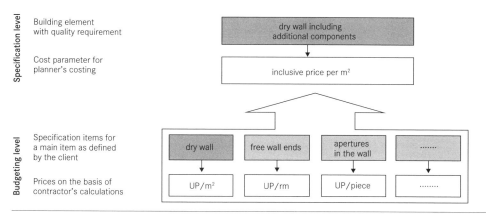

Fig. 9: Connection between building elements and unit prices (UP) in a tender

But building elements also include the whole range of typical additional components. So when setting a price per m² for floor coverings it must include skirting boards, connecting bars, penetrations etc., and a dry wall structure must include doorways, wall ends, connections etc. in the price per m². > fig. 9

Inclusive price

Unit costs are the accounting prices offered by the contractor for each individual item in a tender. The unit cost in agreed contracts after precise calculation (not all-in contracts) forms the contractual basis between client and contractor. It is also possible to work out costs based on unit prices before the contract is awarded. This approach will be preceded by tenders backed up by statistically determined unit prices.

Unit cost

Unit prices offered by a building company will be determined in their turn on the basis of their single cost components. If costs as calculated by the contractor are used, this is known as an <u>estimate</u>. Estimating a tender for building work – regardless of whether it is based on an all-in price or a number of unit prices in a specification – is carried out according to business principles of cost and performance accounting. So a direct distinction is made between costs to be allocated to the work required and supplements for overheads or business expenses. > fig. 10

Construction estimates

Costs that can be allocated directly are known as <u>single partial service costs</u>. These include wages, the cost of materials, equipment and machine costs and where applicable outside service costs that can be allotted to a service and are offered as an item for tender.

Individual partial service costs

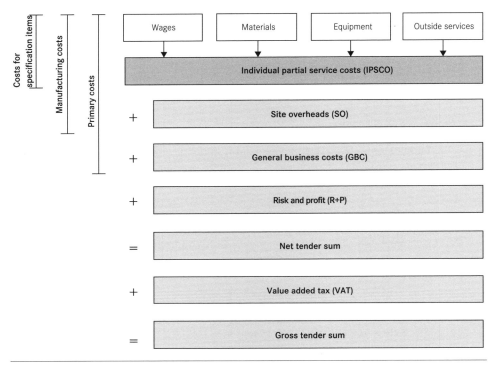

Fig. 10: Structural basis for a contractor estimate

The relevant <u>wage elements</u> within a unit costing are calculated from the average wage and the amount of time needed to produce one square metre of tiling, for example. The average wage includes social and additional wage costs, as well as the actual wage paid to employees. To calculate this, all the costs generated in a year for an employee are divided by the number of effective working hours per year (minus annual leave, sickness, training, public holidays etc.).

The relevant <u>material costs</u> within a unit costing include the purchase price for materials such as tiles, tile adhesive, and grouting cement for tiling, and also additional costs for breakages, waste etc. Auxiliary building materials (e.g. shuttering, supports) and fuel (e.g. fuel for a digger, power for a screed machine) are included in the calculation.

<u>Outside service costs</u> include all costs generated by sub-contractors such as hiring (of a mobile crane, for example, or a concrete pump) or separate contractors (e.g. sub-contracting for pointing by a dry builder).

Once all the above-mentioned costs that can be directly itemised Overheads and business expenses have been calculated, they are added to individual costs within the relevant section of the work. All items are additionally increased by supplements for further costs that may arise. These include building site overheads, general business costs and supplements for risk/profit.

Building site overheads (BSO) include all costs that cannot be allocated directly to the building work but that are nevertheless generated within the building operation. This includes items such as accommodation expenses, site insurance, expenses on the contractors' management side etc.

General business costs (GBC) are the building contractors' non-operative running costs that that have to be covered proportionately across all building sites. These include office rental and upkeep, for example, management salaries, upkeep and security for a builders' yard, and costs for legal and tax advice.

Finally, risk and profit (R+P) represent the commercial result that the building project would like to achieve, over and above the previous prime costs.

Generally speaking, such different levels of detail can be graded from volume-/area-related cost parameters down to detailed business cost elements in the contractors' budgeting. Appropriate parameters are used as a basis according to the costing methods chosen. > chapter on costing methods

COST PREDICTION PRINCIPLES

The point in time at which costings are made is called the cost esti- Cost estimation point mation point. It is possible for there to be some years between the cost estimates made in the early planning phases and the award of the building contract or the final costing for the building work as charged. This makes it difficult to predict future market price changes and include them in the costing.

So in fact costing can be based only on the conditions prevailing at the time, as future developments are speculative and thus of little relevance. But it is important for the client to know how much money will ultimately have to be paid for a project.

The following actions can be taken to reduce this difference:
— Assess and estimate possible variables in future cost movements.
  > chapter on influences on costs

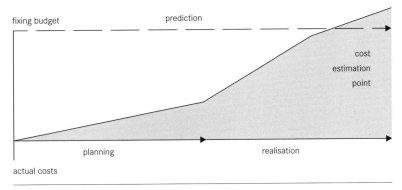

fixing budget   prediction

cost
estimation
point

planning   realisation

actual costs

Fig. 11: Cost prediction principle

— Carry out the best possible risk investigations. > chapter on assessing
   cost risks
— Do not see costing as static but update it throughout the whole
   process and keep adjusting it to current developments. > chapter on
   updating the budget

FACTORS INFLUENCING COSTS

If building costs are to be estimated purposefully and realistically it
is essential to understand the connection between planning qualities and
costs as well as going through a technical costing exercise. Costing
parameters are available for all the levels presented in the chapter on
costing parameters via statistical listings, online platforms or books. But
only the architect responsible can adapt them to suit a particular project.

General influences that may well make the project in question different from your own have to be taken into account, particularly in the
case of parameters that are not directly linked to cost factors. > fig. 12

Scale and context   The scale of a project is highly relevant to the costs per square
metre, as small projects are often associated proportionately with higher
expenditure.

If very difficult sites are involved such as an inner city area that has
to be developed in its entirety, then it will be extremely difficult and
expensive to organise the building site, as it may be that external areas

96

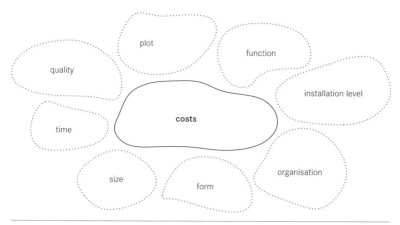

Fig. 12: Factors influencing building costs

will have to be rented and streets closed, which will cost money. If the site is not accessible by a developed road (e.g. a research observatory in a high mountain range), then considerable expenses may well be generated in getting to the building site.

It is goes without saying that different buildings such as dwellings, offices, warehouses or laboratories cannot be compared in terms of volume- or area-related parameters, because the installations required and the complexity of the projects can differ considerably. Building costs depend on the technical installations, particularly for projects needing large quantities of domestic installations. So if volume- and area-related parameters are being applied, then a building with a similar function should be used for comparison.

○ Function and complexity

If the project for which estimates are to be prepared is within the existing building stock and is to be converted or refurbished, considerably greater costs will be involved than for a new building. In the sphere

Projects in existing building stock

● **Example:** If we consider the degree of site preparation and clearing needed to lay screed, this will depend on whether a medium-sized building is to be treated, or just a single room. If calculated by the square metre price for the screed, the relevant building overheads will be significantly higher in the case of a very small project.

of monument preservation, individual finishing and adjustment work is often necessary, with large numbers of personnel involved. Many building contractors work on the basis of higher expenditure simply because the project in question deals with existing building stock. They know from experience that wide-ranging problems and special features will mean that it will not be possible to work as efficiently as for a new building.

Building period   The building period required for a project can also be very important if building has to be carried out very quickly or will be subject to a large number of interruptions. If the contractor can use employees only for short periods – for example because breaks have to be taken in the course of work on projects in existing building stock that continue to be in use – s/he will also have to factor in wage costs for the unproductive intermediate periods. If realisation times are very short, additional costs for personnel and machines will have to be built in. The provision of building site facilities can also be a key factor in terms of overall costs, especially if these costs are not reflected in the physical end result – the fabric of the building.

Quality   The quality of both architecture and the materials is significant in the same way. Products made mechanically in large production runs offer considerable savings over components made by hand. Material prices can rise exponentially in the luxury sector, for example for kitchens, bathroom furniture, tiles, facades etc. In the case of individually designed and produced components such as special facade structures or windows it may be necessary to take further expenses into account, such as individual permits and technical experts, as well as individual manufacturing costs.

Wages and material costs   Generally speaking, the question arises of the extent to which producing a construction element is very labour-intensive and thus dominated by wage costs, or whether its key features are rapid installation and possibly high material costs. In countries with high wage levels it is preferable to opt for industrial prefabrication and simple delivery/installation instead of craft work and raw materials processed on site.

If the component being budgeted for is a work-intensive construction element, changing wage costs may be relevant for price increases in the planning and building process. Additional wage costs may have to be taken into account, as well as general wage scale variations. And some materials may vary considerably in cost as a result of fluctuating raw material prices. Metal prices in particular (e.g. for steel girders, reinforcement or electric cables) are very heavily dependent on world demand,
- particularly from China, India and other rapidly developing markets.

But regional and local market fluctuations have to be taken into account, as well as world trade and international raw material prices. If the building trade is doing well in the economic cycle and building contractors have full order books, prices will be much higher than in times of underemployment when every contractor is desperate for orders. Sometimes prices can fluctuate by 20–30% between recession and growth phases.

Market prices/ economic developments

ASSESSING COST RISKS

The above explanations make it clear that it is sensible or even essential to conduct a risk assessment operation. It needs to be said from the outset that the concept of "risk" should not be seen as negative in the broader sense. In comparison with "security", a risk means first and foremost a lack of knowledge about the state of affairs or uncertainty about whether something is going to happen.

Risks cannot usually be excluded, but simply confined or minimised. Expense incurred in doing this (e.g. general site or contamination tests) are known as <u>due diligence</u>. So a decision has to be made about which costs make sense within a project, so that potentially damaging effects can be kept to a minimum. > fig. 13

Risks in the broader sense are fundamentally assessed on the basis of the <u>incidence rate</u> and the <u>damaging effect</u> in each case. In particular, the risks that are very damaging with disastrous consequences and are very likely to occur have to be limited in advance. The rigour of the examination and the limits to due diligence are fixed for individual projects. It can be helpful to limit risk to a tolerable and above all financially viable level by using the ALARP method (As Low As Reasonably Practicable). > fig. 14

Damaging effects and the incidence rate

Cost risks can be allotted in terms of their origin in various risk areas. As has already been explained, <u>market risks</u> such as fluctuations in the economic cycle can lead to considerable budget changes. <u>Business risks</u>

Market and commercial risks

● **Example:** A few decades ago, attics were still made by carpenters from rough timbers, but now CAD drawings are used to prepare all the necessary purlins and rafters ready for fitting in the factory, using joinery machines. Even though some of the machines are very costly, they are considerably more cost-efficient than hand production.

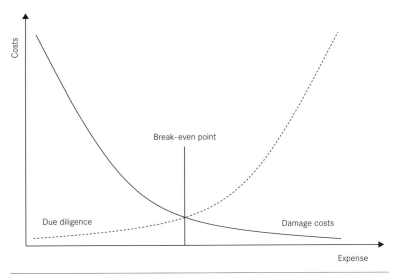

Fig. 13: Connections between damage costs and due diligence

such as strikes or insolvency also represent a high uncertainty factor for the success of the project.

Subsoil risks   Subsoil risks also have to be taken into account. For example, high groundwater levels can require elaborate reinforcement in the cellar and temporary lowering of groundwater levels in the building phase. If the subsoil turns out during the building phase to be non-loadbearing, compensatory measures (pile foundations, soil improvement, anchoring, load distribution slabs etc.), which are usually elaborate and very cost intensive, have to be undertaken.

Risk in existing   Particular risks in existing building stock have to be taken into building stock   account for projects in existing stock. These can include:
— contamination (asbestos, PCB, PAH, AMF, timber protection agents etc.)
— static stability can no longer be guaranteed (non-existent documentation, corrosion, inappropriate interventions etc.)
— data unavailable (missing plans / planning permission for the project, unapproved modifications, building geometry etc.)
— damage to parts of building (damp penetration, mould formation, cracks etc.)

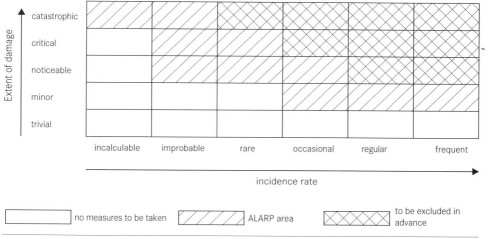

Fig. 14: Riskograph using the ALARP method

— preservation measures not addressed (adaptation to current regulations needed)
— domestic services (ramshackle piping, lack of spare parts, adaptation to current regulations etc.)
— fire protection requirements (upgrading, compensatory measures, replacement etc.)
— and so on

This is why is it necessary to assess the building land and any existing building where appropriate carefully at the beginning of the project, in order to minimise the greatest of these risks.

Major uncertainties in terms of keeping within the costs as fixed frequently arise as a result of setting the project budget early and on the basis of insufficient data. Fluctuation in the area- or volume-related parameters arise because no reference has been made to cost factors as described above, and in addition to this qualities are often described imprecisely in the early stages, e.g. "average quality", which leaves considerable scope for interpretation.

Costing risks

Fig. 15: Example of a risk assessment

Risk	Cost	Effect/ consequence	Percentage risk	Risk costs
Building permission not granted	EUR 70,000	End of project due and previous planning	30%	EUR 21,000
Subsoil not loadbearing	EUR 40,000	Ground improvement needed	25%	EUR 10,000
Steel price rises	EUR 80,000	Tender prices have to be adjusted	10%	EUR 8,000
Shell contractor declared insolvent	EUR 250,000	Increased price as a result of delay and new contractor	3%	EUR 7,500
...	...	...	...	...

Risk assessment methods

The first key basis for assessing cost risks involves addressing possible risk areas. While it is possible to reduce uncertainty through early analysis and expert reports, risks cannot be definitely ruled out until completion and the final invoice. So possible risks areas have to be recorded from the outset, assessed in terms of damage caused and the incidence rate, and then observed throughout the process and the assessment updated in order to guarantee complete risk management. As this involves considerable effort and expense, risk must be assessed in direct relation to the project and an agreement reached about the level of detail and assessment to be taken as a basis.

Now usually only a few potential dangers actually emerge during the planning and building process, so it is not very helpful just to add up the possible risk costs. So the risk budget can be assessed using various mathematical processes, but this depends to a very large extent on the client's risk awareness. One possibility is to present the risks using the following formula:

$$\text{Risk budget} = \sqrt{C_{\text{Risk 1}}^2 + C_{\text{Risk 2}}^2 + C_{\text{Risk 3}}^2 + \ldots}$$

Risk buffer

One typical approach in dealing with costs risks is to build in a risk buffer. This can be placed in the costing as a cost item or planning in optionally as a possibly quality reduction. > fig. 16

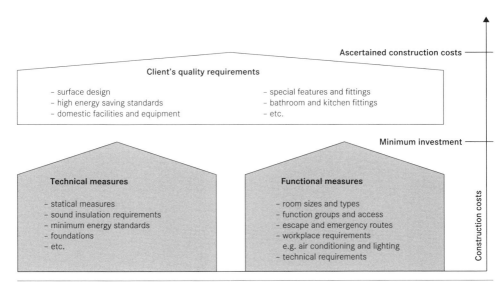

Fig. 16: Buffering cost fluctuations

In this way, modules are identified that can be used for buffering should a risk occur. These are usually based on finishing requirements for the later stages of the project such as floor coverings, external facilities etc. Essential basic requirements for this method are:

— the client's agreement
— the cost relevance of the selected construction elements
  (for example, the quality of the toilet walls offers only a very small buffer in a EUR 20 million project)
— that the contract has not yet been awarded (if parts of an agreed building contract are cancelled, further payments still have to be made to the building contractor)

Unforeseen costs can be dealt with by, for example, building in phases, fixing optional building stages (e.g. developing the attic storey), keeping alternatives open in the case of major cost factors (PVC floors, granite floors etc.). The saving potential of these buffers has to be calculated and a final date set for when each option within the process is freely available. > fig. 17

Fig. 17: Example of modular risk buffering

Cost module	Overall module cost	Saving potential	Available until
Addition of two garages and possibly carport	EUR 18,000	EUR 15,000	March 2014
Extending attic storey, possibly only insulating ceiling	EUR 30,000	EUR 12,000	July 2014
Ashlar floor covering, or linoleum	EUR 25,000	EUR 12,000	August 2014
Exterior garden development, or possibly only grass	EUR 50,000	EUR 20,000	November 2014

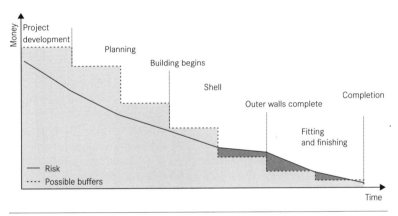

Fig. 18: Risks and buffers compared

Risks and their financial implications, and their savings potential, can be compared directly in this way, and related to a timescale. This also shows up corresponding gaps in cover provision. > fig. 18

Costing methods

There are various ways of drawing up costings. The choice of method depends on the project phase concerned or the depth of planning achieved. The fundamental principle is that costing figures are always multiplied by a unit of quantity in order to be able to make a statement about the costs to be expected. > see chapter on costings For example, the more detailed the available information about the quality of wall and floor surfaces or technical domestic equipment standards, the more precisely this can be taken into account when costings are being drawn up. There is usually not much available in terms of detailed information at the beginning of a project, as this has still to be established in agreement with the client or the various specialist planners in the course of the planning process. But the amount and type of space needed is usually fixed from the outset, as this is clear from the intended use or from the prescribed spatial programme, which means that appropriate cubic capacity and floor areas can be worked out and costs calculated. The more details about the planned building are fixed, the more possible it should be to produce detailed costings. The various costing methods and their application potential for various project phases are described below.

COSTING BASED ON CUBIC CAPACITY

One costing possibility in the very early stages of a project is to calculate the cubic capacity of the building and to multiply it by a cost figure.

Cubic capacity is derived from the area of the building and its height from the foundation of the floor slab to the top edge of the roof covering. In Germany, cubic capacity parameters are defined precisely in DIN 277, which calculates them as gross cubic capacity (GCC). Costing figures can be obtained from national building cost information services (> literature chapter), who record and evaluate these statistically by project type, finishing standard and use. > fig. 20 It is also possible for individuals to devise or set up their own costing systems, provided that a large number of projects of the same type, similar size and finishing standard have been planned, built and budgeted for. In such cases the building costs are finally worked out at the end of the project and then calculated back to the cubic capacity of the building as a rough reference unit. It is essential to ensure that uniform references are made to cost values and quantities. Construction costs calculated from the cubature of the building always remain imprecise, as it is necessary to rely on very rough assumptions about construction quality and to an extent about quantities as well, and it may well be that no definitive building design is available. Direct

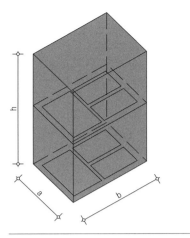

Fig. 19: Calculating the gross cubic capacity

links with cost factors are also not available. > chapter on costings So working out the expected building costs based on gross cubic capacity is simply a planning instrument for defining building targets in terms of quantity and quality.

If the gross cubic capacity needed for a building project has already been fixed, it is then possible to check the essential feasibility or financial viability of a construction project by using product-specific cost figures. Following the minimum principle > chapter on concepts and structures, the quantities here are provided by the gross cubic capacity and the qualities by the choice of the project-specific cost figure. But by the client can follow the maximum principle and name a certain sum for construction expenses as the target cost specification, which will then make it possible to aim for the maximum building size that can be achieved and/or the best possible qualities and finish characteristics within the costs as fixed.

Example 1:
Specifying the gross
cubic capacity An investor wants to erect a new office building. The gross cubic capacity is laid down by the maximum size of building allowed on the plots, which is 3000 m³. The investor provides the architect with rough information about the desired standard of finish and the material quality of the building. But as no definite plans have yet been made for the office building, the architect can draw up a costing only on the basis of the information provided by the investor. The architect has no costings of his or her own derived from similar buildings, and so turns to a information service to find a comparable property that is closest to the design ideas and the requirements for the new building. > fig. 20

Fig. 20: Costings for average standard office and HQ buildings

Office and HQ buildings, average standard
Costings for building construction and technical features and fittings
15 properties for comparison of 30, see property information
GCC of 2,200 m³ to 29,000 m³, GFA of 780 m² to 9,500 m², UA of 580 m² to 7,500 m²

Reference unit	Lower value	Average value	Higher value
GCC	EUR 300/m³	**EUR 375/m³**	EUR 475/m³
GFA	EUR 1250/m²	**EUR 1500/m²**	EUR 1750/m²
UA	EUR 2000/m²	**EUR 2500/m²**	EUR 3000/m²

It is usual to give certain price ranges (from ... to ...) for the cost parameters. If no further clear and detailed information about the building is available it is advisable to use the average cost figures at first and make the client aware of the fluctuation ranges by means of additions and deductions.

Gross cubic capacity × costing = building costs to be expected
3,000 m³ × EUR 375/m³ = EUR 1,125,000

The given cost figures actually lie between EUR 3000/m³ and EUR 475/m³. So the fluctuation is moves between EUR 225,000 downwards and EUR 200,000 upwards.

An investor lays down a fixed investment sum of EUR 800,000 for a new office building. As he wants to let the building later, he wants the architect to provide some information about the maximum built area he can aim to achieve. Costings can be researched via standards fixed as in example 1, and this means that details about the gross cubic capacity that can be realised can also be obtained. The following calculation does not represent an actual costing, but is an important planning instrument in the early project phase.

Example 2: Specifying the construction costs

The GCC that can be realised for the office building is estimated as follows:

Fixed investment sum: cost value =
possible gross cubic capacity
EUR 800 000 : EUR 375/m³ = approx. 2133 m³

The architect should inform the investor about corresponding consequences for the gross cubic capacity that can be realised on the basis of the costs, which extend from EUR 300/m³ to EUR 475/m³ > fig. 20. So the fluctuation range for the estimated possible gross cubic capacity is between approx. 2,666 m³ and 1,684 m³.

Example 3:
Specifying the gross
cubic capacity and
the building costs

It is not unusual for the client to prescribe both the desired cubic capacity and also a fixed budget for the building costs to the architect. If this is the case, a costing can be calculated by dividing the target costs by the desired cubic capacity, and this will give some insight into the quality that can be achieved or whether the project can be realised at all.

The client would like to erect an office building with a gross cubic capacity of 3,500 m³ for EUR 800,000. The following equation makes it possible to calculate a project-specific costing.

Fixed investment sum:
gross cubic capacity = costing
EUR 800,000: 3500 m³ = approx. EUR 228/m³

Now the architect has to set the calculated cost against the other properties available for comparison in order to check whether the client's ideas can be realised at all. The lowest cost for comparable office buildings is EUR 300/m³ of gross cubic capacity. > fig. 20 If the calculated cost falls within the price fluctuations for the comparable properties, the building project can definitely be realised in the form desired. If, as in the sample quotation, the calculated cost falls clearly below that of the comparable properties, then the architect's targets are questionable. In this case the architect and the client can decide whether to concentrate on keeping to the target costs or to the desired gross cubic capacity, as it seems that the project cannot be realised within the target costs. If the desired gross cubic capacity still has to be achieved, the target costs will have to be corrected upwards. If the client is prepared to scale the project down, the architect can follow example 1 and use a realistic costing to calculate the gross cubic capacity that can be realised.

Calculating construction costs by using the cubic capacity of a building, as shown in the examples, is a very flexible planning instrument for
early project phases without a definitive building design. But the results
must always be treated critically, and system-related fluctuations should
definitely be pointed out.

Typical imponderables for this method are:

Information provided by participating specialist planners or local authorities can greatly influence costs at the later stages of the project, and
these are often not predictable in the early stages. Alongside costing fluctuations and unclear definitions of the desired qualities for the standard
of finish, changing the storey heights that have been accepted can have
a great influence on the building costs as calculated. Changed ceiling or
floor heights can influence the gross cubic capacity. It can be necessary,
according to how high the standard for the technical installations in a
building is to be (bus system, ventilation plant etc.), for additional installation levels such as double floors and false ceilings to be required. This
means that, given a planned clear room height of 3.00 m, the necessary
storey height can easily vary between 3.40 and 4.50 m. Without using a
specialist planner who can undertake to set the dimensions for the installation levels, it is not possible to settle the actual storey heights, and
thus the height of the building, finally in the early project phases. But this
considerably affects building costs.

On the other hand, increasing the gross cubic capacity does not have
to go hand in hand with a catastrophic increase in costs.

For a factory hall (e.g. with dimensions of 20 m × 80 m × 9 m), increasing the height of the building by a metre affects the building costs less,
as the cost factors for the foundations or floor slab and the roof structure remain the same, and only the facade area is increased by 200 m².
> fig. 21 So in the building itself it is essentially only the adapted "air space"
that becomes larger, but this cannot be seen as increasing the cost.

○ **Hint:** The costings for gross cubic capacity should not be calculated from an average value for a typical building typology alone. If an office building is being planned, for example, information from building cost information services will usually list several properties for reference, differing in size and design. Here the architect should use the costs for the building project that he or she feels most closely resembles his/her own. Information about individual properties for com-parison can be taken from the property details. Given inadequate links with the actual cost factors at the building elements level, the correct choice of property for comparison is the only way of keeping any state-ment about costs as realistic as possible.

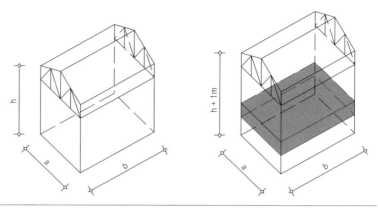

Fig. 21 Factory halls with the same area and different gross cubic capacity

COSTING BASED ON FLOOR AREA AND USABLE AREA

Another way of calculating construction costs involves calculating the floor area or usable area and multiplying that by a relevant cost figure. Here the height of the building is more or less ignored. This makes it all the more important to use costings for comparable properties with similar absolute storey heights (including structural superstructure for foundations, intermediate floors and roofs). In the same way, costing based on floor area and usable area is of only limited usefulness for working out reliable or robust statements about the costs that can actually be anticipated, given that here – as is also the case for calculation based on gross cubic capacity – there is no direct link with the cost factors. It is best to see this costing method in combination with costing based on gross cubic capacity and building- or use-specific conversion factors as a planning instrument for the early phases of the project. In any case it is advisable to compare the results from the volume- and area-related costing methods, as in this way the results can be checked and it becomes possible to aim for a realistic approximation to the actual building costs. Costing based on floor area and usable area is explained with examples.

Costing based on gross floor area   Determining the expected construction costs based on the gross floor area uses similarly simple calculation methods to those used previously for gross cubic capacity.

As has been pointed out already, there is no direct connection between costing figures and the actual cost factors. Factors contributing

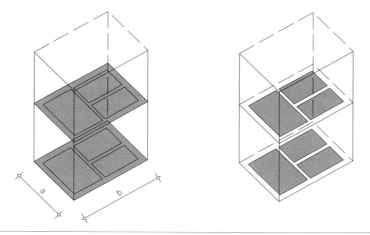

Fig. 22: Calculating floor area and usable area

to increased costs such as additional lift equipment, for example, additional staircase cores providing for shorter routes through the building or especially high ceiling and floor superstructures that are required because the standard of the technical fittings has been raised are not considered separately. As is also the case for the gross cubic capacity method, the costings for gross floor areas can be included in the construction cost planning in a variety of ways.

Here the following possible approaches can be used:
1. The necessary gross floor area is laid down directly by the client or the gross floor area that can be realised on the plot is established and the construction costs are calculated by multiplying them by the costs.

2. The client sets a prescribed target cost. The gross floor area that can be realised within the cost framework is calculated by dividing the target costs by an appropriate cost figure (taking the desired qualities into account).

An investor intends to put up an office building with a gross floor area of 3000 m². He asks the architect to estimate the building costs entailed so that he can raise the finance. The architect researches costings for comparable properties intended for the same use and of the same size (obtaining this information from construction cost enquiry services or from his own experience of such costing), and is thus able to prepare a first rough statement about the building costs. An average price of

Example 1:
Specifying the gross floor area

EUR 1,500/m² GFA is to provide the basis for the calculation, and subsequent fluctuations with additions and deductions are to be considered when estimating the costs. > fig. 20

Gross floor area × costing figure =
expected building costs
3500 m² × EUR 1500 /m³ = EUR 4,500,000

The result of the calculation comes out at EUR 4,500,000 and can deviate up or down by up to EUR 750,000 in each case on the basis of the costings referenced.

But if the client specifies terms based on target costs or the gross floor area and the target costs, simple calculation methods as in examples 2 and 3 can be used based on the gross cubic capacity.

Calculation based on the usable area

■ The calculation of construction costs based on the gross floor area of a building, as described above, is very easy for the architect to use, and also readily comprehensible. But most clients are not property experts, and so can make relatively little of planning costs calculated in this way. In the case of private housing construction and rented office property the areas that can be actually used or let are placed in the foreground, as it is based on these that later use or later income and profit can be determined. A cost estimate relating to the usable area (UA) will be more accessible to the client as he is familiar with his actual use-specific area requirements from his own experience, and can thus evaluate a project better in terms of economic viability in this way. The client can give the architect specifications for the usable area relatively easily by referring to previous area requirements and any increase that is necessary for the future. But it is not unusual for much more abstract specifications to be given, based for example on the necessary number of employees laid down by a company (e.g. at least 1500 employees in single offices), the number of beds required in a hotel, or on a particular number of single or double rooms in hospitals.

> ■ **Tip:** In any costing, the upper and lower values should be listed in the calculation, so that system-related fluctuation ranges in the costing method can be seen. If the architect provides the client with nothing but a single figure for the possible construction costs, that figure is made to seem unduly significant.

If, as mentioned above, the client gives the architect much more abstract specifications, then the architect must establish the area needed in each case and the usable area required for this, as this is the parameter that is relevant for his construction planning. Construction costs calculated by reference to area or cubic capacity can then be recalculated retrospectively to relate to project-specific abstract reference factors, so that the client can always keep an eye on this in the contexts of financial viability checks. Area requirements and conversion calculations made in relation to particular reference points should always be worked out in close agreement with the client.

A client intends to erect an office building for 600 employees. As well as individual offices for the employees, the client says that, exactly as in his present office building, approx. 400 m² of additional area is required for toilets, corridors, foyer, kitchens, storage etc., and a further four conference rooms each of 60 m². The architect works on the basis of simple cubicle offices, each with an area of 14 m². Given the same economical use of space as in the present building and the additional conference rooms required in the new building, the following calculation for the usable area emerges:

Example 1:
Specifying the
number of employees

Area required/employees × number of employees +
additional area required = usable area
$14 \, m^2 \times 600 + 400 \, m^2 + (4 \times 60 \, m^2) = 9040 \, m^2$

Costings for comparable properties come out between EUR 2000/ m² and EUR 3000/m² usable area (average value EUR 2500 /m²). > fig. 20

The expected building costs are calculated as follows:

usable area × costing figure = expected building costs
$9040 \, m^2 \times EUR \, 2500 \, /m^2 = EUR \, 22,600,000$

Regarding the expected building costs, a fluctuation range of EUR 4,520,000 upwards and downwards should be allowed for.

Costing based on the gross floor area of a building is as quick and easy to use as calculation based on gross cubic capacity, but it is equally imprecise. If the usable area required is specified by the client or worked out by the architect, corresponding cost figures can be taken as a basis. But then a decision has to be made when selecting the cost figures about whether similarly economical use of space is possible for this particular project. If the ground plan arrangement and access facilities were to differ significantly, this would create problems in relation to the building costs as calculated. This is why it is particularly important to select com-

Advantages and
disadvantages of
costing based on floor
area and usable area

parable properties correctly. It is also necessary to decide to what extent additional floor space can or may be calculated into the usable area, or the area that can be let out subsequently. Failure to take account of the height of the building when using this method can lead to further imprecision in the case of non-standard storey heights. As almost every building client finds usable area a comprehensible and familiar parameter, it offers the best way of checking specifications and requests, and makes costs readily intelligible. Calculating the building costs to be expected by reference to the usable area can make the result noticeably more precise if applied correctly, as the costing parameters take further information about the financial viability of the space into account. But this concealed information about the financial viability of the space can also bring great imprecision in its wake if no reference objects with appropriately realistic cost parameters are available for concrete comparison, or the depth of planning achieved for the project so far does not make it possible to say anything on this.

COSTING BASED ON COMPONENT ELEMENTS

No reference is made in the above-mentioned calculation methods to the actual cost factors. In the early project phases it is a matter of checking feasibility within a certain cost framework, defining the contract range and developing a building design that conforms to these conditions.

But these rough calculation methods are too imprecise for the later planning stages, which means that a more detailed calculation method is needed. One option here is to calculate the building costs in terms of component elements. But a definitive building design is essential for this, as quantities have to be calculated for the individual structural building components (component elements) needed for the planned building. A uniform procedure must be followed when establishing quantities for the individual component elements. A component element applies to individual parts of the building such as an exterior wall, for example, a ceiling or a roof, and it can be further broken down into <u>construction elements</u>.

○ **Hint:** Basically, the ratio of the usable area to the gross floor area expresses the financial viability of the space. The fewer the construction and traffic areas needed for the same gross floor area, the more economical the building will be.

■ **Tip:** It is rare for a building to use the same component elements all the time. This is why it is necessary to distinguish between possible ceiling, wall and roof structures clearly at an early stage when working out the building costs, as this considerably increases the accuracy of the costing, while only relatively unreliable costing statements can be made without reliable information about the composition of the individual component parts.

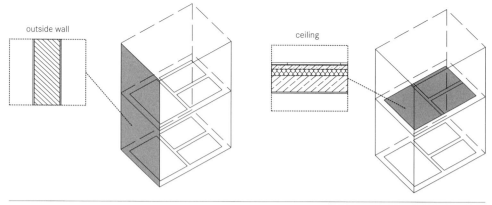

Fig. 23: Outside wall and ceiling as component element

For example, a ceiling as a component element can be made up as follows:

1. tiles, d = 15 mm + adhesive
2. floating cement screed 6.0 cm
3. thermal insulation, footfall sound insulation 5.0 cm
4. reinforced concrete ceiling 25 cm
5. ceiling plaster rendering 1.5 cm
6. paint

The architect proceeds as follows when calculating the building costs to be expected:

The existing design for the building is evaluated by reference to its individual structural components. A table is made of the individual component elements and they are described in more detail if possible. Then quantities are worked out separately for each component element and also entered in the table. > fig. 24 It is possible to use the individual component element descriptions to research appropriately comparable costings through building cost information services, or to use parameters drawn up by the architect or planner. These cost figures now relate to a specific part of the building, rather than simply to a building type. This creates a direct connection between cost factors and cost figures. As well as this, cost figures from various objects for comparison can be cited, as comparability is evaluated by reference to the structural addition. The costings for the individual component elements are multiplied by the established quantities, giving a total for the individual group of component elements (roof, outside wall, inside wall, ceiling, foundations). If individual components are omitted from the quantity survey, this will have a considerable effect on the building costs as calculated. ∎

Fig. 24: Example of a simple costing using component elements allocated to cost groups according to German standard DIN 276.

DIN 276 cost group	Description of component	Quantity, unit of quantity	Cost EUR/unit	Total price in EUR
310	Excavation pit	900 m³	8	7,200
320	Foundations	120 m²	150	18,000
330	Outside walls	200 m²	300	60,000
340	Inside walls	80 m²	150	12,000
350	Ceilings	120 m²	165	19,800
360	Roofs	120 m²	220	26,400
......	....	....	......	....
Total building costs				**230,800**

Advantages and disadvantages of costing based on component elements

Costing based on component elements makes it possible to work out the costs by reference to the cost factors, and is thus considerably more precise than calculation methods using building volumes or areas. But it is difficult to reduce the component elements to a single structural item in each case. The calculation will take a lot more time if the component elements are described and recorded in a sophisticated way, taking all the different structural elements into account. But as has already been pointed out, surface finishes, which affect the cost of a component element significantly, are not specified until much later. Precise building costs can be worked out very quickly and in a very uncomplicated way for very simple buildings with few different structural features. But if a building is planned in a way that is highly individual, technical and architecturally ambitious, calculation by component elements can result in a high potential for imprecision. Like the above-mentioned costing methods, building projects in existing stock are very difficult to illustrate or cost using component elements. A further problem lies in the fact that different specialist areas or craftsmen doing the work are mixed up together when costing for a component element.

The list below shows which skilled workers are already involved in the above-mentioned example of the ceiling:

1. Tiling and slab-work for the floor covering (33%)
2./3. Screed work for the screed including insulation (13%)
4. Concrete and reinforced concrete for the loadbearing ceiling (44%)
5. Rendering and stucco for the interior ceiling rendering (7%)
6. Painting and decorating for the ceiling rendering (3%)

The following skilled work can be needed for an outside wall as a component element:

1. Masonry for the outside wall (65%)
2. Rendering and stucco work for the interior and exterior rendering (27%)
3. Painting and decorating for the facade and for painting the interior wall rendering (8%)

As can be seen from the two examples of component elements for a ceiling and an outside wall, factoring the estimated construction costs into the budget for the individual tendering units is a very fiddly procedure when the project later moves from the planning to the realisation stage. > chapter on work with a skilled-trade oriented costing This is achieved by breaking down the percentage costs of a component element to relate to the individual skills involved. But this approach is questionable, as the percentage cost is very strongly affected by project-specific conditions in the objects chosen for comparison.

COSTING BASED ON CONSTRUCTION ELEMENTS

Costing with the aid of component elements does indeed offer the possibility of working out the building costs based on cost generators, but it leads to imprecision and to problems of application as the project runs its course. This is why a more precise breakdown of the costs, down to the individual construction elements, should be carried out as soon as sufficiently precise information is available about planned structural additions and surface qualities. > see chapter on working with component-oriented costing approaches

Before costing based on construction elements is explained, the concept of a "construction element" should be unambiguously defined. A building element can also be called a fine element, a component, a structural component etc., but these terms cannot be precisely defined. The following explanation is unambiguous: a construction element is a part of a building that can be designated as a component and also assigned to a particular construction skill.

All component elements in a building can be subdivided into individual building elements. An outside wall and a ceiling are shown as examples of component elements in figure 25.

This costing method is based on a building description, which must contain all the construction elements in the planned building. Different costings can be assigned to the individual building elements on the basis

○ **Hint:** This means that a construction element cannot be subdivided further according to its function in the building (e.g. a "wall, non-loadbearing or loadbearing, including doors" can be subdivided into non-loadbearing walls, loadbearing walls, and doors). There are no construction elements that can be assigned to several work areas or tender units – for example, "ceiling plaster with emulsion paint" can be subdivided as construction element one "ceiling plaster, rendering work" and construction element two "emulsion paint, painting and decorating".

○ **Hint:** In the case of a dry construction wall, for example, it is important to have information about the thickness of the wall, details about the materials required for insulation, and also the materials and the thickness required for the planking layers, as this will imply certain fire- and sound-insulation requirements that make a crucial impact on the costs. If a wall consists of two separately constructed partition walls, this also affects costs considerably, as it increases the amount of time needed for the work, and thus the wages to be paid for doing it.

of the qualities as described. As each construction element is defined unambiguously, the costings used for comparison can also be selected very realistically. This construction element catalogue presents all the construction elements in the building in tabular form. In contrast with a room schedule, all the construction elements that are structurally the same are described only once, so that even for large projects the total quantity falls within a manageable framework that is easy to handle. The description should restrict itself to the essential characteristics needed to distinguish between different qualities. But the construction elements must be listed in full, in order to guarantee a precise result for the costing that will be determined later.

Procedure When drawing up the construction element catalogue, the architect goes through the individual cost groups for a building and notes all the relevant construction elements. For example, all the non-loadbearing interior walls are listed and described briefly, along with their qualities and requirements. The same is done for all the other construction elements, such as loadbearing interior walls, loadbearing exterior walls, exterior wall cladding etc. The services required (skill areas needed for the work) should also be identified in this table, not just the cost groups, so that the calculated building costs for individual construction elements can be collated in order to create budgets for the tendering units. In this way, it is easy at any time to move from a building- to a realisation-oriented view within table calculation software. The specified services for the later tender units can be also be summed up project-specifically according to the range of services offered by the contracting firms.

Allocation by rooms It makes complete sense to identify rooms in the construction element catalogue. This is particularly helpful to the client in understanding the planned qualities of the building. Rooms can be identified in groups or by the numbers required. For example, if all the floor coverings in the conference rooms in an office building are identical, floor coverings in other rooms can be unambiguously defined using this description

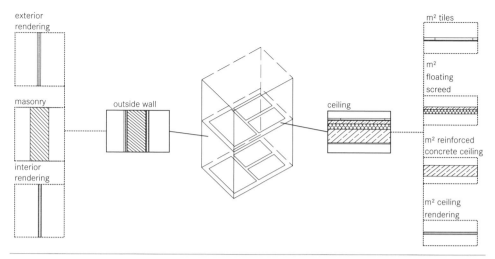

exterior rendering

masonry

interior rendering

outside wall

ceiling

m² tiles

m² floating screed

m² reinforced concrete ceiling

m² ceiling rendering

Fig. 25: Outside wall and ceiling as component elements broken down into construction elements

(e.g. "parquet floor, oak as in the conference rooms"). If the rooms are identified meticulously and fully, the building description will also work as a room schedule, as all the construction elements featuring in a room or group of rooms can be presented clearly. But a table in a construction element catalogue is considerably easier to work with than a room schedule.

Quantities for the construction element catalogue should be established as comprehensibly as possible in a table, so that synergies in deadline planning (duration of all processes) and, above all, quantity calculations can be exploited when going out to tender.

Establishing quantities for construction elements

If the appropriate cost figures are now added to the construction element catalogue, it is possible to proceed with determining the costs. The overall price for a construction element is then arrived at by multiplying the construction element quantity by the cost figure for the building element. The table can then simply be reorganised to calculate either costs for primary component elements or cost group, or also work categories.

Allocating cost figures

The chief advantage of costing based on construction element clearly lies in the additional use that can be made of the calculated costs by re-allocating them in budgets for tendering units for individual craft skills. The building description with construction elements makes it possible to define and adapt the qualities of the building as described more precisely even when the project is under way. Ultimately it forms the basis for draw-

Advantages and disadvantages of costing based on construction elements

Fig. 26: Construction elements catalogue (with cost groups allocated according to German standard DIN 276)

Cost group DIN 276	Construction element Description	Work type
350	**Ceilings**	
351	Reinforced concrete ceiling 20 cm, no requirements for under side of ceilings	Shell
352	Floating cement screed ZE20, thickness 50 mm on footfall insulation 20 mm, rest of structure in thermal insulation PS 20 WLG 035, total height 150 mm	Screed work
352	Parquet, wide oak plank, 22 mm, surface oiled in white	Parquet work
353	Gypsum rendering under the ceiling, average thickness 15 mm	Rendering work
340	**Interior walls**	
341	Reinforced concrete wall 15 cm, no surface requirements	Shell
345	Internal rendering on both sides, average thickness 15 mm	Rendering work

ing up the specifications for individual areas of work. Project-specific qualities, clearly summarised, are easier to understand for the client, as a layperson, than individual items in work specifications, as the construction element always describes the completed structural component and not the work necessary to manufacture it. Despite the high level of detail the structure remains very flexible, as each construction element can be allocated precisely to a cost group (e.g. in Germany according to the third level of DIN 276) and to a work area. > chapter on terms and structures

COSTING BASED ON WORK SPECIFICATIONS

The degree of detail and precision within a cost calculation as described above can be increased considerably by breaking the component elements down into individual building elements. In order to makes things even more precise, it is possible to refine all the information about the individual construction elements that are relevant to cost within the specifications. A specification provides all the relevant information about the individual skills (trades) needed for realising the building, in the form of a set of textual building instructions. The construction element method focuses solely on the completed structure, but costs determined based on work specifications take the way in which the work is realised into account as well. In project-specific terms, the way in which the work is realised can influence costs considerably, as the wages element is correspondingly raised or lowered. These cost factors are not taken into account by the cost determination methods discussed so far.

All the construction elements in a building can be divided into individual service items, which can be summed up in corresponding special-

Fig. 27: Construction element catalogue incl. allocation by room and quantity determination.

| Cost group | Construction element | Work type | Room groups | Quantity |
DIN 276	Description		Room numbers	Quantity unit
350	**Ceilings**			
351	Reinforced concrete ceiling 20 cm, no requirements for under side of ceilings	Shell	Offices and corridors	120 m²
352	Floating cement screed ZE20, thickness 50 mm on footfall sound insulation 20 mm. Rest of structure in thermal insulation PS 20 WLG 035, total height 150 mm.	Screed work	Offices and corridors	120 m²
352	Parquet, wide oak planking, 22 mm, surface oiled in white	Parquet work	Offices and corridors	120 m²
353	Gypsum rendering under the ceiling, average thickness 15 mm	Rendering work	Offices and corridors	120 m²
340	**Interior walls**			
341	reinforced concrete wall 15 cm, no surface requirements	Shell	Staircase	80 m²
345	Inner rendering on both sides, average thickness 15 mm	Rendering work	Staircase	160 m²

ist areas (trades). An example of this is shown in figure 29 for a tile and parquet floor and a loadbearing exterior wall.

○

A specification for laying parquet, for example, would list all the items necessary for preparing the completed floor, including ancillary items (all materials, protective measures, preparing the base, applying adhesive to the parquet, smoothing and oiling the parquet, fitting footboards etc.) for

Example: costing based on specifications

> ○ **Hint:** When determining quantities for individual service items it is essential that the unit prices cited are all based on the same quantity calculation modalities. Different national approaches to calculation can be found here, and a variety of relevant rules can be found. In Germany, calculation modalities are laid down in VOB/C, for example. It may be necessary to convert the unit prices quoted for comparison. In the long term, sustainable documentation and evaluation of unit prices based on individual specification tenders makes it possible for the architect to achieve additional certainty when budgeting.

Fig. 28: Construction element catalogue incl. room allocation, quantity determination and cost figure allocation

Cost group	Construction element	Work type	Room groups	Quantity	Inclusive price	Total price
DIN 276	Description		Room numbers	Quantity unit	EUR/unit	EUR
350	**Decken**					**19,800.00**
351	Reinforced concrete ceiling 20 cm, no requirements for under side of ceilings	Shell	Offices and corridors	120 m²	87.00	10,440.00
352	Floating cement screed ZE20, thickness 50 mm on footfall sound insulation 20 mm. Rest of structure in thermal insulation PS 20 WLG 035, total height 150 mm.	Screed work	Offices and corridors	120 m²	16.00	1920.00
352	Parquet, wide oak planking, 22 mm, surface oiled in white	Parquet work	Offices and corridors	120 m²	47.00	5640.00
353	Gypsum rendering under the ceiling, average thickness 15 mm	Rendering work	Offices and corridors	120 m²	15.00	1800.00
340	**Interior walls**					**12,000.00**
341	Reinforced concrete wall 15 cm, no surface requirements	Shell	Staircase	80 m²	120.00	9600.00
345	Inner rendering on both sides, average thickness 15 mm	Rendering work	Staircase	160 m²	15.00	2400.00

the entire project on all floors. When the specification is complete, the architect can insert average unit prices for the individual items; multiplying them by the quantities determined will then give the total sum required for the parquet work. Once all the specifications for the different work needed to complete the building have been drawn up, the unit prices for the individual services can be added in as well. The individual specification totals then represent one tendering unit at the planning stage before the project is realised. Adding together all the specification totals with their unit prices gives a very realistic view of the total costs to be expected

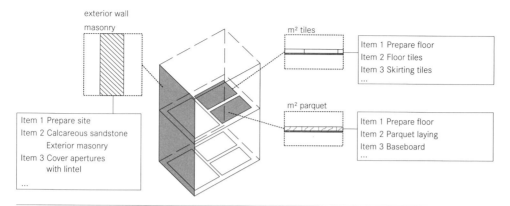

Fig. 29: Construction elements broken down into individual service items

for the project as a whole. The specifications can then also be drawn up in a simplified form, with all the items defined by short titles only.

Costing based on specifications guarantees a reliably realistic statement about the costs to be expected. But this approach assumes that all the qualities and detailed requirements for the planning process have been finally fixed and that all the quantities have been listed without omissions. This means that the method cannot be used or does not provide reliable results in the absence of precise information about the realisation of the project. If planning for the project has not progressed far enough, another costing method should be used instead.

Account must also be taken of the fact that drawing up all the necessary specifications takes a comparatively long time, so the architect has to look at each project phase and decide whether the construction element or component element method might not be the right tool for determining the costs in this case. But if the planning is at a very advanced stage, no additional time will really be needed. On the contrary, costing based on specifications in fact anticipates planning work that the architect has to do anyway as part of putting building work out to tender. The work can be cut down to some extent by using simplified specifications, but the individual work items have to be expanded and adapted subsequently so that they can be used as a basis for seeking tenders from contractors.

In particular cases, costing based on specifications can also be used in combination with other cost determination methods. Individual areas

Advantages and disadvantages of costing based on specifications

123

Fig. 30: Costing for parquet work using a specification

Item no.	Work item Description	Quantity Unit	Unit price EUR	Total EUR
1	Clean the subsurface, remove of sinter layers	500 m²	5,00	2500
2	Glue oak planks 14 cm wide, 22 mm thick, light oak	500 m²	85.00	42,500
3	Oil parquet surface with white-pigmented oil	500 m²	10.00	5000
4	Fit footboard, 20 × 50 mm, MDF, white	500 m²	5.00	2500
5	Fixing skirting boards, 20 × 50 mm, MDF, white	100 m	12.00	1200
6	Cover completed parquet with protective cardboard	500 m²	2.50	1250
7	Apply tolerance compensation filler to concrete steps (110 × 30 cm)	50 Stk.	25.00	1250
8	Glue risers and steps, light oak, 3 cm × 110 cm × 30 cm or 17.5 cm, to match parquet	50 Stk.	150.00	7500
9	Smooth steps	50 Stk.	10.00	500
10	Oil steps with white-pigmented oil	50 Stk.	5.00	250
Parquet work total				**64,450**

of work for which wide-ranging information and thus certainty about planning are available can be described and priced sufficiently precisely based on specifications, whereas cost determination based on construction methods can make sense in other areas.

○ **Hint:** If the architect is unable to find prices for rare or unusual construction elements in the literature, cost determination based on specifications still offers a possibility for putting one's own figure on a cost. In this way the individual items necessary for creating the construction element are determined and an inclusive price is reached using all the unit prices.

Continuing the budgeting process

There are no circumstances in which a building cost calculation that is set too low from the outset can produce a satisfactory outcome, as it will not be possible either to deliver the desired quality or to complete the full number of rooms required. This is why it is essential to conduct cost planning continuously and in stages in order to work within the project budget and thus keep the client satisfied. The foundation stone for this is laid when the project budget is first fixed. The following describes the project phases into which cost planning can be divided meaningfully and how the insights or results provided should be updated in the next project phase.

BASIC PRINCIPLES FOR CONTINUING AND MAINTAINING THE COST PLANNING PROCESS

As already described in the basic principles for cost planning chapter, the specified cost of keeping to the project budget is usually a key factor in the success of the project. Generally speaking, few points of detail have been settled at the time the decision to go ahead with the project is taken, so costings have to be updated throughout the planning and building process. Almost all the decisions made as the process continues – whether in terms of agreement about design, details, qualities or retrospective changes – will alter the cost structure of the process.

Costs must be fully presented at the point of each key decision by the commissioning client as the project proceeds and handed over as a basis for decisions along with the actual project documents such as plans, for example. The usual decision levels are:

Costing stages

1. Cost framework: deciding to go ahead with the project

The first step the architect takes is to establish whether the general conditions laid down by the client (site use, usable area, cost framework, timeline etc.) can be implemented in terms of the given requirements. In order to establish this s/he uses the development plans to examine whether the plot is suitable for such building and possible exploitation, and checks whether the costings and timeframe provided are realistic – without going as far as to produce a design. If it really is possible to realise a building within these project parameters, the necessary aids to decision-making are submitted to the client, who decides how the designs should be drawn up. This has major financial consequences, because the given parameters will form a basis for consulting and commissioning various building and specialist planners, and also experts in particular fields.

It is essential to check at this stage whether the specified cost and the desired usable area are statistically realistic, by reference to sample projects for which budgets have been calculated.

2. Estimating costs: deciding about the design idea/ the preliminary design

After the architect has developed a first design idea s/he will present this to the client and, where appropriate, provide alternatives to help in making the decision. The client now has to decide whether to go ahead with the preliminary design, or which alternative should be pursued. In order to do this, s/he needs information about whether the design that has been devised can be realised within the specified cost, or which alternative will generate which construction costs. Fixing the design idea will make a considerable financial impact to the extent that approving the design represents a move towards design planning that might be acceptable for realisation, but basically is not being questioned in full.

So at this stage architects draw up the costs in with reference to the design by using volume- or area-related costings, or better by using costings that have already been compiled with reference to construction components/elements backed up by quantity surveying.

3. Calculating costs: deciding about submitting the application to build

Once the design has moved forward and been thoroughly planned to the extent that it is "adoption-ready", the client has to decide whether s/he wishes to realise it as presented, and so is ready submit the building application to the responsible authorities. In this respect, the building application generates facts, as the building permission granted on the basis of it reflects the design as it is to be realised, so if changes are required they have to be submitted to the authorities for approval.

At this stage, costs are compiled with reference to the design using cost figures based on construction components/elements backed by quantity surveying. This compilation is more detailed than at the last stage, as considerably more information about the project and the shape it is taking is available as a basis for costing.

4. Estimating costs: deciding to go to tender and fix the agreed construction work

After building permission is granted, preparations are made to put the building work out to tender, and for the actual realisation of the building. This is done drawing up descriptions of the work needed and where necessary providing final plans/details according to the chosen tendering and awarding procedure. Planning precision is enhanced by the degree of detail provided by the quality requirements in the tender's global description sections, and then by drawing on the detailed specifications, and this can lead to marked changes in the costs. After the documents have been submitted there is very little scope for making relevant changes, particularly in the case of public commissions. Thus fixing the "agreed construction work" is crucial within the tender process.

At this stage the costs are presented in terms of construction elements. This is based on structural components at first, by analogy with the level of detail in the tender documents, and is then reformulated with a view to contract award. So when single assignment awards are being made, budgets presented using single award units are easy to break down and easy to check when offers are submitted.

5. Comparing prices: deciding how to award the building work contract

After all the responses to the tender have come in and are available for consideration, the client has to decide which contractor s/he is going to commission to carry out the building work. The architect's examination of the tenders provides a basis for this: the client compares the prices and assesses deviations, variant solutions etc., and then makes a recommendation awarding the contract. Awarding the contract to a single contractor or to several single craft firms (trades) represents a significant milestone in the cost development, because after the contract has been awarded, any changes to the building programme have to be accounted for financially in consultation with the building firm. If the client takes out or cancels single items of work, payment still usually has to be made to the contractor, as the latter must receive either complete payment minus any saved expenditure or at least a profit claim based on the sum contracted.

The architect usually processes the tenders by comparing the single tender prices offered by the various contractors against each other. > fig. 31

6. Establishing costs: determining the actual costs

Once all the building work is finished and audited and final accounts have been presented, the lead architect brings all the costs generated together in a cost statement. This is useful for the architect's own work on concluding the project, and also as information for the financing individuals or institutions or the client's auditors. So for example the bank providing the finance or an internal auditor on the client's side can check whether the monies that have been transferred have been used for the correct purposes in the building programme.

Fig. 31: Example of a price comparison

			Tender 1		Tender 2		
Item	Work involved	Quantity	Unit price	Total price	Unit price	Total price	...
01.001	Site preparation	Flat rate	EUR 200.00	EUR 200.00	EUR 450.00	EUR 450.00	
01.002	Ceiling rendering	60 m²	EUR 19.00	EUR 1140.00	EUR 22.00	EUR 1320.00	
01.003	Interior wall rendering	40 m²	EUR 25.00	EUR 1000.00	EUR 20.00	EUR 800.00	
01.003	Exterior wall rendering	40 m²	EUR 42.00	EUR 1680.00	EUR 46.00	EUR 1840.00	
01.004	...	...	...	...	...	...	...
...	...	...	...	...	...	...	...
...	...	...	...	...	...	...	...
	Total price						...

Fig. 32: Example of a list of decisions and changes

No.	Date	Decision/change	Approved/ rejected	Affects costs	Costs increased (+) Costs reduced (−)
1	10.03.14	Patterning on the tile product by client	yes	yes	EUR −1535.00
2	20.03.14	Change of tile colour	yes	no	0.00 EUR
3	25.04.14	Amendment 01 for compensating for the uneven ground	no	yes	EUR +2670.00
...	...	...	...	...	...

Cost control   Every cost determination stage is bound to deviate from its predecessor because new information has come to light, changes have been made or matters have become more concrete. So it is necessary to reconcile the current cost determination stage with the one before it and with the costs as originally specified. Here detailed reasons have to be supplied for any changes to the overall costs and how they can be picked up again if necessary. One way of presenting this via the planning and construction process is to produce a decision list and a list of changes, in which the main events after commissioning relevant to costs are listed chronologically. > fig. 32

Sometimes the client or the project managers will insist that every decision or request for change by the client that is relevant to costs must be assessed and shown to the client. This makes for precise documentation of the cost-relevant processes.

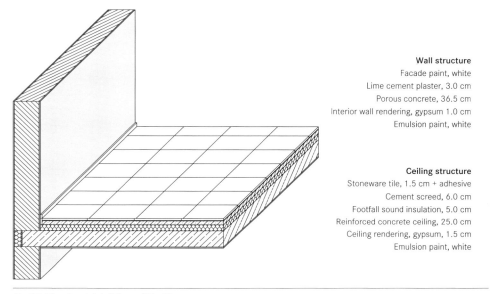

Wall structure
Facade paint, white
Lime cement plaster, 3.0 cm
Porous concrete, 36.5 cm
Interior wall rendering, gypsum 1.0 cm
Emulsion paint, white

Ceiling structure
Stoneware tile, 1.5 cm + adhesive
Cement screed, 6.0 cm
Footfall sound insulation, 5.0 cm
Reinforced concrete ceiling, 25.0 cm
Ceiling rendering, gypsum, 1.5 cm
Emulsion paint, white

Fig. 33: Structural detail for wall/ceiling

The aim is to put the client in a position to think over his or her deci- Controlling
sions, and where appropriate to compensate for them by taking other interventions
measures. For example, this could entail reducing the quality of finish
elsewhere, reducing the usable area or providing additional financial
resources. It is essential here that the client be informed immediately or
at a time close to the decision about which past arrangements have led
to which consequences, and not simply be given a summary in a later
project revision. So this work is not restricted to particular cost determination stages, but must accompany the process and be carried out
continuously.

WORKING WITH COST DETERMINATION BASED CONSTRUCTION ELEMENTS IN THE PLANNING PHASE

If a costing relating to construction elements is drawn up during the Groundwork in the
design process, it will not usually contain much specific information about preliminary design
precise qualities and surface finishes. This is because materials and surface qualities tend to be decided on successively in the course of the
planning process. So in the first place costs are worked out by working
on general assumptions about quality. > figs. 33 and 34

Fig. 34: Simple costing based on construction elements for figure 33

Component		Quantity	Unit	Inclusive price (EUR/unit)	Total price
Ceiling					
	Tiles	60	m²	80	EUR 4800.00
	Floating screed	60	m²	25	EUR 1500.00
	Reinforced concrete ceiling	60	m²	115	EUR 6900.00
	Rendering	60	m²	19	EUR 1140.00
	Paint	60	m²	4	EUR 240.00
				Total	**EUR 14,580.00**
Wall					
	Facade paint	40	m²	13	EUR 520.00
	Exterior rendering	40	m²	42	EUR 1680.00
	Masonry	40	m²	105	EUR 4200.00
	Interior rendering	40	m²	25	EUR 1000.00
	Interior paintwork	40	m²	4	EUR 160.00
				Total	**EUR 7560.00**

Clients will often have said nothing at all about individual materials or quality, so that the architect has to set a first general quality standard. The client will then see from these listings what standard the architect is working from, and what general quality standards the architect has used when determining the construction costs.

Continuing the planning process

Decisions are made and details are regularly clarified throughout the planning process, in meetings with the client, for example, so that these can then be incorporated into the current costing. > fig. 35 Cost changes can then be identified directly and passed on to the client by matching

● the qualities laid down in the list to the relevant costing figures.

● **Example:** In the exploratory phase of the preliminary design, decisions made by the client and the architect are usually based on broad creative themes within the design. But then the client says that she or he wants to see a "good average standard". Then the architect, when determining costs, will accept simple parquet as a floor covering, without any further specific details at first, tiles costing an average sum, and gypsum rendering, painted white, for the surface finish.

Fig. 35: Concrete detail for cost determination based on construction elements

Component	Construction element	Quantity	Unit	Inclusive price (EUR/unit)	Total price
Ceiling					
	Stoneware tile 30 × 60 cm, anthracite, laid using the thin bed method, grouting in tile shade, skirting tiles	60	m²	80	EUR 4800.00
	Cement screed as floating hot screed, d = 6 cm, on 5 cm footfall sound insulation	60	m²	25	EUR 1500.00
	Reinforced concrete ceiling, in-situ concrete, d = 25 cm, shuttering, reinforcement, underbeams	60	m²	115	EUR 6900.00
	Sprayed ceiling rendering, gypsum rendering, d = 1.5 cm, pre-treatment of floor	60	m²	19	EUR 1140.00
	Indoor emulsion paint, ceiling, white	60	m²	4	EUR 240.00
				Total	**EUR 14,580.00**
Wall					
	Exterior paint for mineral substrates, white	40	m²	13	EUR 520.00
	Exterior wall rendering, lime cement plaster, d = 3.0 cm, pre-treatment of floor	40	m²	42	EUR 1680.00
	Masonry wall, porous concrete, d = 36.5 cm	40	m²	105	EUR 4200.00
	Interior wall rendering, gypsum plaster, d = 1.5 cm, pre-treatment of floor	40	m²	25	EUR 1000.00
	Interior emulsion paint, wall, light colour	40	m²	4	EUR 160.00
				Total	**EUR 7560.00**

With this approach the continuation of the costing becomes an iterative planning component because planning decisions are constantly checked, adapted and modified by feedback from the cost management process until a viable solution is found that does justice to the budget. Continuation to the end of the planning phase produces a final project target as a basis for going out to and awarding tender.

Fig. 36: Costing based on contract award

Trade	Construction element	Quantity	Inclusive price (EUR/unit)	Total price
Shell				**EUR 11,100.00**
	Reinforced concrete ceiling, in-situ concrete, d = 25 cm, shuttering, reinforcement, underbeams	60 m²	115.00	EUR 6900.00
	Masonry wall, porous concrete, d = 36.5 cm	40 m²	105.00	EUR 4200.00
Rendering work				**EUR 3820.00**
	Sprayed ceiling rendering, gypsum rendering, d = 1.5 cm, pre-treatment of floor	60 m²	19.00	EUR 1140.00
	Sprayed ceiling rendering, gypsum rendering, d = 1.5 cm, pre-treatment of floor	40 m²	25.00	EUR 1000.00
	Exterior wall rendering, lime cement plaster, d = 3.0 cm, pre-treatment of floor	40 m²	42.00	EUR 1680.00
Painting				**EUR 920.00**
	Interior emulsion paint, wall, light colour	40 m²	4.00	EUR 160.00
	Indoor emulsion paint, ceiling, white	60 m²	4.00	EUR 240.00
	Exterior paint for mineral substrates, white	40 m²	13.00	EUR 520.00
Screed work				**EUR 1500.00**
	Cement screed as floating hot screed, d = 6 cm, on 5 cm footfall sound insulation	60 m²	25.00	EUR 1500.00
Tiling				**EUR 4800.00**
	Stoneware tile 30 × 60 cm, anthracite, laid using the thin bed method, grouting in tile shade, skirting tiles	60 m²	80.00	EUR 4800.00
			Total	EUR 22,140.00

WORKING WITH TRADE-ORIENTED COST DETERMINATION IN THE TENDERING PHASE

Tender-oriented view   The continuing process of establishing costs changes once the tender documents are drawn up. Up to this point the design and the construction components associated with it have essentially provided the focus, but now definite building jobs are being assigned to one or more contractors, and they will determine the relevant structuring for the costing process.

Fig. 37: Matching up budgets and contract award sums

Trade	Construction element	Quantity	Inclusive price (EUR/unit)	Total price/budget	Contract award price	Deviation
Shell				**EUR 11,100.00**	**EUR 11,460.00**	**EUR +360.00**
	Reinforced concrete ceiling, in-situ concrete, d = 25 cm, shuttering, reinforcement, underbeams	60 m²	115.00	EUR 6900.00	EUR 7140.00	EUR +240.00
	Masonry wall, porous concrete, d = 36.5 cm	40 m²	105.00	EUR 4200.00	EUR 4320.00	EUR +120.00
Rendering work				**EUR 3820.00**	**EUR 3620.00**	**EUR −200.00**
	Sprayed ceiling rendering, gypsum rendering, d = 1.5 cm, pre-treatment of floor	60 m²	19.00	EUR 1140.00	EUR 1020.00	EUR −120.00
	Sprayed ceiling rendering, gypsum rendering, d = 1.5 cm, pre-treatment of floor	40 m²	25.00	EUR 1000.00	EUR 1080.00	EUR +80.00
	Exterior wall rendering, lime cement plaster, d = 3.0 cm, pre-treatment of floor	40 m²	42.00	EUR 1680.00	EUR 1520.00	EUR −160.00
...	...	...	...	...	...	...

So the costing table, which has previously been based on structural components, is re-sorted so that the individual structural components are subordinated to the contract units or trades. As described in the chapter on costing methods, costing based on construction elements, the essential requirement is that each construction element can be properly allocated as a structural component, or to a trade as a contract award unit.

Summing up the individual structural elements as a contract award unit makes it possible to create contract award budgets that can be compared directly when submitting and assessing the offers. This listing forms the basis for keeping an eye on costs throughout the building phase.

Creating contract award budgets

If a contract is awarded to individual craftspeople, then over- or under-spending on the contract award budget as calculated can be compensated for by subsequent contract awards during the building process. > fig. 38

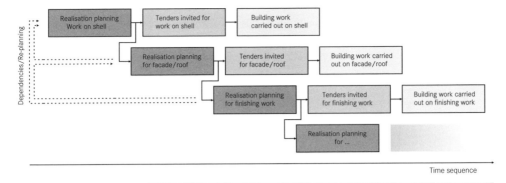

Fig. 38: Typical sequence for planning and contract award during the building phase

COST CONTROL IN THE BUILDING PHASE

When the building contract is awarded the building costs are fixed via the contractual payment agreement as a lump sum, or a provisional one (in the case of settlement or unit price contracts).

This makes it necessary to update and check costs throughout the building period. The client must be informed of significant cost changes immediately so that she or he can intervene to direct matters where appropriate. But minor cost changes are normal, and do not necessarily ○ need intervention and direction.

Structuring cost control
The following cost control sequence is triggered by each award unit: see chapter on working with trade-referenced cost determination in the contract award phase
1. Fixing the budget
2. Invitation to tender and submission of offers
3. Assessment and checking of the contract award sum with the budget specification
4. Cost predictions and cost control during the building process

○ **Hint:** In the case of a unit price contract, payment is made according to the amount of work done. Consolidating payment into a lump sum shifts the risk in relation to quantities to the contractor. This depends on the degree of detail provided in the description of the agreed construction work.

● **Example:** Quite often the ground to be built on is checked only by random test drillings prior to the work. The resultant assumptions about quantities can turn out to be wrong once soil starts to be excavated. If this occurs, the costs should be adjusted correspondingly in the case of unit price contracts.

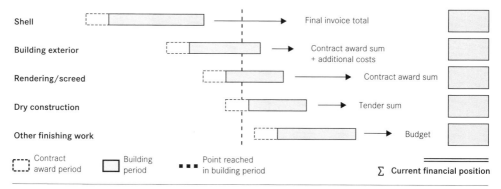

Shell	Final invoice total	
Building exterior	Contract award sum + additional costs	
Rendering/screed	Contract award sum	
Dry construction	Tender sum	
Other finishing work	Budget	

┌┄┐ Contract award period   ☐ Building period   ■■■ Point reached in building period   Σ Current financial position

Fig. 39: Working out the current financial position during the building phase

5. Following up changes in the scope or content of work
6. Cost statement after checking the final invoice

If contracts for the building work are awarded to several firms, this scheme makes it possible to check on each individual contractor in terms of costs. This is because the contractors are all appointed at different times. So it can come about in the course of the building process that individual items of work (e.g. earthworks, shell construction) have been paid off, but later items have not yet even gone out to tender and been awarded. Other jobs may still be in progress. If a current cost estimate is to be made now, then very different situations in terms of contracts awarded and work completed will have to be taken into account. If work has been completed, the final invoice sum will be used here, but where work is still in hand the contract award sums plus known additional costs and deviations from the original agreement in terms of work done will form the basis. Work that has still not gone out to tender will continue within the budget as calculated. As soon as offers or a commission are available, the appropriate sums will be taken from the contract. > fig. 39

Sequence of events with single tenders

This produces a <u>work-related table of costs</u> that can be continued on the basis of the contract-award related costing. The most up-to-date cost data for a piece of work are listed in the last column, so that the sum of this column reflects the current financial position. > fig. 40

Checking contractors' invoices can reveal that the bills of quantities as originally accepted clearly differ from the quantities invoiced. Any quantity deviations for items affecting costs should feature in the table of costs.

Information gained from checking the invoice

●

Fig. 40: Structure of a costs table during the building phase

Job/ contract award unit	Structural elements	Quantity/ units	Budget cost estimate	Contract award sum	Additional costs/Cost prediction	Final invoice	Current financial position
Job 1	Construction element 1						
	Construction element 2						

Incorporating additional sums It is not unusual for work to be listed that is not included in the "agreed construction work", perhaps because it was forgotten when the work went out to tender, was not open to identification, came to light only in the building phase, or was ordered by the client at a later stage. Sums that deviate from the "agreed construction work" (also know as additional payments), can be generated as modifications to work required or delays during the building period, as well as by the above-mentioned quantity deviations. Changes to work required include all changes ordered by the client, plus necessary work, exclusions/partial terminations etc. Costs generated by delays during the building period mean all the additional costs resulting from obstacles to the building process, extending or speeding up the building period.

Demands from contractors for additional payments are checked against the grounds for the claim, whether it is justified, and the amount involved. As a rule, the additional price must correspond with the contract price level. This means that if a contractor has stated a very reasonable price in the tender, the additional price must be correspondingly low. Additional charges are then included in the table of costs, and here it is also possible to distinguish between checked, unchecked and assigned charges. For large projects, separate lists of additional charges are usually kept, and these record and evaluate all additional charges so far incurred chronologically. The totals for all these lists of additional charges are then transferred into the statement of costs.

Cost predictions But it is not only additional costs that make the building process more expensive. Often the site manager will notice things that have not yet been addressed but will or could generate additional costs as the building process moves on. For example, if items were omitted from the invitation to tender, then the costs generated should be built into the cost predictions as soon as they are identified – even if the contractor concerned has not yet made an additional charge.

Fig. 41: Established costs for the client based on contracts as awarded

Job/contract award unit	Total final invoice
Work on shell	EUR 512,134.50
Roof waterproofing work	EUR 64,478.42
Windows	EUR 83,210.00
Rendering	EUR 51,619.36
Rendering work	EUR 12,820.00
Dry construction	EUR 21,143.67
Painting	EUR 10,405.50
Heating/plumbing	EUR 134,685.08
...	...
Total construction costs	**EUR 1,105,680.05**

ESTABLISHING AND ASSESSING COSTS

Once the project has been inspected, approved, and any necessary corrective measures taken, the contractors involved in the project will present their final invoices within a contractually agreed period. These will include all the costs generated by the project on the basis of contractually agreed additional payments, and those that have emerged subsequently. The final invoices are checked for correctness by the architect and amended where applicable.

The costing that documents the actual project costs (> chapter on the basic approach to updating and serving cost planning) is made up of the sum of all the costs incurred and thus represents a survey of all the costs already generated, and represents the final cost determination stage. Usually a list of all the costs in the final invoices is drawn up here and presented as a total sum, and this is usually sufficient information in terms of the client's interest.

Total of all final invoices

If the table structure for the planning and construction process had been updated systematically, the contract-based totals can be re-allocated to the original construction elements without a great deal of effort. This has distinct advantages for the architect, as it means that he or she can assess the project as a whole and thus draw conclusions and determine costs for future projects.

Re-organisation based on structural components

To do this, the sums actually invoiced, including all changes, additional charges etc. are divided by quantities invoiced. When compiling cost figures based on construction elements, care must be taken that all

Compiling cost figures

Fig. 42: Determining costing figures

Job/contract award unit	Heading	Sum due under heading	Quantity invoiced	Inclusive price cost figure
Dry construction				
	Dry-built walls	EUR 24,154.50	517.56 m²	approx. EUR 47.00/m²
	Firewalls	EUR 3468.36	46.50 m²	approx. EUR 75.00/m²
	Suspended ceilings	EUR 11,210.42	214.67 m²	approx. EUR 52.00/m²
	...	...		

the additional constituent elements are added in again. This can be done most successfully if all the essential building components including relevant secondary items are listed under their own headings in the invitations to tender. In this way the specific value can be derived from the invoiced sum under this heading and the total quantity under the main item. > fig. 42

If specific values are to be prepared for component elements, the relevant costs should be totalled from a retrospective cost breakdown based on building parts. To compile costings relating to volume or area, the invoiced construction costs should be divided by the areas and gross cubic capacity that will usually have been determined previously for the building application.

○ **Hint:** It is important for planning practices to set up their own costing databases. Costs derived from their own projects define costs according to the individual quality requirements, constructions and degrees of detail customary for the practice, and are therefore significantly more precise than average statistical values that are generally accessible.

■ **Tip:** Costings should always be entered in a personal database without value added tax, in case this is altered by law. It also makes sense to name the construction year as well, so that cost values can still be used by allowing for inflation and statistical adjustments. Statistics offices in almost all countries keep records of significant price fluctuations in the building sector.

In conclusion

Construction costs are a key element for the client in almost all architectural projects, and determine their success or failure. The aesthetic quality of a building is very important, but it is governed by subjective evaluation criteria – as a layperson, the client can judge a building technically only to a limited extent. But apart from the user-friendliness of a building, keeping to costs and where necessary to deadlines are fixed factors that are extremely important for the client, who can also assess them very readily. Keeping within the planned building costs can always be checked in terms of concrete figures. High creative ambitions and good architectural concepts can be realised and implemented attractively only if they are based on professional budgeting. This ensures that the desired quality will be delivered, but also guarantees that the project as whole is financially viable, and no architecture can be realised if this does not happen. So it is essential for architects to see the subject of costs as an essential planning element, to tie the emerging designs and projects together in a structured way, and to cost them carefully.

Even though the subject of costs is often not an important feature of architectural studies, a competent approach to costs is essential if architects are to be successful in their later professional lives. For this reason the methods and practical procedures are an important building block in architectural studies as a preparation for their subsequent professional lives. Understanding creative design, technical construction, holistic co-ordination and competent budgeting as an iterative process constitutes a good architect's repertoire. Just as the design process cannot be schematised, budgeting is also a project-related heterogeneous process that adapts itself both to the client's special needs and spheres of interest and also understands how to illustrate the shape of a particular project and its specific idiosyncrasies.

Bert Bielefeld

Construction
Scheduling

Introduction

The translation of an initial idea into a completed building is a lengthy and extremely complex undertaking. The large number of people involved – construction contractors, planners and owner-builders – make it necessary to coordinate all the different contributions to the process closely.

Architects and project planners represent the owner in technical matters and must work to ensure that the entire process runs as smoothly as possible. Looking after the owner's interests, they coordinate all the participants in the planning process and monitor the contractors on the construction site. Larger projects often entail twenty to thirty participants or more in the planning and construction processes, which results in complex links and interdependencies. The various participants are often unable to understand or judge how their specific work is linked to the project workflows as a whole. As a result, architects have a special coordinating responsibility since their planning encompasses the entire range of specialized tasks involved in a project, and they are therefore the only participants in the process who have the "big picture."

Scheduling is a tool that is used in all stages of this process. The present book explains its foundations and applications, addressing all forms and depths of representation and providing practical information on typical processes. Its goal is to give students a quick, real-world introduction to the material. Yet coordination work is not over once a schedule has been created. It is a work process that must be constantly updated and made more precise. A good deal of preliminary consideration and refinement of detail is required in order to specify the phases into which work on a site is ultimately organized. The following chapters describe which participants and steps need to be taken into account when creating a schedule.

Creating a schedule

SCHEDULE ELEMENTS

To begin with, a description of a few key terms and the various elements of a schedule is in order.

Planners distinguish between a deadline and a time period. The word <u>deadline</u> describes a specific point in time, such as the day on which part of a project must be completed, while a <u>period</u> is a span of time (e.g. completion of a job within fourteen days).

Period and deadline

<u>Tasks</u> are the very foundation of the schedule and refer to self-contained work units (e.g. tiling the ground floor). If several tasks are combined (e.g. tiling and plastering), the result is a <u>summary task</u> > Chapter Creating a schedule, The structure of the project schedule

Tasks

<u>Task duration</u> is the time needed to complete a task. It is a factor of production quantity and productivity. > Chapter Creating a schedule, Planning task duration

Planning the duration and sequence of tasks

The calculation of duration is referred to as <u>duration planning</u>. Establishing the dependencies between activities is referred to as <u>sequence planning</u>. Taken together, duration and sequence planning form the basis of <u>construction scheduling</u>. > Fig. 1

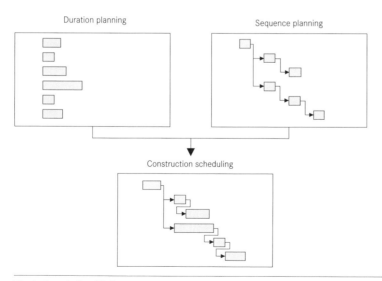

Fig. 1: The relationship between duration planning, sequence planning and construction scheduling

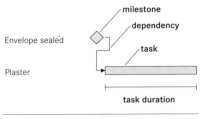

Fig. 2: Typical scheduling terms

Construction methods and resources

Construction method refers to the technical procedure for carrying out a task.

The equipment and labor necessary to perform a task are called resources. While preparing for a building project, construction companies plan their resources in order to calculate costs precisely and define construction methods. The result serves as the foundation for their bid. While calculating resources has only limited significance for the architect doing the scheduling, smooth workflow requires a realistic assessment of task durations, for which resource planning provides a foundation. > Chapter Creating a schedule, Depth of representation

Milestones

A milestone is a task without a duration. It is a special event entered separately into the schedule. Typical scheduling milestones include the start of construction, completion of the building structure, sealing the building envelope, final inspection and putting the building into operation. > Fig. 2

Dependencies between tasks

In most cases, tasks are not isolated items on the schedule but are integrated into a web of dependencies with other tasks. There can be several reasons for this. The normal case is a sequential dependency: task B can only begin once task A is finished (e.g. ground-floor walls → ground-floor ceiling → upper-floor walls).

> ● **Example:** In any construction process there may be many ways to achieve the desired results. For instance, a reinforced concrete ceiling may be built of prefabricated elements or cast on site. Wall tiles can be laid in a thin bed on plaster or in a thick bed on a rough wall.

That said, some tasks can only be performed jointly in a parallel process (e.g. setting up scaffolding floor by floor as the structure of a multistory building goes up). Often these process dependencies can be broken down into sequential dependencies by using a higher level of detail.

By contrast, it is often impossible for finishing contractors to work in parallel during a number of construction phases (e.g. screed and plastering work). In this case we speak of one task <u>interfering</u> with another. This is why it is essential for planners to examine mutual dependencies between specialized tasks and, if necessary, to divide the project into optimal construction phases. > Chapter Creating a schedule, Planning task sequence and Chapter Workflows in the planning and construction process

Various types of relationships play an important role in the graphic representation of dependencies between two tasks. Construction scheduling distinguishes between four types: > Fig. 3

Types of relationships

■

— <u>Finish-to-start</u>: Task B can only begin after task A is finished. This is the most common type of relationship and may apply to activities such as the construction of interior walls (A) and interior plastering (B).
— <u>Finish-to-finish</u>: Task A and task B must be completed by the same time. This type of relationship exists when tasks A and B provide the foundation for an additional task. Examples are installing windows (A) and sealing the roof (B), which create the airtight building envelope necessary for interior work.
— <u>Start-to-finish</u>: Task B must end when task A begins. In this type of relationship, one task can be scheduled at the latest possible point in time before it interferes with another task.
— <u>Start-to-start</u>: Task A and task B must start at the same time. This makes sense if the work can be performed in parallel – if, for instance, workers from one trade can use a crane that is operated by another contractor to deliver large building elements.

○ **Hint:** If sequential dependencies are not examined in detail during scheduling work, the result can often be disruptions and delays in the construction process. If, for instance, a disabled-accessible, steel-framed door needs to be installed, the required electrical outlets must be installed before plastering is done. Overlooking such dependencies may result in further work being required on finished surfaces.

■ **Tip:** The most popular construction scheduling programs support the types of relationships described above. As a rule, they assign each task its own number, which can be used to denote dependencies. For example, if a task needs to begin after task no. 5, the previous task is marked 5FTS, where FTS stands for a finish-to-start relationship.

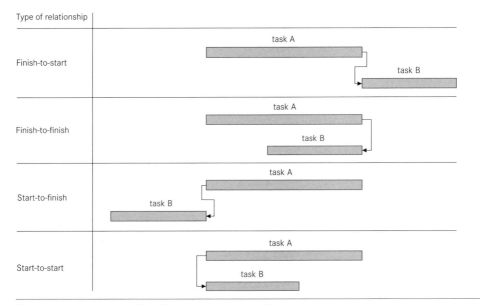

Fig. 3: Schematic diagram of the different types of relationships

FORMS OF REPRESENTATION

There are different ways to represent a schedule graphically. The following forms of representation are used to communicate schedule contents in a clear and useful manner, depending on the goal and purpose of the schedule: > Fig. 4

— Bar chart
— Line diagram
— Network diagram
— Deadline list

Bar chart   In building construction, schedules are normally shown as bar charts, also called Gantt diagrams. Time is charted along the horizontal axis, and the various tasks are listed along the vertical axis. The duration of each task is recorded as a horizontal bar along the corresponding time axis. > Fig. 5

The time axis can be divided into months, weeks and days, depending on project scope and the required degree of detail. In addition to graphically representing activities, this form of schedule commonly in-

146

Bar chart

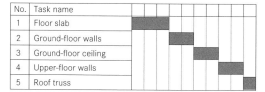

No.	Task name
1	Floor slab
2	Ground-floor walls
3	Ground-floor ceiling
4	Upper-floor walls
5	Roof truss

Line diagram

Network diagram

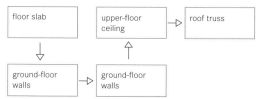

Deadline list

Task	Start	End
Bottom slab	June 1	June 22
Ground-floor walls	June 23	July 7
Ground-floor ceiling	July 8	July 22
Upper-floor walls	July 23	Aug. 6
Roof truss	Aug. 8	Aug. 14

Fig. 4: Different schedule forms

corporates related information in the left-hand column to facilitate easy reading (e.g. task description, starting date, completion date, duration and, if necessary, dependencies with other tasks). Dependencies are often shown graphically as arrows between different bars.

The basic structure of a <u>line diagram</u> differs from that of a bar chart in that the units executed are shown on the second axis next to the timeline. The tasks are depicted by lines in the coordinate system. The following types of line diagrams are commonly used in the construction industry:

Line diagram

— The space-time diagram, which shows the quantity as a geometric segment (e.g. a stage in highway construction);
— The quantity-time diagram, which scales the amount to 100% and shows what percentage of the task has been completed, independent of the actual quantity.

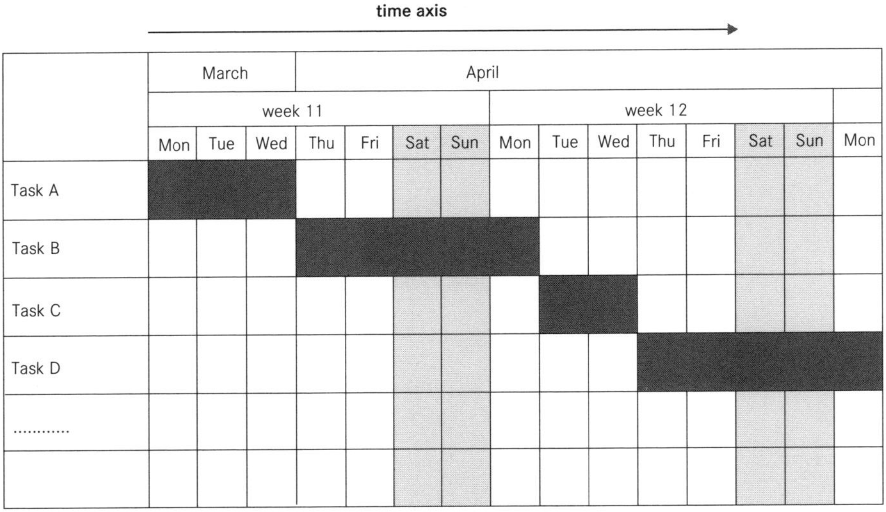

time axis →

	March			April											
	week 11							week 12							
	Mon	Tue	Wed	Thu	Fri	Sat	Sun	Mon	Tue	Wed	Thu	Fri	Sat	Sun	Mon
Task A	■	■	■												
Task B				■	■	■	■								
Task C								■	■						
Task D											■	■	■	■	■
....															

Fig. 5: Bar chart principle

The line diagram is generally used less frequently in building construction than in areas involving linear construction sites such as streets, tunnels and sewage systems, in which the construction steps follow each other in regular cycles. In building construction, many tasks, particularly those done by the finishing trades, must be performed in parallel and cannot be clearly illustrated on a line diagram. Nevertheless, the line diagram does have the advantage of being able to represent target-performance comparisons more clearly. > Fig. 6

A network diagram represents scheduled tasks as networks rather than as items along a time axis. Using this form of schedule, planners can effectively map out the reciprocal links between tasks, but it provides only a limited sequential overview of the entire process.

There are three types of network diagrams; the activity-on-node network is the most popular:

— Activity-on-node: Activities are represented by nodes and dependencies by arrows.
— Activity-on-arrow: Activities are represented by arrows and dependencies by the links between the nodes.
— Event-on-node: Arrows symbolize the dependencies and nodes represent the results (without durations). > Fig. 7

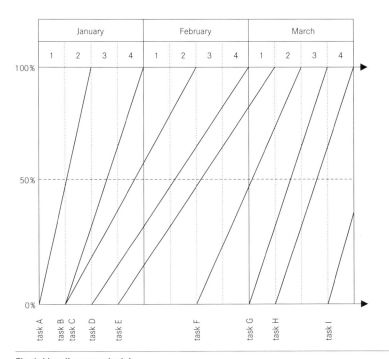

Fig. 6: Line diagram principle

Network diagrams are rarely used to represent construction schedules, but they are often featured in premium construction scheduling software as an additional means of displaying bar charts. As such, they fulfill an important function in schedule creation. Since they allow for more enhanced graphic representation of dependencies between tasks than a bar chart, planning specialists can switch between these two display modes to better orient themselves within the schedule. Tasks can be recorded and assigned durations using bar charts, while mutual dependencies can be checked and represented using network diagrams.

A deadline list is a very simple form of representation. As used in construction scheduling, it presents important deadlines and periods in table form and therefore offers only a limited view of the project. The more deadlines the list contains, the harder it is to read and the more difficult it is for project participants to grasp the interconnections between the individual deadlines.

Deadline list

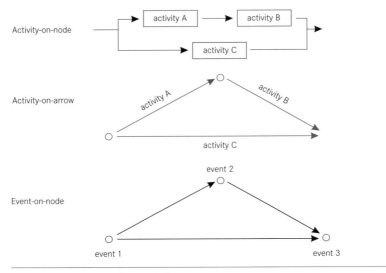

Fig. 7: The various types of network diagrams

Deadline lists are often excerpted from the schedule for the different participants in the planning and construction process in order to inform these parties of important deadlines and time periods. Such information may relate, for instance, to the time needed by planners or experts to do their work or to the contractual specifications of the individual contractors. Lists including construction deadlines are often submitted along with tenders, and they may afterwards be incorporated into the construction contract as contractual deadlines. Many scheduling programs can output deadline lists in separate files based on construction schedules.

DEPTH OF REPRESENTATION

A schedule should always meet the specific requirements of the project concerning clarity, functionality and degree of detail. These requirements may vary widely depending on the perspective taken on the construction project. There are generally three levels of detail in construction processes, all of which reflect this perspective:

— The owner's perspective: establishing deadlines with the help of framework scheduling
— The planner's perspective: coordinating participants with the help of project scheduling

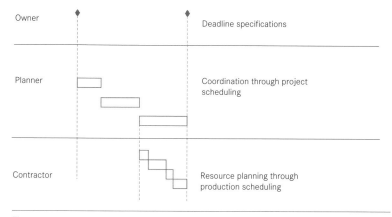

Owner — Deadline specifications

Planner — Coordination through project scheduling

Contractor — Resource planning through production scheduling

Fig. 8: Diagram of deadline specifications, as well as project and production scheduling

— The construction contractor's perspective: preparing work and planning resources with the help of <u>production scheduling</u> > Fig. 8

Furthermore, schedules are also categorized in terms of their time frame (short-term, medium-term, long-term), the person creating them (owner or contractor), and their level of detail (rough, detailed, highly detailed).

Owners usually have a clear idea of when they want or must begin using a building. A department store may need to be completed by the next Christmas season, or the owner may already have given notice on his or her lease and must be out by a certain date. Planners must take into account the <u>deadlines</u> specified by the owner. Often the financial backers of a project (banks) are also the source of deadline constraints. In order to check the owner's ideas about deadlines and roughly structure the entire process, planners create a <u>framework schedule</u> as an initial overview. It contains the broader sets of tasks and the intermediate deadlines of planning and construction. Typical tasks are: > Fig. 9

Framework schedule

— Project preparation
— Design
— Building permit application
— Preparing for construction work
— Start of construction work

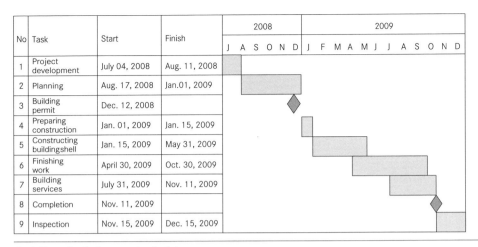

No	Task	Start	Finish	2008						2009											
				J	A	S	O	N	D	J	F	M	A	M	J	J	A	S	O	N	D
1	Project development	July 04, 2008	Aug. 11, 2008																		
2	Planning	Aug. 17, 2008	Jan.01, 2009																		
3	Building permit	Dec. 12, 2008																			
4	Preparing construction	Jan. 01, 2009	Jan. 15, 2009																		
5	Constructing buildingshell	Jan. 15, 2009	May 31, 2009																		
6	Finishing work	April 30, 2009	Oct. 30, 2009																		
7	Building services	July 31, 2009	Nov. 11, 2009																		
8	Completion	Nov. 11, 2009																			
9	Inspection	Nov. 15, 2009	Dec. 15, 2009																		

Fig. 9: Example of a framework schedule

— Building structure
— Building envelope
— Various finishing jobs
— Completion

Project schedule

The <u>project schedule</u> is usually created by the architect, and its objective is to coordinate all the participants in the planning and construction of a building. In order to link the different activities and effectively coordinate the work, the project schedule must have a higher level of detail than the framework schedule. > Fig. 10 The most important factor in combining or separating out tasks is their interdependence. For instance, the building shell often requires a low level of detail since the related tasks are not carried out by different trade contractors and only serve the purpose of deadline control. By contrast, the construction of a drywall may require electrical installations, sanitary installations, door assembly and painting work, which make it necessary to break down the task into several steps. > Chapter Workflows in the planning and construction process, Finishing work As mentioned above, the most effective level of detail in a project schedule generally depends on the project's complexity and time frame.

Moreover, the project schedule should cover the execution of construction work and also integrate the planning phase so that it covers all interfaces. Ideally, the project schedule should be designed in such a way that the various users at the architectural office (construction planning,

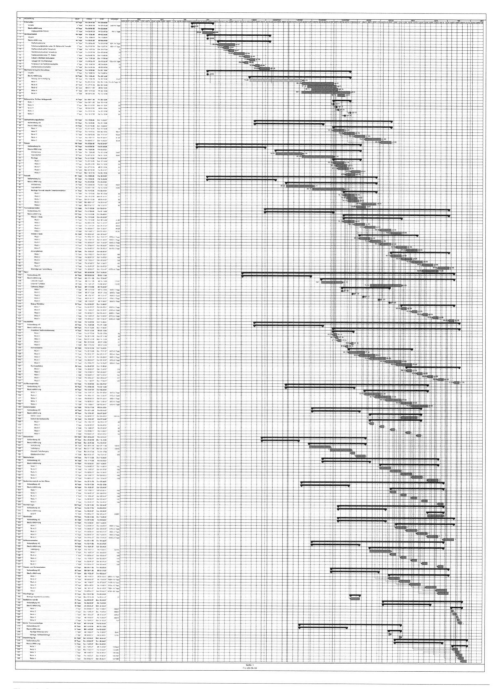

Fig. 10: Sample project schedule

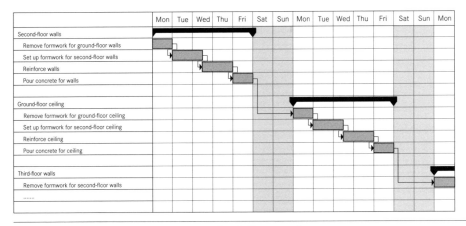

	Mon	Tue	Wed	Thu	Fri	Sat	Sun	Mon	Tue	Wed	Thu	Fri	Sat	Sun	Mon
Second-floor walls															
Remove formwork for ground-floor walls															
Set up formwork for second-floor walls															
Reinforce walls															
Pour concrete for walls															
Ground-floor ceiling															
Remove formwork for ground-floor ceiling															
Set up formwork for second-floor ceiling															
Reinforce ceiling															
Pour concrete for ceiling															
Third-floor walls															
Remove formwork for second-floor walls															
......															

Fig. 11: Example of a repetitive schedule for building shell construction

tendering, construction management) can concisely and clearly display those deadlines that are relevant to their work. > Chapter Workflows in the planning and construction process, Coordinating planning

Production scheduling

Production scheduling has a different objective from project scheduling. While project scheduling is used to coordinate all the project participants, production scheduling is carried out by construction companies to plan personnel, material and equipment resources.

The production schedule adopts deadline specifications from both the framework schedule and the project schedule, and translates them into individual steps in the construction work. This form of schedule enables planners to determine the required number of construction workers and to promptly allocate both equipment and sufficient quantities of material in order to avoid bottlenecks.

The task which the construction company adopts from the project schedule (e.g. a concrete ceiling installed over the ground floor) is broken down into individual steps (placing forms, adding reinforcing steel, pouring concrete, drying, removing forms). It is also assigned the necessary resources. > Fig. 11 Construction companies working on the building shell normally create production plans that can be described as repetitive schedules due to the cyclical nature of the individual work steps. In this case, the construction project is divided into several identical construction phases. Since quantities are identical, companies only need to

154

develop a production schedule for the steps in a single phase and apply it to additional cycles.

Production schedules are used less often in the finishing trades since there are many links between the specialized tasks that place limits on the finishing contractors' ability to organize and schedule the work themselves.

CREATING A FRAMEWORK SCHEDULE

The usual objective of the framework schedule is to examine the feasibility of the owner's deadlines and integrate participants roughly into a plan. When project managers or professional owners participate in larger projects, the framework schedule is often created by the owner and given to planners as a set of parameters.

Depending on the owner's preferences, deadline specifications will take the form of either a directly specified completion deadline or indirectly defined deadlines and periods that participants must observe (e.g. the start of construction in the current fiscal year to give tax advantages). The time span from the start of planning to the completion of the building marks out the framework for the entire planning and construction period.

Deadline specifications from the owner

Dividing the project into planning and construction periods is a crucial step that allows planners to examine whether both parts of the project can be implemented. While the construction period can usually be streamlined using a cushion and it is also possible to optimize the planning period time-wise, there are limits to such optimization efforts. The two phases must meet basic requirements, and related deadlines can be missed by only a narrow margin.

Dividing the project into planning and construction

The start of construction is determined by the availability of the building permit, the related lead times for planning and approval, and the contractual agreement with the construction company. This agreement usually presupposes construction drawings, a call for bids, and the submission of bids from construction companies.

Construction work cannot bypass the typical sequences of the construction process to any significant extent, and there are also limits to the ways it can be organized in parallel sequences.

If a deadline is specified by the owner, the necessary construction period should be calculated backwards from it, or it should be estimated using comparable projects. This approach allows planners to determine when construction needs to start. They must then examine whether plan-

ning requirements can be met in the time remaining between the start of the project and the start of construction. Even when making comparisons with other projects, they should always keep the complexity of the
● project in mind.

If there are grounds for believing that a project is not viable, various alternatives must be considered. For instance, construction time can be shortened by using alternative construction methods (pre-manufacturing, prefabricated parts, materials with short drying times). If the completion deadline is still unrealistic, the problem should be discussed with the owner at an early stage.

Organizing tasks   In addition to dividing the project into a rough planning and construction period, the framework schedule covers a few central planning steps and work sections, presenting them as individual tasks or milestones. > Chapter Creating a schedule, Schedule elements It provides a general overview of the project and ensures that the participants are deployed punctually. Project scheduling generally adds a higher level of detail, but the boundaries are fluid and additionally influenced by the owner's interest in information.

THE STRUCTURE OF THE PROJECT SCHEDULE
Since the project schedule coordinates participants, its rough structure is tailored to their work. The schedule integrates each planner and construction company separately, together with the jobs they do.

Hierarchical structure   Individual tasks are combined to form <u>summary tasks</u> in order to
based on contract   structure the schedule and create a schedule hierarchy. For example,
work packages   individual tasks can be assigned to a component group or to a construc-
■   tion phase group. > Fig. 12

The highest hierarchical level should always be the respective <u>contract work package</u>. The term "work package" refers to the construction jobs that have been contracted out in an agreed planning or construction contract. If a work package involves several trade contractors, each must individually be subordinated to the work package. The advantage of this

● **Example:** It is much easier to evaluate the planning scope and the construction period of a simple hall as opposed to a laboratory building of the same size that will contain sophisticated technical equipment. An additional problem is that a larger number of planners must be coordinated for the laboratory, which increases the risk of disruptions.

■ **Tip:** In most scheduling programs, planners can use summary tasks to structure the schedule by "inserting" tasks at lower levels. The respective lower-level task automatically becomes a summary task, the duration of which is determined by the sum of its subordinate tasks.

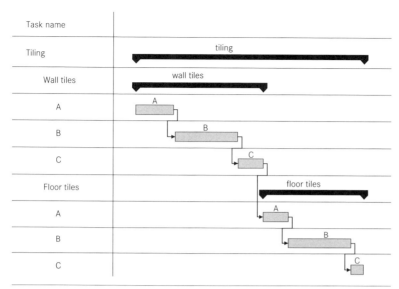

Task name				
Tiling			tiling	
Wall tiles		wall tiles		
A	A			
B		B		
C			C	
Floor tiles			floor tiles	
A			A	
B				B
C				C

Fig. 12: Summary tasks in a schedule

approach is that the hired contractors can be clearly monitored in terms of their individual deadlines and construction jobs. Furthermore, contract award schedules can be created without additional effort and used to establish the deadlines of contract award processes. > Chapter Workflows in the planning and construction process, Coordinating construction preparation, and Chapter Working with a schedule, Updating and adjusting a schedule

The work packages are usually arranged in chronological order according to the progress of construction work. If the construction process is divided into segments, it may include the following broad phases:

Rough phases of an implementation schedule

1. Preparatory measures
2. Building shell
3. Building envelope
4. Interior finishing
5. Building services
6. Final work

These broad chronological phases can be matched to individual work sections (sometimes with overlaps) in order to produce an initial schedule structure. Afterwards, the construction jobs are categorized under the contract work packages as sets of tasks. > Tab. 1 and Chapter Workflows in the planning and construction process

Allocating tasks to the work sections

Tab. 1: Typical work sections in each rough phase

Rough phase	Possible work section
Preparatory measures	– Preparing the construction site (construction fences, construction site trailers, utilities, etc.) – Demolition work – Clearing – Excavating
Building shell	– Excavating – Dewatering – Reinforced concrete work – Masonry work – Structural steelwork – Timber work – Sealing – Ground drainage – Scaffolding
Building envelope	– Sealing – Roofing/roof waterproofing – Plumbing (rainwater drainage) – Windows – Shutters/sunscreens – Facade work (plaster, natural stone, masonry, curtain wall, etc., depending on building envelope)
Finishing	– Plastering – Screed work – Drywall construction – Metalwork (e.g. railings) – Natural/artificial stonework – Tiling – Parquet – Flooring – Painting/wallpapering
Building services	– Ventilation systems – Electrical work – Sanitation/plumbing – Heating/hot water systems – Gas installations – Lightning protection – Transportation and elevator systems – Fire protection – Building automation – Security technology
Final work	– Carpentry (furniture) – Locking systems – Final cleaning – Outdoor facilities

The next steps involve linking the tasks with one another and calculating their duration. > Chapter Creating a schedule, Planning task sequence, and Planning task duration While dependencies in the construction process usually determine the links between tasks, planners should also take outside influences into account. For instance, they might have to observe deadlines specified by the owner or integrate events such as topping-out ceremonies that need to be scheduled before the start of summer vacations. Finally, events taking place in the area around the construction site may have an effect on the schedule (e.g. street or city festivals, utility connection dates specified by the authorities). If at all possible, planners might also find it advisable to schedule critical tasks in a period of more clement weather outside the frost season.

Planning task sequence and duration

Dividing the work into construction phases is one of the most important steps in organizing the sequence of the different work sections and generally streamlining the schedule. Tasks such as laying floor screed are organized for the different building sections (ground-floor screed work, second-floor screed work, etc.). Smaller phases help produce overlaps between sets of tasks and are advisable since it would "straighten out" the construction process too much if, for instance, the schedule required plastering throughout the building before screed was laid. The tasks are assigned to construction phases in order to inform construction companies where they are to start and in what order the work will proceed. > Fig. 13

Dividing the project into construction phases

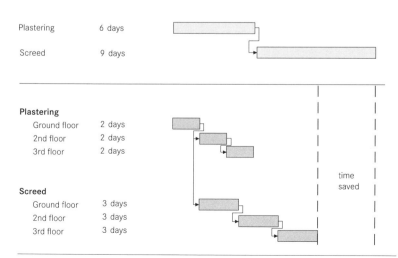

Fig. 13: Shortening construction times through construction phases

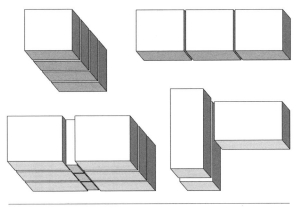

Fig. 14: Typical ways to divide a project into construction phases

Planners must consider carefully how they divide the project into construction phases when they structure the schedule since changes made to these phases at a later date can result in a great deal of extra work. The rule of thumb is, the smaller the building sections that forms the basis of construction phases, the shorter the construction time. However, depending on the project scope and time constraints, this division must not be too intricate since it is difficult to create a schedule and use it on the construction site if the building has been divided into too many sections. > Chapter Working with a schedule, Updating and adjusting a schedule

While it may not be necessary to divide the smaller projects (home extensions) into phases, large projects may require several phases for the participants to complete construction within an appropriate period.

Finally, the project should also be divided into construction phases that make sense and are easy to communicate. Following the geometry of the building, they can be based on floors, building sections accessed by stairs, units located on both sides of a stairwell, subsequent rental units, etc. > Fig. 14

Important factors to consider for construction phases are separate accessibility, the ability to close off areas, identical production quantities in construction phases, and production processes.

Separate accessibility by means of a stairway or other access route is particularly important for tasks such as laying screed or flooring since

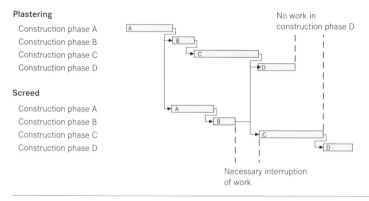

Plastering

Construction phase A
Construction phase B
Construction phase C
Construction phase D

No work in
construction phase D

Screed

Construction phase A
Construction phase B
Construction phase C
Construction phase D

Necessary interruption
of work

Fig. 15: The problems caused by construction phases of different length

it ensures that the different contractors do not get in each other's way and are not prevented from reaching their work stations by closed-off areas.

Even so, closing off areas can help to protect completed building sections and surfaces from damage. If areas are closed off or only open to the contractors currently working on them, on-site damage, dirt and theft can be limited, and the responsible party can be identified more easily.

As regards production quantities, planners should define the various construction phases so as to ensure that each phase and work section involves an identical volume of work. This creates continual cycles and avoids long waiting times for the different contractors. > Fig. 15

An additional factor to be considered when dividing a project into construction phases is the various production processes used by the individual contractors. As a rule, a building structure is built floor by floor (from bottom to top), but there are a number of building services contractors that work either along installation paths such as sewage pipes (from top to bottom) or in self-contained cycles (e.g. subdivisions in a rental unit). This is a constant source of misunderstanding and mutual disruptions.

PLANNING TASK SEQUENCE

In order to gain a better understanding of the different tasks, we will systematically follow a single project participant through the typical sequence of the work he or she performs. This sequence can usually be divided into three rough phases:

- Lead time (necessary planning time, lead time for contract awards and trade contractors)
- Execution period (planning period or construction, depending on the participant)
- Lag times (drying and curing times) and follow-up periods

Lead times cover tasks or milestones that must be scheduled before construction work is performed. For example, before windows are installed on site, it may be necessary to take measurements and plan and prefabricate the windows. In contrast, lag times are periods, like drying times, that must be observed after the completion of a task and before additional work can be done on the building section.

Lead time for awarding contracts

Schedulers must take into account the time needed to award a contract, which falls between the planning and implementation period. A basic distinction must be made between private-sector and government procedures. The government usually awards contracts on the basis of strict guidelines or regulations with legally established deadlines. In the private sector, these regulations are not binding. The contract award process can therefore be organized along less formal and more direct lines, yet it should nonetheless adhere to certain minimum periods in order to allow all participants to respond in the proper manner. The deadlines in government regulations are therefore a good foundation for the private sector.

○

Schedule milestones

The contract award process involves several steps > Fig. 16 and Chapter Workflows in the planning and construction process, Coordinating construction preparation The schedule should, at the very least, include the following tasks or milestones:

> ○ **Hint:** A lead time for awarding contracts should also be taken into account for planning services in order to find the planning specialists who are best suited and have the most experience for the job (e.g. those with expertise in fire protection for conversions of existing buildings). Public invitations to tender may also be necessary when awarding planning contracts.

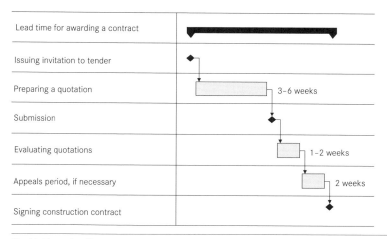

Lead time for awarding a contract		
Issuing invitation to tender		
Preparing a quotation		3–6 weeks
Submission		
Evaluating quotations		1–2 weeks
Appeals period, if necessary		2 weeks
Signing construction contract		

Fig. 16: Example of lead time for awarding a contract

— Publication, which is necessary for most government procedures
— Issuing invitations to tender: the deadline by which the planner must complete all documents
— Submission: the deadline by which companies must submit their tenders
— Signing the construction contract: a deadline for the building owner
— Start of construction

When scheduling the lead time for the award of each contract work package, planners calculate backwards since the lead time is usually scheduled to that construction work begins promptly on site.

A period of at least two weeks must be scheduled between the signing of the construction contract and the start of construction since the contracting company must first make plans before it can begin the construction process (material requirements, transportation to the site, construction site facilities, etc.).

The construction contract and the start of construction

Sufficient time must also be left between the submission of a tender and the signing of the construction contract – at least one or two weeks, depending on the complexity of the work. During this period, planners examine all the tenders and compile a price comparison list that will be used by the owner as the basis for deciding which construction company to hire. Any unclear items or deviations in the tenders must be discussed

Submission

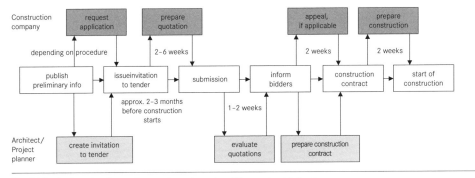

Fig. 17: Typical contract award procedures based on EU award guidelines

with the participants. Government procedures often stipulate an appeals period for bidders who have submitted less favorable offers. The owner's decision-making process may at times be arduous, making a period of more than two weeks necessary.

Sending out the call for tender

Once the planner <u>issues the invitation to tender</u>, the tendering construction company must put together a <u>solid offer</u> by the submission deadline. Depending on the complexity of the required construction work, the company may require a good deal of time and effort to calculate its offer. It must therefore be given sufficient time to do so – usually around six weeks. The reason for this is that the construction company will have to ask suppliers for their prices or create its own call for tenders in order to get information from subcontractors on sections of the construction work. Even if there is great urgency, construction companies are usually unable to put together a tender in less than two weeks.

Publication

Depending on national regulations and the contract award procedure selected, a government agency that contracts out work must publish its intention to award the construction contract in advance. Advance <u>publication</u> of the information enables construction companies to request the tender documents and apply on time. > Fig. 17

Lead times for trade contractors

Not every construction job can be started immediately after the contract is signed. Construction companies must often carry out additional steps before they can perform the work on the construction site. Planners must also take this <u>lead time for trade contractors</u> into account, especially for jobs that require planning work by the contractor, as well as off-site prefabrication and extensive procurement of materials.

To ensure a secure financial framework when <u>procuring materials</u>, companies generally only place orders after signing a contract. For many construction tasks such as plastering and screed work – which use standardized and readily available building materials – companies can do so in the abovementioned two-week period between the signing of the construction contract and commencing construction.

Planning material requirements

But if companies require materials that cannot be purchased in standard forms at wholesale outlets, planners must consider and check in advance the time involved in <u>planning material requirements</u>.

●

If the owner wants to inspect samples (e.g. bricks, tiles, windows, colors and similar items) > Figs. 18 and 19 before orders are placed, planners must leave sufficient time for the following steps:

Inspecting samples

— Procurement of samples
— Inspection and approval of samples
— Modification or procurement of additional samples (if necessary)
— Material delivery periods

In addition to the time needed to procure materials, some construction work requires planning by the construction company and involves <u>prefabricating</u> components before the work can be carried out on the construction site.

Prefabrication

Depending on the construction job, the construction company may have to take on-site <u>measurements</u> in order to prefabricate and install components precisely. Measurements can only be taken once there has been sufficient progress in the construction process (e.g. completion of floors or openings in the building shell).

● **Example:** In large companies, the staff in charge of construction work may not be able to finalize a decision if contract volume exceeds a certain limit. A higher-level body such as the management board must first approve the contract award. This may entail a long period of time, depending on how often this body meets.

● **Example:** If natural stone tiles are needed in specific sizes from foreign countries, they must first be ordered, manufactured and imported by ship. If particularly large quantities of a special material or component are needed, or if single parts must be produced, production may take some time due to the lack of supplies at wholesale markets.

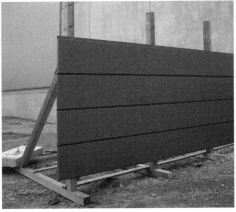

Fig. 18: Inspecting a facade system   Fig. 19: Inspecting the design of the roof edge

Based on these measurements, the construction company creates its own <u>working drawings</u>, which provide a foundation for prefabricating the necessary components. If stipulated in the contract, the architect approves technical aspects of the working drawings before components are manufactured. In this case, planners must schedule inspection and <u>approval</u> times in addition to the periods needed to create and work on the working drawings. > Fig. 20

After the architect gives the green light, <u>prefabrication</u> can begin. Depending on the trade contractor and the component, it can take six to eight weeks or more before the component is ready for assembly. However, the actual on-site assembly process usually takes a relatively short amount of time.

Elements that typically require prefabrication are:

— Facades, windows and doors
— Glass roofs and skylights
— Precast concrete units
— Steel structures (e.g. loadbearing hall structures, stairs, railings)
— Timber structures (e.g. roof trusses)
— System elements (e.g. office partition walls)
— Ventilation systems
— Elevator systems
— Built-in furniture and interior installations

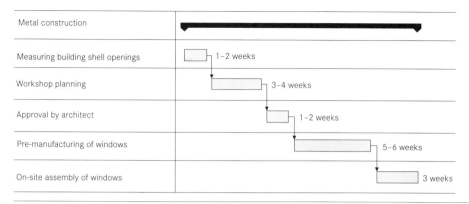

Metal construction	
Measuring building shell openings	1–2 weeks
Workshop planning	3–4 weeks
Approval by architect	1–2 weeks
Pre-manufacturing of windows	5–6 weeks
On-site assembly of windows	3 weeks

Fig. 20: Typical lead times for metal windows

Construction period

The construction period encompasses all the tasks covered by the contract work package. When structuring such tasks, planners must consider the dependencies between components and trade contractors, as well as task duration and the assignment of work to construction phases. > Chapter Creating a schedule, Planning task duration As a rule, the construction company should be allowed to schedule its work on a detailed level if there are no dependencies with other crews. In areas of the building where several trade contractors intermesh, the work should be organized in such great detail that each contractor can see its own working periods and interdependencies.

If the different jobs performed by one trade contractor are separated by longer periods and are not structurally linked, it can be effective to divide the skilled tasks into two contract work packages so that both an adequate planning lead time and self-contained, coherent construction contracts are ensured. ●

● **Example:** Steel and metal construction often involves a number of jobs that extend through the entire construction process. These include the construction of steel structures, windows, exterior wall cladding, doors, railings and stairs. Since in most cases these jobs do not build upon one another and the companies usually specialize in certain fields, it is advisable to plan partially separate contract work packages.

The tasks and dependencies that are typical of the planning and construction process are described in the chapter "Workflows in the planning and construction process."

Lag and follow-up periods
These periods can be divided into periods relating to construction work and those relating to contracts.

Of fundamental importance for sequence planning are component curing and drying times, which must be planned as interruptions before additional jobs can begin. Such lag times include curing periods for screed, since screed surfaces cannot bear weight or be walked on directly after pouring. This means that individual areas of the facility are temporarily off limits. Drying time is also needed before additional work can be done on a component. In other words, if tiles, paint or other surfaces are applied to plaster or screed, sufficient drying times must be taken into account so as to prevent subsequent damage to the completed surfaces caused by dampness. In there are many components, curing times and thus accessibility are shorter than the full drying times required before additional work can be performed.

Follow-up work that is typically required for individual trade contractors influences the contractually stipulated construction period of a contract work package. Examples of follow-up work are:

— Building shell: closing wall openings after building services are installed, removing site installations after completion of the building (if contracted out with the building shell)
— Windows and doors: assembly of windows and door handles before completion of the building
— Plastering: plastering flush with doors, stair coverings, window sills
— Building services: detailed installation work for switches, heating elements and sanitary fixtures; launching technical systems
— Painting: additional coat of paint after tiling, detailed installation work and assembly of fixtures on finished walls and ceilings

Planners should enter such follow-up work into the schedule as separate tasks in order to eliminate the possibility of claims from construction companies that have exceeded contractually defined work times. Also of relevance are the guarantee periods that start with inspections. The sooner both the contractually stipulated work ends and the inspection takes place, the earlier the guarantee periods end that give owners the right to have damage repaired.

Follow-up periods in the field of planning primarily entail information and advisory services that become necessary when designs or conditions change during the construction process (e.g. unexpected discoveries in existing buildings or on the building lot).

PLANNING TASK DURATION

Once planners have recorded all the tasks of the various trade contractors and planning participants, they must now estimate how long tasks will last. Architects usually use empirical values from past projects or question trade associations and construction companies about typical task durations.

Another way to calculate durations is to use defined quantities and quantity-related time values. Here an important distinction must be made between unit production time and unit productivity rate.

The <u>unit production time</u> (UPT) indicates how many person hours are needed to produce a unit of work. It is calculated as follows: Unit production time

Unit production time = required person hours/quantity unit (e.g. 0.8 h/m^2)

The <u>unit productivity rate</u> (UPR) is the reciprocal of the unit production time. It indicates the quantity produced per time unit: Unit productivity rate

Unit productivity rate = executed quantity/time unit (e.g. 1.25 m^2/h)

In construction, <u>unit productivity rates</u> are used primarily for equipment (e.g. the performance of a power shovel expressed as m^3/h), while unit production times are applied to labor (e.g. the number of hours needed to make a cubic meter of masonry, expressed as h/m^3). ○

Estimations of quantities are based on the <u>quantity units</u> of the underlying unit production times and productivity rates (m, m^2, m^3, or piece). If a productivity rate is expressed in terms of cubic meters of earth, excavations must also be calculated in cubic meters. Determining quantity

> ○ **Hint:** Unit production time and unit productivity rate are always dependent on the type of construction company, its working method, and the workers involved. Furthermore, on-site work is often influenced by the specific conditions there. It is therefore never possible to calculate precise task durations in advance using these approximate values.

Since the quantity units are often the same as those in other stages of the planning process (costing, tendering, etc.), the quantities can be adopted directly from these other stages. If no quantities are available, they must be calculated from scratch. When choosing the degree of detail in quantity calculations, planners should keep in mind the imprecision of unit production times and unit productivity rates. A rough calculation is normally sufficient.

■

Establishing task duration

The total number of work hours necessary to perform a task – known as person hours (PH) – can be calculated on the basis of the required quantity and either the unit production time or unit productivity rate. If person hours are divided by both the number of workers (W) and the daily working time (DWT), the result is the probable task duration (D), expressed in workdays (WD):

●

$$D = \frac{PH(UPT*quantity)}{W*DWT} \quad D = [WD]$$

Number of workers

The daily working time is usually set by the regulations in collective wage agreements. Overtime must be allowed for in special circumstances, such as significant deadline pressure. All things considered, an optimal number of workers should be allotted so as to ensure an effective construction process. Some jobs such as window assembly require a minimum number of workers – otherwise they cannot be done properly or cannot be done at all. Nevertheless, worker numbers cannot be randomly increased since there is a chance that the workers will then no longer be effectively deployed. One example is screed work, where the number of workers depends heavily on the availability of equipment, the productivity of which can be only slightly increased using more personnel.

The specification of staffing capacity is merely an internal calculation method used to achieve a reasonable implementation duration. Normally planners leave it to the construction companies themselves to deploy an adequate number of workers for the available construction

---

■ **Tip:** Depending on construction conditions, published time values and real values may deviate by up to 50%. Smaller quantity differences in calculations can therefore be seen as negligible. If precise information is required, planners should compare several sources for time values. The appendix contains a summary of many typical unit production times as a basis for calculation.

● **Example:** If the unit production time is 0.8 h/m², the quantity 300 m², the number of workers 5, and daily work time 8 hours, task duration is:

$$D = \frac{0.8 \times 300}{5*8} = 6 \text{ WD}$$

period. However, such calculations can help site managers determine whether a site is understaffed to the extent that problems will arise in meeting final deadlines. The reverse of the equation can be used to figure out the number of workers necessary to complete a job in the given time frame.

$$W = \frac{PH(UPT*quantity)}{D*DWT}$$

Such calculations can also be used to evaluate contract awards with reference to the on-site performance capacity of construction companies. ■

It is an advantage for the scheduler if worker numbers are tailored to task durations in the given construction phase. If several trade contractors work one after the other in one construction phase and then gradually switch to the next phase, identical task durations will ensure that work is constantly being performed in each phase and that crews do not have to wait for each other. > Fig. 21

It is not necessary to calculate task durations precisely for every single schedule and every single task. Often all that is needed is an estimate based on empirical figures. The main reason is that every construction project is subject to small modifications of task durations, and in most cases these have only a limited effect on the completion deadline for the entire building. What are much more important for meeting overall deadlines are task sequences, which are described in the next chapter. Here errors can cause structural displacements and have far-reaching consequences for the project.

The results of duration planning

Nevertheless, task durations must not be overlooked since they provide a basis for the implementation deadlines that are agreed upon in the contracts with construction companies. It is therefore crucial to use realistic, viable task durations in order to facilitate smooth execution of the various construction contracts.

● **Example:** If a total of 240 person hours is required to do a job and the given time frame is limited to five working days, the number of workers required is calculated by dividing 240 PH by 5 × 8 (PH / D × DWT). The result is 6 workers.

■ **Tip:** When determining task duration, planners should not only take a mathematical approach, but also consider other factors that keep the construction work from proceeding at the same rate as during the rest of the year (holidays, typical vacation periods, frost periods, etc.). This is typical of the time around Christmas and New Year's Eve, despite the fact that a sufficient number of working days are available.

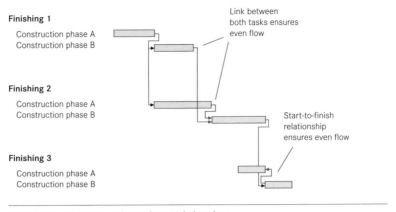

Finishing 1
Construction phase A
Construction phase B

Link between
both tasks ensures
even flow

Finishing 2
Construction phase A
Construction phase B

Start-to-finish
relationship
ensures even flow

Finishing 3
Construction phase A
Construction phase B

Fig. 21: An approach to pacing various task durations

The results of duration planning

It is generally impossible to calculate planning services using unit production times, since intellectual and creative work cannot be grasped in terms of hours per quantity unit. The durations of planning tasks are usually determined in conversations with planners and experts when they are hired and as the project progresses. This approach optimally exploits the planners' personal experience and available time. By illustrating the effects of possible delays in planning stages, it also makes the participating parties conscious of their own contribution to completing the project on time.

Workflows in the planning and construction process

The following chapter describes typical tasks performed by the participants in the planning and construction processes and discusses the dependencies of these tasks on one another. Its goal is to use this background information to examine projects, identify relevant tasks and depict them in a real-world schedule.

PLANNING PARTICIPANTS

The various parties that need to be coordinated in the planning phase can be roughly categorized as follows: > Fig. 22

To begin with, the owner or client must be mentioned, as the initiator of the building project. The owner may be a single person or a complex web of people and institutions. These different constellations can result in significantly different perspectives on the part of owners, project developers, financial backers (banks), and subsequent users. For example, if the owner is a company or a public institution, the project supervisor must answer to committees and departments that have both influence and decision-making power and that must be integrated into the owner's decision-making processes.

Owners and
affiliated parties

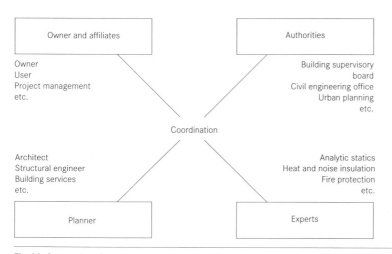

Fig. 22: Categories of participants in the planning phase

In efforts to coordinate the people involved in the owner's company or organization, it is important for planners to understand the decision paths and to estimate the time involved so that they can make punctual
● preparations for decisions.

Authorities   Further, every newly erected building requires interaction with the authorities that decide on the legality of the project, grant permits under public law, and monitor the project using tests. The extent to which authorities intervene in the process depends largely on the function of the planned facility, the building type, the legal regulations, as well as local conditions. In addition to building supervisory boards, the project may involve the following authorities:

— Civil engineering offices (connecting the property to public infrastructure)
— Urban planning authorities (analyzing the urban planning context)
— Environmental authorities (the environmental effects of the project)
— Occupational safety and health authorities (worker safety on the construction site and later in the completed building)
— Historical preservation offices (for historical buildings)
— Land surveying offices (maps, site plans)
— Registry and property authorities (property management, encumbrances and restrictions on the property)
— Trade authorities (in the event of subsequent commercial use)

Since these authorities normally exercise a control function or serve as decision-makers, planners must understand the steps and durations of their decision-making processes. For example, a realistic time period should be built into the schedule for the authorities to award a building permit – to begin after documents have been submitted.

● **Example:** If, for the additional planning process, architects require an decision from the owner on floor coverings or other surfaces, they should provide the owner at an early stage with samples of viable alternatives with corresponding advantages and disadvantages (costs, life cycle, sensitivity, etc.). Owners may have to discuss these alternatives with other persons in their organization or with subsequent tenants.

The planning staff consists of various <u>project planners</u> and <u>planning specialists</u>. The project planner (usually the architect) brings them together and resolves any possible conflicts between the different requirements. The three most important integrated planning areas that extend through the entire planning process are the <u>architecture</u>, <u>structural engineering</u> and <u>building services</u>. However, in practice, a large number of planning specialists may be involved:

— Structural engineering
— Interior architecture
— Electrical engineering
— Drinking and waste water engineering
— Ventilation systems
— Fire protection engineering
— Data technology
— Elevator engineering
— Kitchen planning
— Facade engineering
— Landscape and open space planning
— Lighting systems
— Facility management

Along with the planning participants, experts are required to assess and submit reports on the different specialized tasks. At the very least, this group of experts includes specialists who assess and test heat insulation, noise protection, fire protection and statics.

The experts' assessments must be taken into account in the schedule, primarily in connection with the submission of results. For example, specific expert opinions must be submitted for the construction permit and the start of construction. Experts must therefore be hired and given the work documents with an appropriate lead time.

COORDINATING PLANNING

The intensity of coordination during the planning phase is very much dependent on the size and complexity of the structure in question and on the scheduling constraints imposed by the owner. In the case of a residential building, which is largely planned exclusively by the architect, only a few deadlines are usually relevant, such as the application and award of the building permit and the start of construction. In larger structures, such as laboratories and specialized production facilities, input from a range of specialists is often required.

The way in which the planning phase is divided up is only partly dependent on the sequence of architectural planning, since other participants will have structured their particular areas differently. The best way to approach the organization of planning is by making an initial link between the three most important planning areas – architecture, structural engineering and building services – since, as a rule, planners in these areas have a constant integrated influence on the planning process as a whole. Planning should take into account the fact that planning specialists require an appropriately advanced state of overall planning in order to be able to make their particular contributions. This networked approach is typified by the following sequence:

1. Advance development of an appropriate foundation for planning specialists by the project planner
2. Forwarded to planning specialists
3. Worked on by planning specialists
4. Results returned by planning specialists
5. Integrated by project planner and coordinated with results of planning by other participants
6. Mutual coordination of specialist planning and (if necessary) further revision

The schedule should allocate enough time after the submission of responses by planning specialists to resolve inconsistencies between specialist planning and project planning or other areas of specialist ■ planning. > Fig. 23

Integration
of other
participants

Integrating other participants is generally simpler, since their work is not as closely linked with that of the planners referred to above. It is often sufficient simply to include a period in the schedule in which planning specialists will be given time to react to particular results of the overall planning process. This will clarify when the various participants need to be given the information they require for planning their specific input into the project, and when the results will be integrated into the overall planning process.

> ■ **Tip:** Typical information exchanges between the architect, structural engineer and building services engineer relating to different project phases can be found in the appendix. However, the details of such exchanges differ according to the specific project and depend on the function and design of the building and the people involved.

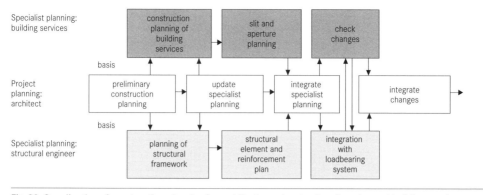

Fig. 23: Coordination of construction planning for architecture, structural engineering and building services

The most important aspect of the scheduling process is the identification of milestones that can be passed on to the various participants (building owners, planners, experts) in order to provide them with a basis for their respective input into the project. > Chapter Creating a schedule, Schedule elements Established and agreed deadlines ensure that all parties adopt the discipline of a fixed time frame and help avoid the delays in the planning process that can occur when participants are included in the process too late.

Planning milestones

COORDINATING CONSTRUCTION PREPARATION

When it comes to awarding contracts, planning deadlines must be particularly well thought out. Construction preparation is a time-consuming process that can easily take several months. If it is clear when a building company has to begin work on the construction site, this deadline can be used as a basis for scheduling the different steps in the preparation process. > Chapter Creating a schedule, Planning task sequence If owners are public bodies, legally prescribed deadlines mean that planning can include only limited provisions for delays, which will thus directly affect the start of construction.

Since a range of companies are usually involved in a building project, the construction preparation phase must make provision for a range of different deadlines. It is therefore wise to organize the respective steps in the preparation process to ensure that all preliminary work, such as securing owner decisions, construction planning, and organizing and announcing tenders and contract awards, can be punctually initiated in relation to each trade contractor involved.

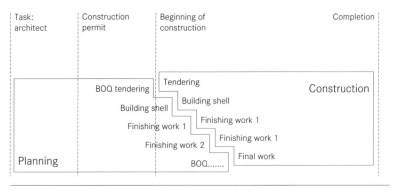

Task: architect	Construction permit	Beginning of construction		Completion

Fig. 24: Dovetailing between planning and construction

Dependencies generated by construction workflows also give rise to planning requirements.

Planning during construction Many rough schedules present planning and construction as separate phases, but in reality, construction planning and construction itself largely proceed in parallel. This is because deadlines are often very tight, and planning does not necessarily have to be completed when building commences. Although it is important that documentation is available in good time before the relevant construction work commences, many types of work (such as painting and laying flooring) tend to commence once the building process is quite advanced, which means that relevant planning and contractual documents can be completed after construction has begun. In such cases, owe refer to planning that accompanies the construction process. > Fig. 24

In planning that accompanies construction there is always a risk that specific planning details that are developed later in the process will have an influence on aspects of construction that have already been completed. Many building elements interface with other parts of the building in terms of statics, building services, structure and aesthetics.

Since individual building elements such as windows, doors and dry construction work are increasingly integrated with other work sections, planning for such elements needs to be sufficiently advanced in order to avoid the need for subsequent modifications. > Fig. 25

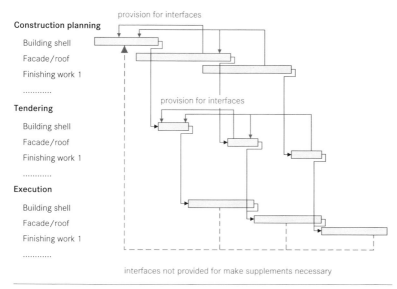

provision for interfaces

Construction planning

Building shell
Facade/roof
Finishing work 1
....

provision for interfaces

Tendering

Building shell
Facade/roof
Finishing work 1
....

Execution

Building shell
Facade/roof
Finishing work 1
....

interfaces not provided for make supplements necessary

Fig. 25: Provision for interfaces in planning that accompanies construction

PREPARING THE CONSTRUCTION PROCESS

During the construction process the building planner or site manager needs to coordinate all companies operating under a separate contract with the building owner. The goal is to ensure that work proceeds in an integrated and trouble-free manner. A central aspect of this coordination involves the interfaces between individual tasks and trade contractors. A description of typical interfaces is given below; it should however be remembered that these can vary significantly between different construction projects.

● **Example:** When the building shell is planned, consideration needs to be given to the subsequent effects of facade connections, ceiling and stairwell heights, as well as the surface treatments of concrete walls and their associated requirements. Drainage underneath the bottom slab also needs to be clarified at a very early stage.

Fig. 26: Manual demolition on projects involving existing buildings

Fig. 27: Mechanical demolition of entire buildings

Prior to the erection of the building shell, a number of preliminary tasks relating to the preparation of the construction site need to be considered. First, the site needs to be in a condition that actually allows construction work. Vegetation must to be removed and the ground reinforced, pre-existing piping and drainage systems must be located and protected, and pre-existing constructions (walls, fences, etc.) need to be demolished.

Preparing the construction site

The required preparatory measures include setting up the construction site. This process involves installing the construction trailers from which construction is supervised, connecting utilities, and putting up fences to prevent unlawful entry. Further work may be required to improve access (e.g. access roads) and to shield the site from the external environment (e.g. blinds and noise protection).

Demolition measures

For new buildings, preparatory measures can often be completed within a few days or weeks. However, in projects involving existing building stock, the need for extensive demolition work may require scheduling a significantly longer preparatory phase. At the same time, the unpredictability of the demolition process often makes it extremely difficult to estimate task durations. The choice of the demolition method decisively influences task durations, since mechanical demolition with heavy equipment cannot be compared with manual demolition using light machines. > Figs. 26 and 27 Routes for waste transport within the building and access to dumps also need to be taken into consideration. Because

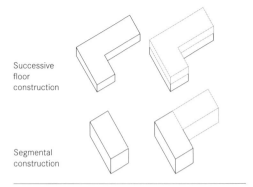

Successive
floor
construction

Segmental
construction

Fig. 28: Schematic representation of building shell
construction floor by floor and in segments

demolition measures precede construction, delays in the demolition
phase directly affect all subsequent work.

BUILDING SHELL

Constructing the building shell entails a range of tasks, all of which
contribute to creating the building's basic skeleton. In the case of concrete construction these tasks include:

— Excavation
— Masonry
— Pouring concrete
— Putting up scaffolding
— Sealing the building to protect against rising damp
  and groundwater
— Separate roof construction (if required)

Depending on the type of construction, structural steelwork and tim-
bering may also be needed. As a rule, building shell construction is organized by the construction contractor. Of primary concern for architects
are the interfaces with subsequent work sections that commence after
the shell has been completed.

The sequence of tasks involved in the construction of the building
shell is usually highly structured and easily comprehensible. Once the
foundation and drainage systems have been completed, the floors are

Fig. 29: Construction of a concrete wall using prefabricated elements

Fig. 30: Construction of bottom slab and concrete supports cast on site

added in succession. However, where large floor areas are required, building shell construction may involve working in vertical segments as well as successive floor construction. > Fig. 28

Pre-manufacturing in the building shell phase

If a building is made up of elements such as prefabricated concrete units and steel or wooden structures, these components are usually pre-manufactured off site, delivered ready for assembly and quickly mounted on site. > Fig. 29 and Chapter Creating a schedule, Planning task sequence Apart from the different floors, this usually also applies to roof structures made of wood or steel. These structures may have to be contracted out separately from the building shell, and this needs to be taken into account in the construction schedule.

BUILDING ENVELOPE

Envelope sealed

Directly after the completion of either the building shell (including roof structure) or the individual segments of the shell, the building needs to be sealed off from its surrounding environment. Sealing the building envelope is a basic precondition for all subsequent finishing work. For this reason the "envelope sealed" stage should be reached as soon as possible after completion of the building shell. The relevant functional requirements are:

— Rainproofing (protection for finishing elements, drying out the building shell)
— Windproofing (above all in winter, to retain heat in the building)
— Security (protection against theft of finishing elements)
— Heatability (only necessary during winter months)

Fig. 31: Assembly of continuous windows   Fig. 32: Assembly in attic area

The most important precondition for reaching the "envelope sealed" milestone is the sealing of openings and roofs. This is achieved either by installing windows and doors immediately or by blocking off openings using temporary seals such as guard doors. Depending on the type of construction, builders can add insulation and the facade of the closed external wall immediately after the "envelope sealed" stage. Where additional, thick outer-wall features are added, it may be necessary to modify or shorten scaffolding.

Windows and doors

The covering of steep roofs and the sealing of flat roofs must be completed in order to seal the building envelope. This also applies to skylights and roof-light domes and includes the completion of plumbing and roof-drainage work. For drainage embedded within a flat roof, builders must also ensure that once the envelope is sealed, water is actually drained out of the building.

Sealing roofs and drainage

Before scaffolding for facade and roofing work is removed, lightning protection work also needs to be carried out and lightning conductors must be earthed.

Lightning protection

FINISHING WORK

Coordinating finishing work is the most demanding segment of the construction supervision process. Precise scheduling is essential since tasks are closely linked and the different types of work being simultaneously carried out are often not restricted to one or a few companies – in contrast to the building shell and envelope.

Most contractors will not be able to coordinate their own work with that of other contractors because of the complexity involved. For this reason, the schedule must define the relevant dependencies in detail.

Plastering work is generally carried out soon after the building envelope has been sealed. Since in most cases wall installations need to be concealed behind plaster surfaces, they must be in place before plastering begins. In this context care should be taken not to overlook features such as drive mechanisms for doors, fire protection installations and emergency lighting. In industrial buildings, cables are usually laid on the outside of walls, which means that plastering can be done before building services are installed.

Plastering   Door frames are a typical interface in this context, since the type of door frame chosen determines whether it is mounted before or after plastering. For instance, steel corner frames should be mounted prior to plastering, because embedding frames and intrados later on usually generates additional costs. Dual section closed frames should only be installed late in the construction process to protect against damage. Interfaces that can influence the sequences of all types of work take place wherever building elements intersect with one another, as is the case with windows, window sills, stairway access points and stairway railings.
> Figs. 33 and 37

In order to ensure that surfaces are ready for further work (e.g. painting), the schedule needs to include a drying period appropriate to the type and thickness of the plaster used.

It is also helpful to include a post-plastering section in the schedule to ensure that surfaces damaged by other work can be repaired at a later date.

Screed work   Schedules usually make special provision for screed work, because no other work can be carried out while screed is being laid or is curing. As a consequence, the schedule must not only cover screed application but also include a curing period appropriate to the type of material used. Cement screed has a curing time of three to ten days (depending on the aggregate, weather and thickness), and it is significantly more economical than, for example, poured asphalt screed. However, the latter is ready for use and further work after only two days.

Apart from curing time and readiness for use, another important aspect of screed work is drying time. Flooring can commence only after screed has dried sufficiently and moisture content is low. The drying time is primarily dependent on the type and thickness of the screed and on

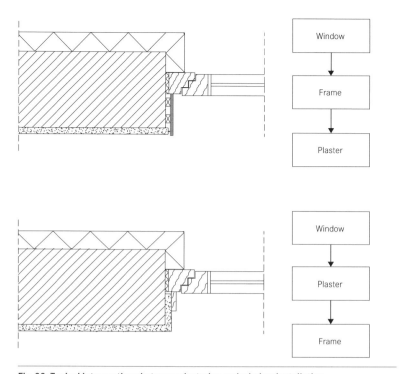

Fig. 33: Typical intersections between plastering and window installation

environmental factors such as temperature and humidity. In many cases flooring is only installed late in the construction process to avoid such problems. In cases where deadlines are tight, the drying time can be reduced by using additives or drying equipment, although such measures generate additional costs.

When scheduling screed work, planners should also consider installations laid under screed, such as floor heating, heating distributors, floor power outlets and electrical conduits. > Fig. 34 Due to the inaccessibility of building sections containing freshly applied screed, interconnected workflows need to be checked in terms of possible system bottlenecks, walkways (and escape routes), transport routes for materials, as well as intersecting installation areas (such as electrical conduits).

The sequence in which drywall construction and screed work are car- Drywall
ried out also depends on whether more priority is given to noise insulation (walls attached to the unfinished floor) or flexibility (walls attached to the screed). Where a large proportion of the walls and ceilings in a

Fig. 34: Installations prior to application of elevated screed

Fig. 35: Rough installations prior to closing a suspended ceiling

building are constructed using the drywall method, the coordination of this work with many other work sections is one of the most important tasks in the scheduling process.

Due to these dependencies, plasterboard walls are usually constructed in two steps. First, the substructure is erected and sealed on one side. This is followed by all installation work related to building services (electricity, sanitation, heating, ventilation). The drywall contractor only seals the second side of the wall once this work has been completed.

The construction of suspended ceilings also involves close integration of installation work and drywalling. All raw installations must be completed before the ceiling is mounted, and planners need to consider possible geometric dependencies between installations and the suspension and screening of the ceiling. > Fig. 35

In addition, some building-services elements require specific preparation of drywall surfaces and subsequent sealing once they have been installed (e.g. recessed lighting, access panels, fire detector covers). > Fig. 36

Doors and partition walls   With plasterboard walls, frames are often installed while the wall is being constructed, because they must be screwed to and aligned with

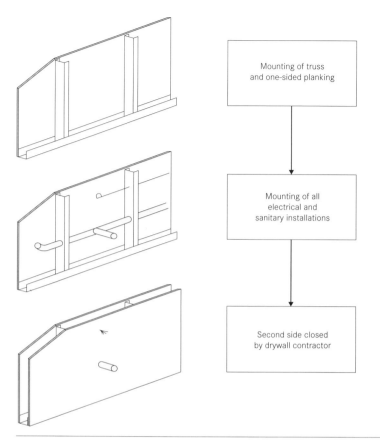

Mounting of truss
and one-sided planking

Mounting of all
electrical and
sanitary installations

Second side closed
by drywall contractor

Fig. 36: Typical sequence in the construction of plasterboard walls

lateral profiles. In the case of solid walls, the frame is usually fitted before or after plastering in the form of a corner, profile or dual section closed frame. > Fig. 37

In addition to affecting the way doors are mounted (in the building shell and the drywalling work), the type of frame or door construction is a significant factor in determining the point at which mounting should take place. For normal doors, frames are installed before or after plastering or during drywalling depending on the particular situation, and the door leaf is mounted as late as possible to avoid possible damage. Metal frame doors and system elements as well as standardized steel doors and panels are often supplied and installed as complete units, including the frame and door leaf.

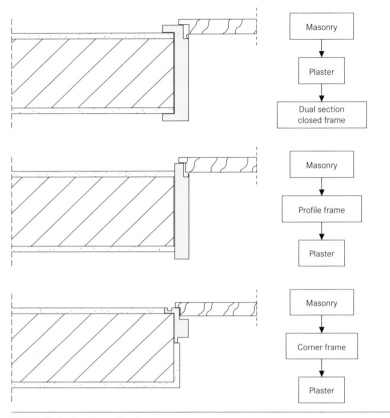

Fig. 37: Methods of mounting frames

In many cases, door details have a decisive effect on the time period allocated for installation:

— Door frame installation with or without floor recess (dependent on screed)
— Door structures with or without surrounding frames (dependent on screed)
— Frame geometry: frame over plaster or plaster applied to frame (dependent on plastering) > Fig. 37
— Permit requirements application of plaster to fire doors
— Electrically operated doors with access surveillance, escape route functions, accessibility for disabled people, automatic door openers (dependent on electrical systems and fire alarm installation)

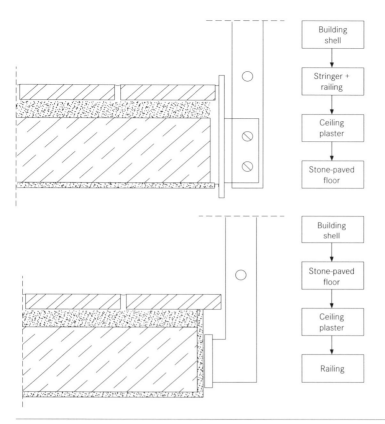

Fig. 38: Typical plaster connections in balustrade area

In principle, sensitive installation elements should be planned as late as possible in order to avoid damage to finished surfaces.

In addition, depending on the type of door, delivery times often must be taken into consideration. Standardized steel doors and frames can be delivered quickly and installed as complete units. Special structures such as fire doors and complete metal-frame door units are manufactured to order, and delivery times can easily be 6 to 8 weeks or more.

A fundamental requirement for laying tile and stone surfaces is the completion of the underlying foundation. However, a distinction must be made here between using a thin bed of plaster on a level foundation, and a thick bed on the building shell surface.

Tiling, parquet laying, stonework and flooring

189

Different surfaces, such as screed, building shell surfaces, masking, plaster, drywall, etc., can serve as the foundation for all coverings and coatings. For stairs, the sequence in which a covering is applied will also depend on the way the stair railing is attached, the possible addition of a stringer, and in some cases the presence of scaffolding in the stairwell.
> Fig. 38

Integrating different surfaces, such as plaster around door frames and different types of flooring, requires careful attention to task sequences. Relevant details need to be clarified in invitations to tender, including bracket and seal requirements. In many areas, particularly bathrooms and kitchens, interdependencies with building services installations need to be taken into account:

— Sanitation installations: rough installations such as toilet cores, ground outlets, downpipes, water connections, access openings
— Heating installations: heating pipes, heating elements
— Electrical installations: switches, floor outlets, etc.

It should be noted that special surfaces such as flooring in elevators and tiled backsplashes in kitchenettes are often overlooked in the planning process.

Wherever possible, floor surfaces should be applied in an order that ensures the least risk of damage. For instance, carpet, plastic and linoleum floors should be installed as late as possible, since they are more susceptible to soiling and damage than parquet, stone or tile. They can also be laid quickly. Laying such floor coverings is often one of the last tasks in the construction process.

Painting and wallpapering Painting and wallpapering require dry level surfaces. For this reason, schedules need to include adequate drying times for mineral-based surfaces such as plaster. As a rule, painting and wallpapering work is relevant to all wall and ceiling surfaces that are not covered by other surfaces such as tiles or prefabricated ceiling elements. Planners also need to

● **Example:** Heating elements represent a typical interface problem. Planners need to be aware that heating is required on the construction site over the winter months in order to ensure that sub-surfaces and paintwork dry properly. However, in some cases heating elements must be removed again later on, to allow the wall areas behind them to be painted.

consider smaller-scale tasks such as the application of varnish to stair rails, frames and steel doors, dust-binding and oil-resistant coatings to elevator shafts prior to elevator installation, and fire- and rust-resistant coatings to steel structures. As with plastering, provisions should be made in the schedule for follow-up work.

BUILDING SERVICES

Building services include all installation work involving heating, water supplies and drainage, sanitation units, ventilation, electrical installations, data technology, fire prevention installations, elevators and other building-specific installations. Coordination of building services and their integration with interior finishing work are generally based on collaboration between building and building services engineers. In this context, it is important that building planners understand where the interfaces are located between different building services contractors and integrate these interfaces into workflows. > Fig. 39

Heating installation involves a range of different construction elements. The order in which these elements are installed during a particular project must be determined on the basis of the different systems and distribution networks. Typical elements are: *Heating installation*

— Energy supply (gas pipes, solar collectors, pipes, etc.)
— Storage facilities (e.g. hot water and oil tanks)
— Heat stations and heat generation
— General distribution and sub-distribution within the building (duct installations)
— Distribution per heating unit (heating unit connection)
— Heating unit installation

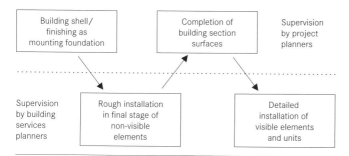

Fig. 39: Typical workflows in building services work

191

Planners need to coordinate the installation of the heating system with relevant interior finishing work on a range of surfaces. If the heating system is to be used to heat the construction site during the winter months, parts of the system need to be installed in advance and then temporarily removed to permit work on surrounding surfaces (plastering and painting).

Sanitary installations   Like heating systems, sanitation systems require closed and sometimes pressurized circuits and networks. For this reason, the workflows involved are similar to those in the installation of heating systems. Apart from the connection of the building to the local water provider, planners dealing with the installation of the drinking water supply need to understand how it is distributed throughout the building via feed pipes, ascending pipes in installation shafts or wall slits, and connections to individual use points in bathrooms, kitchens and similar rooms. Analogous planning must be performed for sewage disposal.

The rough installation phase is followed by the detailed installation of sanitation facilities (sinks, toilets, faucets, etc.). This work is often scheduled well after the completion of tiling and painting work > Fig. 41 in order to avoid the risk of theft or damage. Elements such as bathtubs and shower trays that are to be tiled on the outside need to be installed before tiling work commences.

Typical interfaces requiring coordination between work sections:

— Piping underneath the bottom slab (often installed during building shell construction)
— Wall and ceiling openings (which in some cases need to be closed after installation during building shell construction)
— Ventilation ducts running through the roof (connection of sewage disposal pipes to fans in the roof area)
— Water and sewage connections to the building (requiring coordination with public providers)
— Installation of pumping systems below the backwater level
— Heating water (installed centrally with a parallel piping configuration or decentrally at the point of use)

○ **Hint:** Further information on drinking water and sewage system components can be found in: Doris Haas-Arndt, *Basics Water Cycles*, Birkhäuser Verlag, Basel 2008.

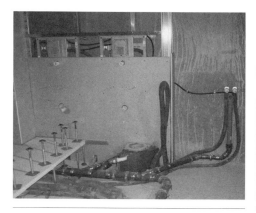

Fig. 40: Drinking water and sewage installations in the toilet core with hollow floor

Fig. 41: Tiled surface ready for detailed installation of sanitation facilities

Electrical installation work is also divided into rough and detailed phases. Depending on the method used, rough installations can be concealed beneath plaster or left exposed. If, as in residential buildings, cabling is not supposed to be visible, completion of the entire electrical network must be scheduled between the building shell and plastering phases. The visible (exposed) mounting often encountered in industrial buildings is usually carried out only after all wall surfaces have been finished. Exposed concrete walls are a special case, in that ductwork must already be laid in the wall when it is reinforced in order to allow for later electrical installations. > Fig. 42 Typical stages in electrical work are:

Electrical installations

— Building connection and main fuses (coordination with electricity provider)
— Earth connection (coordination with building shell work)
— Battery and transformer installations (if required)
— Distribution within building and sub-distribution to individual points
— Detailed installation of lights, outputs, switches, etc.

Due to the increasing integration of structural elements with electrical systems, scheduling electrical work is becoming an increasingly complex task. In order to avoid having to open finished surfaces for additional installation, planners need to systematically check construction elements detailed in the building design for possible interfaces with the electrical system. Typical examples are:

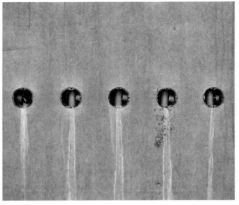

Fig. 42: Electrical installations in exposed concrete walls

Fig. 43: Example of distribution cables in floor

— Specific connections for stoves, tankless water heaters, heating systems and particular structural elements
— External lighting
— Emergency lighting
— Fire alarm units
— Ventilation units
— SHEV units (window, roof opening, smoke extraction)
— Disabled access (switches, automatic overhead door closers) and access monitors
— Alarm system components (outer doors and emergency exits, window burglar alarms, surveillance cameras, etc.)
— Facade control (electrical ventilation, sun and glare protection, rain and wind detectors, overhead lights, etc.)

Data technology   Data technology is a special aspect of electrical installation and is particularly complex in buildings used for administration and communications. Data technology refers to all forms of telecommunications and media technology such as telephone connections, television technology, computer networks, server rooms, etc.

In order to provide flexible access to every workstation in administrative buildings, server rooms and wiring closets are often installed either centrally or on each floor. Planners need to take into account dependencies with installation channels in floors, ceilings and walls.

Planning the installation of ventilation or air-conditioning systems must also cover the installation of extensive ductwork for incoming and outgoing air. As a rule, ventilation ducts, whether exposed or concealed, are laid in shafts, floor structures and ceiling areas, and planners must ensure that such installations are properly integrated with relevant structures and surfaces. It is critical in this context to take into account aspects such as supply conduits (cooling pipes, electrical cables, inlet vents), penetrations from the outer surface (caulking by roofer or facade construction contractors) and fire compartments (mortaring by the building shell contractor or fire-retardant sealing by the drywall contractor).

Along with the individual interfaces between the distribution system and the ventilation plant, the schedule for later work in the construction process needs to accommodate the detailed installation of features such as exhaust outlets, grating, covers and screens. Such installation is generally carried out after surfaces have been finished.

An important consideration when scheduling the installation of large ventilation and air-conditioning systems is lead time for prefabrication. Apart from a few standardized duct cross-sections, the dimensions of ducts, intersections and units must usually be calculated on site during building shell construction and represented in an independent working drawing. The components are only manufactured once this drawing has been approved, and the entire process can take several weeks. It is therefore important that the ventilation system contract be awarded to a specialist company at an early point so that the work on the building site can be carried out punctually.

Conveyor technology such as elevators and escalators usually re- quires a large number of electrical connections. Planners also need to take into account interfaces with floor coverings (inner covering of an elevator car, connection to door sills) and walls (elevator door embrasure).

In most cases, the anchorage points for a planned elevator must be defined by anchorage channels already installed within the shaft during the building shell construction phase. This enables planners to select the elevator construction contractor or manufacturing system at the earliest possible stage. Once the building shell has been completed, the shaft is measured precisely, and a working drawing for the elevator is made. Following the pre-manufacturing phase, installation often proceeds in several steps. First the load-carrying system is installed in the shaft, then the elevator car is mounted, and finally the electronic control system is put in and connected with the electrical system.

Scheduling also needs to consider whether the elevator will be used to transport materials during subsequent construction. However, such use of elevators is usually not advisable because damage to the interior of the elevator car is inevitable. As a result planners often make a conscious decision to complete all work on elevators in a late phase of construction.

FINAL WORK

Final contract awards
prior to completion
Apart from the follow-up work by individual participants already referred to (painting, detailed installation etc.) there are also entire sets of tasks that are concluded only at the end of the construction process. These can include:

— Final cleaning following the completion of all work and prior to handover to users
— Locking systems (delivery and installation of the final locking and access systems for later users)
— Completion of outside space (access routes, garden and lawn design, parking areas, signage, lighting and other outdoor installations)

Inspections
stipulated by law
In principle it is wise to schedule in a period at the end of a project for the correction of defects and for formal inspections, since these take time and inspection should be completed before the occupation date.

Inspections include both contractually stipulated inspections and inspections as prescribed under public law. In the latter case the building supervisory board checks that the completed building observes construction regulations, and approves the building for use. Such inspections also cover technical installations such as fire prevention facilities and heating and air-conditioning systems, which in some cases have to be checked by outside experts.

Working with a schedule

Even though a schedule may present a detailed and coherent arrangement of the tasks making up a construction project, it is not a static framework that, once formulated, will necessarily remain unchanged until the completion of work. The construction process continually gives rise to particular situations that make it necessary to adapt the deadline structure. A construction schedule should therefore be seen as a tool that accompanies the entire construction process.

UPDATING AND ADJUSTING A SCHEDULE

Real conditions on a construction site often look different from the situation envisaged in the schedule. There are many reasons for disruptions and necessary structural changes. > Chapter Working with a schedule, Disruptions to the construction process Schedules, which are usually printed on paper and displayed on the construction site, age quickly, resulting in work that no longer reflects their constraints. This makes updating the schedule essential. Ideally, a schedule is not seen as a set of imposed obligations that need to be repeatedly adapted to the actual construction situation, but as a daily tool that helps planners monitor, organize and, if necessary, adapt the actual construction process.

Conception versus reality

When formulating a schedule, planners should therefore structure it in a way that allows them to make effective and sensible adjustments and additions during the construction process. In large-scale projects, schedules are often confusing due to the range and complexity of the tasks involved. In such cases the individual tasks should be hierarchized using a clear structure of summary tasks. > Fig. 44 This enables the construction phases and workflows to be presented in detail and also to be seen within the overall deadline structure.

Structuring the schedule

This approach makes for easier comprehension of the schedule in its entirety. It can also be represented in different ways depending on the specific user. Typical modes of displaying the schedule include:

User-oriented schedule versions

— Overview for project manager and clients: shows major summary tasks; does not show individual tasks
— Planning and contract award deadline schedule for the planning office: shows all individual planning tasks and award lead times: does not show construction tasks
— Construction schedule for site managers: does not show planning and award lead times; shows all contractor lead times and construction tasks

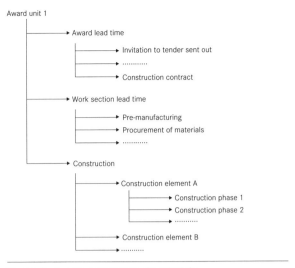

Fig. 44: Typical hierarchy levels of a schedule

— <u>Construction schedule as a guide for individual participants</u>: shows the participant's tasks only

By showing only those tasks that are relevant to a particular target group, the schedule provides a clear basis for participants in terms of planning and execution.

An important criterion for the relevance of all modes of display is that they be based on a single coherent schedule. If different schedules are used in parallel, the various users and multiple influences make synchronization difficult at a practical level. Integrating modifications from a single point and then passing them on to all participants using the hierarchical structure described above facilitates their application to the relevant parts of the overall process.

Integrating modifications

Apart from hierarchization, the usability of a schedule in practice is greatly improved when planners establish a clear connection between all sets of tasks. Identifying the effects of a modification requires the integration of all the tasks into a single context that allows the entire schedule to be updated automatically. At the same time it should be noted that not every delay or adjustment affects the deadline for completion.

198

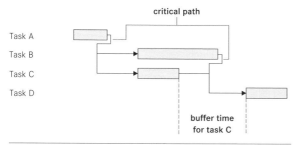

Fig. 45: Tasks without a buffer time on the critical path

Usually there is only one dependency running through the project   Critical path
from start to finish – a dependency that, if subject to delays, has an immediate effect on the deadline for completion. This is referred to as the
critical path. In the case of other tasks, a buffer time can be used to prevent delays influencing the critical path. > Fig. 45

Every task that is not on the critical path has a buffer time that can   Buffer time
be calculated by modern scheduling programs. This means that planners
can directly monitor the degree of flexibility at their disposal when faced
with a potential delay, and also see how much additional time they can
allow the construction contractors involved.   ■

DISRUPTIONS TO THE CONSTRUCTION PROCESS

Most of the modifications planners find it necessary to make to a
construction schedule are based on disruptions to the construction process. Disruptions can be caused by clients (owners and planners and
construction firms contracted by them), contractors or by third parties.

Typical examples of disruptions from the client side are:

— <u>Changes made by the owner</u>: owner requests retroactive changes based on new user specifications, structural alterations to planning, etc.
— <u>Lack of contribution by client</u>: failure to give approval, non-payment, etc.
— <u>Mistakes by planners contracted by client</u>: mistakes in planning, planning not submitted in time, incomplete calls for tenders, unrealistic schedule, insufficient construction supervision, etc.
— <u>Mistakes by contractors engaged by client</u>: preparatory work is not completed in time and the client is therefore unable to make the site available to contractors.

Different events can also lead to disruptions caused by contractors. In the worst case, a contractor becomes insolvent and is forced to declare bankruptcy. The client is then forced to find and engage a new contractor to complete the remaining work, which causes significant delays to the construction process. On the other hand, construction firms that have taken on a large number of contracts often have problems meeting their contractual obligations with the workforce at their disposal. This can produce delays on the individual construction sites. Strikes and flu epidemics, for example, can also significantly reduce the number of staff that construction firms can allocate to a particular contract.

Capacity planning is often also faced with problems. Construction firms plan their staffing capacities at regular intervals (e.g. weekly) and allocate their available workforce across different construction sites. Firms cannot usually vary the size of the workforce they allocate to individual construction sites from day to day. If schedules demand daily variations in workforce provision, there will be a high probability of disruptions. > Fig. 46

■ **Tip:** In order to ensure that firms have a constant level of work, tasks are linked not only to other job areas but also to one another within the same work section. This allows schedulers to preplan a range of teams that can successively work on individual aspects of the same work section.

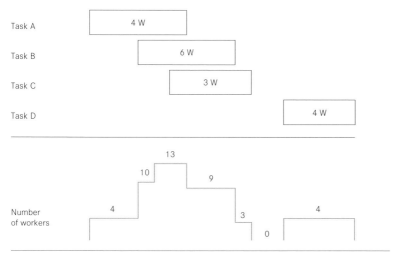

Fig. 46: Schedule with pronounced variations in workforce size

For this reason, in order to avoid problems at a later stage, planners should endeavor to schedule work sections in way that allows staff capacity to remain relatively constant. ■

Apart from clients and contractors, third parties contractually engaged in the construction process can also cause disruptions. These can range from constraints and conditions imposed by authorities, strikes, and theft of clients' and contractors' property, to force majeure. If disruptions by third parties influence the client's situation, contractors have the right to claim an appropriate extension of the time scheduled for construction. If the influence of third parties affects the contractor's level of risk, the construction firm in question is nevertheless obliged to meet its obligations punctually. In the case of force majeure such as storm damage, flooding, etc., the construction firm is usually granted a time extension. > Tab. 2

Disruptions by third parties

Even in large-scale projects, unfavorable weather conditions in the winter months and other times of the year often lead to delays in meeting schedules. Although declines in performance over the winter months or in holiday periods can generally be offset by longer buffer times and task durations, predicting winter weather conditions precisely is impossible. Depending on the location of the construction site, frost and other adverse conditions can bring construction to a standstill for a long pe-

Effects of weather

Tab. 2: Contractual consequences of disruptions for construction process

Influence of the client (CL)	Influence of the contractor (CN)	Example of influence	Can CN claim time extension?	Can CL claim additional payment?
Direct	No	Directive by the CL, e.g. work stoppage due to lack of funds, or changes to construction	Yes	Yes
Indirect	No	Lack of CL involvement, e.g. late submission of approval	Yes	Yes
Indirect	No	Third-party influence on CL, e.g. preparation delays mean site not be ready for construction work	Yes	Yes
No	No	Force majeure, e.g. storm, war, environmental disaster	Yes	No
No	Indirect	In-house disruption to CL, e.g. flu epidemic or strike	No	No
No	Indirect	Third-party influence on CL, e.g. theft of equipment	No	No
No	Direct	Refusal to fulfill contract, e.g. too few workers on site	No	No

riod. Early installation of heating or site-heating facilities can remedy this situation. However, planners need to note that, despite adequate temperatures inside the building, materials such as ready-mixed concrete, poured asphalt and ready-mixed plaster cannot be applied if external temperatures are too low.

Types of disruptions   Disruptions relevant to the schedule can basically be divided into three categories: > Fig. 47

— Delayed completion: A task begins at a later time but is
   completed within the prescribed task duration.
— Extended construction time: A task requires longer than the
   planned task duration.
— Structural change to the construction sequence: The construction
   process, or rather, the interdependent tasks, are arranged in a
   sequence that differs from the one planned.

DEALING WITH DISRUPTIONS

Should disruptions occur that require "critical path" intervention due to structural changes or because they could cause the project to miss its completion deadline, planners must endeavor to deal with these problems within the prescribed construction period. Possible forms of intervention include:

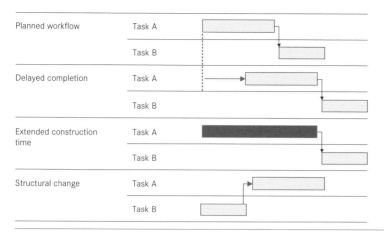

Fig. 47: Types of schedule disruptions

The figure shows four groups of paired task bars:

- Planned workflow — Task A, Task B
- Delayed completion — Task A, Task B
- Extended construction time — Task A, Task B
- Structural change — Task A, Task B

— Checking necessary dependencies
— Structural changes in the construction process
— Changing the method or quality of construction
— Shortening construction phases
— Accelerating construction work

Not every dependency is absolutely necessary, even if it makes sense. Necessary dependencies
Work can sometimes be done retroactively if sufficient consideration is
given to the subsequent tasks and if the connections to other components can be subsequently reworked.

Planners must first check whether a dependent relationship is com-
pulsory with an eye toward additional work steps (plastering → painting),
or whether they can organize the work in other sequences. It is probably
best to discuss any related problems with the participating construction
companies.

If it is impossible to avoid interventions in obligatory dependencies Structural changes
due to the scope disruptions and the need to meet the completion deadline, planners need to consider the possibility of structural changes to
the construction process. If there are many consecutive tasks, it is possible to change the structure of components. For instance, light partition
walls can be installed on an unfinished floor or on finished screed, and

electrical lines can be laid beneath or over plaster. As a rule, though, these decisions must be discussed with construction companies and the building owner since they often influence the properties and visual impression of the completed component.

Method and quality of construction ●

Schedules can be partially streamlined by changing the method and quality of element construction. This may avoid long lead times in the pre-manufacturing process and long curing and drying times.

Shortening construction phases

One method of process optimization is to shorten the construction phases. As described above > Chapter Creating a schedule, The structure of the project schedule construction periods can be reduced if back-to-back work is organized into cycles. If the first contractor completes work on a floor only after the next contractor begins, more construction time is needed than if the floor is divided into smaller construction segments. In the latter case, one or several contractors can work on the floor at the same time. In case of doubt, a delayed contractor must be called upon to finish parts of the construction area in order to allow the subsequent contractor to start work there.

Accelerating construction

In general, the client may ask a contractor to work more quickly, but distinctions must be made between the causes of the delay. If the contracting company is responsible, it must take all the necessary measures – including overtime and deployment of additional workers – in order to meet the agreed deadline, and it must do so on a cost-neutral basis. However, if the client or the site manager requests a third company that is not responsible for the delay to speed up work, the client must pay for any additional costs.

Preventing additional costs

Since the measures described above often produce additional costs, the owner must be involved in the decision-making process. It is ultimately the owner who must decide what funds he or she is prepared to mobilize to ensure that the building is completed on time.

● **Example:** Work that produces a lot of dirt such as plastering, laying screed or putting in cut stone floors, should be scheduled before jobs such as carpeting and painting where surfaces are easily soiled. This is not to say that a stairway cannot also be laid with stone at a later stage in a project as long as areas with carpeting are closed off until the stone work has been completed and the stairway has been cleaned.

● **Example:** If planners are confronted with tight deadlines and wish to avoid curing and drying times for a cement screed and thus work holdups in the areas in question, they can, as an alternative, install poured asphalt or dry screed, which can be walked on one day later. It should however be noted that this is more expensive than cement screed.

Even in the initial phase of creating the schedule, planners are well advised to integrate delay periods. Problems almost always arise – insufficient preliminary work, delivery delays, theft of materials, etc. – and they will have to be dealt with. The time cushions in a schedule are an important way to ensure completion deadlines are met. If no cushion exists when planners create a schedule, it is usually a sign that the completion deadline is unrealistic.

Furthermore, at an early stage in the project, planners should also consider the latest point at which they will still be able to select an alternative construction method without violating the contract or incurring additional costs (e.g. cast-in-place concrete vs. prefabricated solutions, plaster vs. plasterboard, cement screed vs. dry screed, plaster flush with doorframes or closed frames). The deadline conditions should be analyzed in good time, and corresponding decisions discussed with the owner.

Considering alternatives

SCHEDULING AS PROCESS DOCUMENTATION

Scheduling is not only a method for organizing the construction process. It also performs an important function in documenting the project. Since it evolves over the entire planning and construction process, it can be used in retrospect to prove or disprove the occurrence of disruptions. This is important if there are unresolved claims between the owner and construction companies (e.g. compensation for damages) that need to be settled. Further, the schedules of completed projects are a source of data for future schedules and therefore represent important knowledge gained by the planning architect in the process.

The main task of scheduling in this context is to record actual task durations as compared to the target task durations estimated by the scheduler. Disruptions and their causes should also be jotted down. One method is to document current events on the construction site by making handwritten entries into the current schedule. The paper copies, which should be filed at regular intervals, provide a basis for updating the schedule. Ideally, site managers will enter the deadlines directly into a scheduling program that will keep the schedule data constantly up to date. However, after each change, the previous version and its associated data should be archived under the proper date.

Recording actual deadlines and disruptions

In conclusion

Complex building projects require a great deal of organization and coordination. Without solid scheduling, it is impossible to achieve effective time management of large construction projects. For both the architect in charge of this coordination and the site manager, it is extremely important to organize all the planning and construction processes in advance in order to remain in control of the situation. If these parties only respond to events and are unable to actively control the process, the self-organizational attempts of project participants will often result in disruptions, coordination problems, mutual interferences and delays.

Nevertheless, managing the planning and construction processes is not a matter of giving project participants written-in-stone deadlines that they must strictly follow. Planning specialists must consider all their concerns and integrate them into the management process in order to find solutions that everyone can implement.

A schedule is not merely a contractually agreed service between the building owner and the architect. It is also an effective instrument for the daily management of planning and construction processes. The creation of a realistic and implementable schedule involves effort, but keeping the entire planning and construction process in mind, planners will find that it makes later coordination and conflict resolution a good deal easier. It also lays the groundwork for short construction periods. The more architects devote themselves in advance to sequences in the construction process, the easier the work of site managers becomes.

Tables

INFORMATION REQUIRED FOR PLANNING

Tab. 3: Information typically required by the main planner in the initial project phase

From:	To:	Required information
Structural engineer	Architect	– Relevant structural systems and materials – Full range of component dimensions
Building services engineer	Architect	– Type of installations required for building use – Location of utility and wiring rooms – Route of main lines, required routes for main distribution lines – Initial sizing of installations and lines
Architect	Structural engineer	– Site plan, building form, floor height – Maximum and most common width of columns – Rough specifications
Architect	Building services engineer	– Site plan, building form and size – Use, user numbers (e.g. number of employees if used as office) – Building services requirements – Floor plans

Tab. 4: Information typically required by the main planner in the design phase

From:	To:	Required information
Structural engineer	Architect	– Main and secondary axes of loadbearing elements – Preliminary dimensions
Building services engineer	Architect	– Initial sizing of installations and lines – Openings necessary for building services – Cost estimate
Architect	Structural engineer	– Dimensioned design development drawings (plans and sections), ready to be submitted for the building permit
Building services engineer	Structural engineer	– Location of the main lines, location and loads of the installations
Architect	Building services engineer	– Final design development drawings (plans, sections, views)
Structural engineer	Building services engineer	– Design of loadbearing structure (girders, columns, loadbearing walls) – Openings and slits in loadbearing elements

Tab. 5: Information typically required by the main planner to prepare for construction

From:	To:	Required information
Structural engineer	Architect	– Formwork drawings – Reinforcement drawings – Connection details – Bills of material
Building services engineer	Architect	– Electrical, ventilation, heating, sanitary planning – Drawings of wall openings and slits for building services – Tendering documents, e.g. main lines for the invitation to tender for the building shell – Defined responsibilities for other planning specialists
Architect	Structural engineer	– Updated dimensioned plans and sections – Working drawings, design details, specifications – Specifications from the preliminary building notification or the building permit
Building services engineer	Structural engineer	– Location of the main lines, location and loads of the installations – Drawings of wall openings and slits
Architect	Building services engineer	– Approved plans and perhaps specifications from the authorities – Specifications – Construction drawings
Structural engineer	Building services engineer	– Formwork drawings, steel structure drawings and timber structure drawings – Location of steel reinforcement for wall openings

UNIT PRODUCTION TIMES

Tab. 6: Sample unit production times to roughly estimate task durations

Work	UPT	Unit
Preparing the construction site		
Setting up crane	10–50	h/unit
Steel-lattice fence	0.2–0.4	h/m
Connecting utilities (electricity, water)	0.2–0.5	h/m
Excavation		
Excavating building pit	0.01–0.05	h/m^3
Excavating individual foundations with power shovel, including removal	0.05–0.3	h/m^3
Excavating individual foundations by hand	1.0–2.0	h/m^3

Concrete

Rough estimate for complete building shell (700–1400 m³ gross volume and 3–5 workers)	0.8–1.2	h/m³ GV
Binding layer, unreinforced, d = 5 cm	0.2	h/m²
Bottom slab, reinforced cast-in-place concrete, d = 20 cm	2.0	h/m²
Ceiling, reinforced cast-in-place concrete, d = 20 cm	1.6	h/m²
Precast and partially precast concrete ceilings	0.4–0.9	h/m²
Entire building, prefabricated	0.3–0.7	h/t
Casting concrete elements (without formwork or reinforcement)	0.4–0.5	h/m³
Casting walls (without formwork and reinforcement)	1.0–1.5	h/m³
Casting columns (without formwork and reinforcement)	1.5–2.0	h/m³
Cast-in-place concrete stairway (without formwork and reinforcement)	3.0	h/unit
Large-panel formwork	0.6–1.0	h/m²
Single formwork	1.0–2.0	h/m²
Reinforcement	12–24	h/t

All types of sealing — 0.25–0.40 h/m²

Scaffolding (assembly and disassembly) — 0.1–0.3 h/m²

Masonry

Loadbearing masonry wall	1.2–1.6	h/m³
Non-loadbearing interior wall	0.8–1.2	h/m³

Carpentry work

Rafter roof, including joining and mounting (based on roof area)	0.5–0.7	h/m²

Roofing

Flat roof (gravel), including complete mounting of non-insulated roof	0.5–0.7	h/m²
Pitched roof with roofing tiles	1.0–1.2	h/m²
Metal roofing	1.3–1.5	h/m²

Cladding for exterior walls

Metal facade cladding	1.0–1.3	h/m²
Facing brick leaves	1.1–1.5	h/m³
Composite heat insulation system	0.6–0.8	h/m²
Assembly of precast concrete facades	0.5–0.7	h/m²
Exterior wall cladding with natural stone, slate, etc.	0.5–0.8	h/m²

Window construction

Installing individual windows	1.5–2.5	h/unit
Installing roller shutter housing	0.6–1.5	h/unit
Roof windows	2.5–3.5	h/unit
Interior window sills	0.3–0.5	h/m

Plaster

Exterior plastering	0.5–0.7	h/m^2
Interior plastering, done by machine	0.2–0.4	h/m^2
Interior plastering, manual	0.3–0.6	h/m^2
Ceiling plaster	0.3–0.4	h/m^2

Screed

Laying cement screed and anhydride screed (without membranes, insulation, etc.)	0.1–0.3	h/m^2
Laying mastic asphalt screed (without membranes, insulation, etc.)	0.3–0.5	h/m^2
Floating floor screed, including insulation layer	0.6–1.0	h/m^2
Terrazzo screed, polished	2.0–2.5	h/m^2

Dry construction

Drywall with plasterboard	0.2–0.5	h/m^2
Prefabricated walls or wall paneling, single layer, including substructure	0.7–0.8	h/m^2
Covering slanted ceilings	0.3–0.5	h/m^2
Suspended ceiling structures	0.6–1.1	h/m^2
Plasterboard stud wall, single panel	0.4–0.8	h/m^2
Plasterboard stud wall, double panel	0.6–1.5	h/m^2

Doors

Installing steel frames + door leaves	1.9–2.5	h/unit
Installing wooden doors	1.0–1.5	h/unit
Exterior doors	2.5–4.5	h/unit

Tiles, paving stones, cut stones

Floor tiling	0.5–1.8	h/m^2
Wall tiling	1.3–2.5	h/m^2
Natural and concrete paving stones	0.8–1.2	h/m
Baseboard made of tile or natural stone	0.3–0.4	h/m

Flooring

Creating level surface, filling holes	0.05–0.2	h/m²
PVC, linoleum and rolled flooring materials	0.3–0.6	h/m²
Needle felt or carpet on screed	0.1–0.4	h/m²
Baseboards	0.1–0.2	h/m²
Parquet floors, including surface treatment	1.2–1.8	h/m²
Sanding parquet floors, surface treatment	0.2–0.3	h/m²
Natural stone floors	0.9–1.2	h/m²
Stairway coverings	0.5–0.7	h/m²

Painting and wallpapering

Putty work	0.1–0.2	h/m²
Standard wallpaper (wall chip wallpaper, thick embossed wallpaper, etc.)	0.1–0.4	h/m²
Special wallpaper (velour, textile, wall images, etc.)	0.3–0.8	h/m²
Painting interior wall, single coat	0.05–0.2	h/m²
Painting interior wall, three coats	0.2–0.5	h/m²
Plastering and painting exterior wall	0.2–0.8	h/m²
Painting window, per coat	0.2–0.6	h/m²
Painting metal surface, all required coats (doors, sheet metal walls, etc.)	0.3–0.6	h/m²
Painting metal elements, all required coats (frames, sheet metal covering, etc.)	0.6–1.0	h/m²
Painting metal railings	0.1–0.3	h/m

Electrical work

Rough estimate for all electrical installations (700–1400 m³ gross volume and 2–3 workers)	0.2–0.4	h/m³ GV
Assembling cable tray + electrical lines	0.3–0.5	h/m
Assembling lights	0.3–0.8	h/unit
Assembling sub-distribution board	0.5–1.0	h/unit
Detailed installation of switches, outlets, etc.	0.02–0.05	h/unit

Heating, plumbing and sanitation installations

Rough estimate for complete heating installation (700–1400 m³ gross volume and 2–3 workers)	0.1–0.3	h/m³ GV
Rough estimate for complete gas, water and wastewater systems (700–1400 m³ gross volume and 2–3 workers)	0.15–0.4	h/m³ GV
Rough assembly of pipe routes	0.4–0.8	h/m
Rain and wastewater pipes	0.10–0.50	h/m
Detailed installation and assembly of sanitary fixtures	0.3–1.0	h/unit

Tim Brandt –
Sebastian Th. Franssen

Tendering

Introduction

Planners – this includes architects, civil engineers and specialist engineers – have to involve another group of people by the end of the plan submission and planning permission process at the latest. The earlier phases of the process focused on communicating with the client and the authorities, but now planners have to turn their attention towards the firms who will be responsible for realizing the project: craftsmen and women, building contractors, specialist companies.

From planning to realization

All the information needed for realizing the project is provided to building firms as part of an invitation to tender, in the form of descriptions or drawings of the work to be done and services needed. The invitation to tender must contain all the information the bidding firms need to perform the necessary services and to submit a bid for the contract and, where appropriate, for planning the work.

Tender content

○

○ **Hint:** The tender becomes part of the contract that the client concludes with the building contractor. Planners can incur penalties for errors and omissions in the bid.

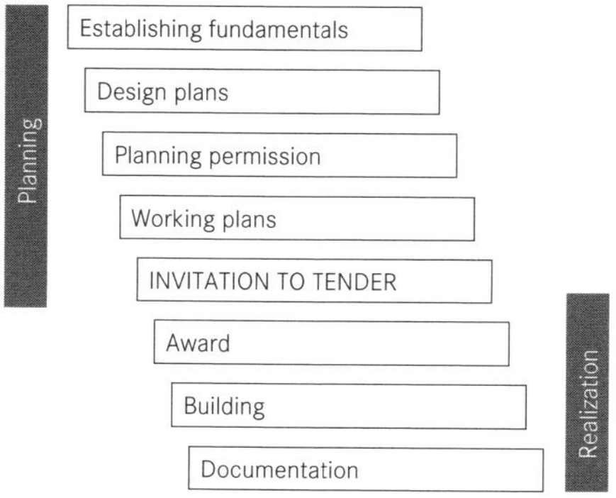

Fig. 1: Planning phases

The tendering process aims to attract as many appropriate bids as needed to form a broad view of the market. The invitation to tender is compiled by the planner and submitted to suitable contractors, who then calculate prices and submit a bid, which is binding. This is then examined by the planner and compared with other bids. The comparison gives the planner an insight into current prices and enables the client to commission the work from the bidder who has submitted the most reasonable offer for the particular project.

TENDERING REQUIREMENTS

The invitation to tender collects all the requirements that have come to light in the planning phase. These requirements are essentially laid down by the client, but they may also relate to legal or technical matters. They can be categorized as follows: > Fig. 2

— Costs
— Deadlines
— Function
— Scope
— Quality

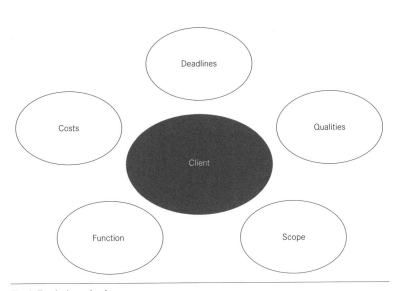

Fig. 2: Tendering criteria

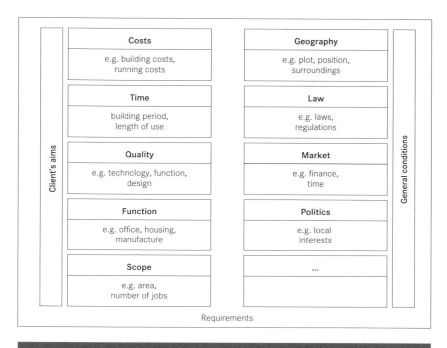

Client's aims			General conditions
	Costs e.g. building costs, running costs	**Geography** e.g. plot, position, surroundings	
	Time building period, length of use	**Law** e.g. laws, regulations	
	Quality e.g. technology, function, design	**Market** e.g. finance, time	
	Function e.g. office, housing, manufacture	**Politics** e.g. local interests	
	Scope e.g. area, number of jobs	...	

Requirements

Building commission

Fig. 3: Definition of requirements

These criteria are used to fix the realization phase and to identify any planning services that are still required. > Fig. 3

Costs

In most cases cost is the key criterion for or against a realization bid, or even for or against the building project itself. Planners are obliged to spend a client's money on the project in the client's best interest. Planners generally have a prescribed budget, and must set all the costs arising from the building work against this. This will mean drawing up separate budgets for the various service packages or award units. > Chapter Organizing the tender, Fixing bid units

Cost range

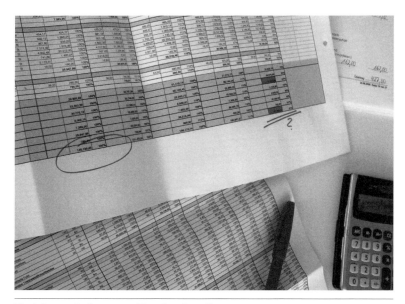

Fig. 4: Range of prices as an aid to choosing a firm

For the client, keeping to the prescribed budget is often crucial to the success of the entire project. The contractors' concrete bids are the first check on the planner's suggested costs in relation to real market prices.

■ **Tip:** Bids submitted in response to the first invitation to tender are crucially important in establishing the client's confidence in the planner's costing competence. If even the first bids come in outside the planned cost framework, it is possible that the client, anxious about keeping within the overall budge, might make radical adjustments at an early stage that could affect all the other criteria, e.g. a marked reduction in the standards for the finished building.

An overview of the individual budgets makes it possible for planners to control costs. If the bid for a particular unit is above the budget allocated to it, planners will have to cut the budget for other units and take this into consideration when drawing up invitations to tender, for example by reducing quality standards or the scope of the work required. Conversely, if an item comes in under budget, planners can, for example, include clients' requirements that had previously fallen outside the cost framework.

Cost control

Clients can best ensure that costs are firmly fixed by attempting to eliminate all cost risks arising from unpredictable events during building, from market developments, and from submitting a series of individual tenders. One possible way of doing this is for a single contractor to take on the whole operation, which guarantees completion costs and deadlines. > Chapter Organizing the tender, Fixing bid units, Package awards

Cost guarantees

Deadlines

Clients will generally set firm deadlines, or at least express their wishes about them. Once deadlines are agreed, they are binding.

■

Constraints on deadlines arise mainly from the planned use of the building concerned. For example, completion dates, and thus possible moving-in dates, are crucially important for private clients building their own home, who need to give appropriate notice on their previous, rented accommodation. Renovation work in schools can often be carried out only in the school holidays. Here both the starting and completion dates are deciding factors.

Deadline constraints

> ■ **Tip:** Planners must establish that the client's ideas about deadlines are realistic. This affects the services that can be delivered by the firms involved, and the planners' own ability to deliver. Some events that occur in the course of building can be influenced only slightly or not at all. These include gaining permission from authorities, the weather, and some product delivery times.

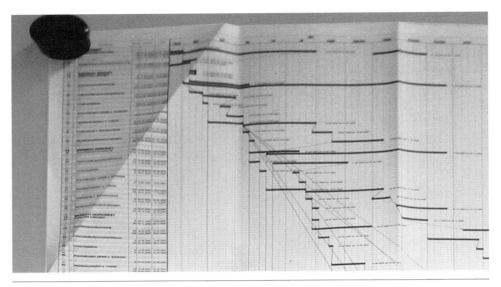

Fig. 5: Example of a deadline plan as a bar chart

<table>
<tr><td>Deadlines as a cost factor</td><td>Deadline requirements also influence possible construction processes and thus costs. The only realistic way of working faster is to employ a larger workforce, more machines and materials. Contractors could then be compelled to hire equipment or to complete the work in overtime, working at weekends or even at night. This will result in high bid prices, as the company factors the extra costs into the bid price.</td></tr>
</table>

Deadlines as a cost factor

Deadline requirements also influence possible construction processes and thus costs. The only realistic way of working faster is to employ a larger workforce, more machines and materials. Contractors could then be compelled to hire equipment or to complete the work in overtime, working at weekends or even at night. This will result in high bid prices, as the company factors the extra costs into the bid price.

Effects on tendering

Deadline requirements also affect the way planners submit their tenders. Robust and detailed planning involves investing a great deal of time, so planners have to consider whether they will be able to submit such plans at the appropriate time. If they cannot do so, they can transfer some of the planning services to the contractor, by defining some aspects in terms of functions, rather than in full detail. > Chapter Organizing the tender, Tendering style, Tendering by function

Function

Realization range

The client's requirements establish the extent and bandwidth of the realization variants. For example, if a private client wants to buy land and build a home on it, this can be a terraced house, a semi-detached house or a detached house. Function is thus one of the factors determining the form the building will take. It is also possible to decide on particular building methods from a function description. When building a warehouse with

Fig. 6: Various functions

no special requirements, a choice will usually be made between favorably priced variants (e.g. reinforced concrete or steel construction). Thus function is linked with a particular range of possible solutions, modified by the client's individual requirements.

The more strongly clients identify themselves with a commission, the more influence they will wish to exert on planning the invitation to tender. If the project is their dream house, the client could well wish to be involved in every last detail of the planning process. The invitation to tender will thus have to be correspondingly detailed, so that the client's ideas can be implemented in full. > Chapter Organizing the tender, Tendering style, Detailed tendering

Client profile

If the finished building is intended as a for-profit project, however, clients will be mainly interested in minimum costs for maximum yield. They will want to scale their requirements down as much as possible at first, and will be prepared to raise their technical or aesthetic sights only if there is a prospect of higher profits or greater marketability. If clients are simply after a box to put something in (e.g. a warehouse or an industrial production hall), they will also tend to see the commission pragmatically in terms of function, and not want to bother themselves with too much detail.

Fig. 7: There are various ways of meeting requirements for a building.

Range of services

Minimum scope   The range of services derives from clients' wishes. For example, when building an office block, clients can state how many office workstations are intended and what other spaces are needed to serve the desired function (foyer, conference rooms, server areas, etc.). The more precise the requirements, the more precisely the minimum project range can be determined.

Rationalization   If the project range is inappropriate to the desired cost framework, planners can reduce costs by rationalization (for example, by using a large number of identical elements and focusing on the same service provider as much as possible): facade design can match the facade panel format the manufacturer produces, so that large quantities of a particular panel format can be used without cutting or having to order special formats.

Factors open to influence   As well as the scope set by minimum standards, there are also variable quantities that affect the quality of the building as a rule. For example, planners can minimize the window area, which is more expensive than a closed facade, at the expense of user comfort, or reduce the number of workstations at the expense of subsequent flexibility.

Fig. 8: The relationship between function and quality

Quality

Function also affects the quality expected. Here we can speak of technical and aesthetic criteria. > Fig. 9 Technical requirements include building law provisions (e.g. statutes relating to assembly of persons or the fire prevention concept), or health aspects (e.g. ventilation or hygiene); aesthetic requirements relate to the visual impact, form and characteristics of the building as a whole, down to individual details such as door handles.

There are fixed minimum standards for most building services, intended to guarantee the use of appropriate materials and professional execution. Clients will have requirements for their property that go beyond minimum quality. As soon as the planned finish deviates from the standard quality, planners must mention this expressly in their service description and describe the finish or the desired result. Standards of quality

If requirements relating to quality of finish exceed the normal standard, costs will rise as well. For example, the amount of work and cost involved in dry-building a wall with a high level of overall finish on the plasterwork is considerably greater than for one that is simply smoothed and finished at the joints.

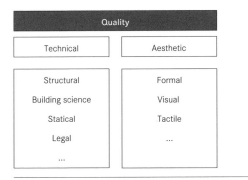

Fig. 9: Division into technical and aesthetic criteria

Longer-term planning Long-term considerations should always be included in relation to quality. For example, installing a more expensive but higher-calibre heating system can easily compensate for its greater cost through lower energy costs over the period of use.

TENDER ITEMS

Building services and construction products The building process involves choosing and coordinating an enormous range of structural elements. Here, planners have a very wide range of prefabricated items at their disposal (e.g. doors and door frames), but can also work with individually manufactured elements (e.g. hand-crafted door fittings). A building can be planned down to the position of the last screw, and the shape of its head. Invitations to tender for building services relate both to parts of the planning process and also to the whole realization process. They summarize all the services needed. The scope of the invitation to tender will vary according to the scope of the building project and the nature of the tender. > Chapter Organizing the tender, Tendering style For example, if tenders are being invited for a complete building project, starting from scratch to the very end, they can include all construction services from digging the foundations to cleaning at the end of the construction phase and handing the key over to the client. Invitations to tender may also be issued for replacing a single window.

Fig. 10: Everything can be built into an invitation to tender

Complementary planning and services can also be included in an invitation to tender, as well as classical construction work or products. So it is possible to invite bids for specialist planning such as preparing a sound insulation report, or services such as organizing a topping-out party.

Planning and other services

Organizing the tender

The possible scope of the project, and the diversity and complexity of the invitation to tender, mean that it makes sense to divide the building process into significant phases. To do this, planners must be familiar with events within the construction process and the individual events' interdependence, so that they can arrange them in the correct time sequence.

Fundamentals of organization

○

TIMETABLING THE INVITATION TO TENDER

Deadlines are an important element of the tendering process. Planners have to know what periods of time are realistic for realizing the project. A timetable for the planner's and the bidding companies' work on the tender can be drawn up with reference to the realization deadlines, bearing possible preliminary planning periods for specialist firms and for the awarding procedure in mind.

Deadlines and tendering

○ **Note:** The process following the invitation to tender, collecting in bids and subsequently commissioning of firms by clients, is called the awarding procedure. Information about awarding tenders can be found in Building projects in the *European Union* by Bert Bielefeld and Falk Würfele, Birkhäuser Verlag, 2005.

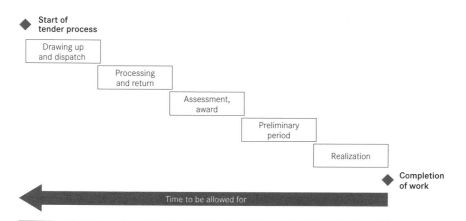

Fig. 11: Timetabling an invitation to tender

Time invested by participants

Time invested
by planner

Planners need sufficient time to draw up an invitation to tender. > Fig.11 Once they have compiled a list of all the client's wishes and requirements, they must take time to organize the invitation to tender and think how to convey the requirements in such a way that the invitation can be formulated meaningfully. Planners must establish quantities needed, to define the scope of the services required. Any question arising must be cleared up with manufacturers, specialist organizations or other appropriate contacts. It is often necessary to provide any experts approached with documents about the general conditions, and drawings, to ensure that responses are robust and appropriate for describing the services required. If difficult installations or complex construction processes are involved it often makes sense for planners to cover themselves by asking manufacturers for written statements or opinions.

Once planners have drawn up their lists of services needed, they must compile a list of bidders, i.e. the names of all the firms invited to tender, in consultation with the client where appropriate. The tender documents have to be duplicated and sent out to the companies concerned, allowing an appropriate length of time for processing by the companies.

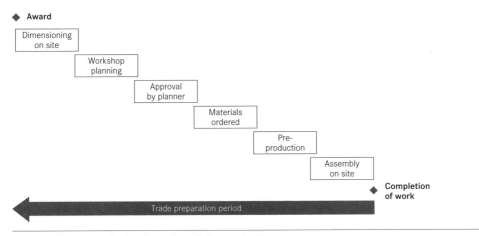

Fig. 12: Preliminary trade planning period: window production

Construction companies submitting bids who receive a description of the services required have to familiarize themselves with a new building project, and thus need an appropriate period to work on the invitation to tender. In some cases, the nature and scope of the tender may require additional planning work before the price can finally be calculated; manufacturers or other firms and their internal price enquires may need to be considered in their turn. The calculation must take wages, materials, equipment and outside services into account. As well as these factors relating directly to the building commission, general overheads and possible profit have to be built into the bid price. Preparing the bid can take anything from a day to several weeks, according to the complexity and scope of the tender. The necessary processing period is extended correspondingly if the invitation to tender also covers planning services or technical tests.

Time needed for processing the bid

The time span from commissioning to the actual delivery of the services (start of building work) on the building site is the preliminary planning period for specialist firms. > Fig. 12 During this period, the firms being commissioned can construct working plans or samples and submit them to the planner for approval. Construction elements are often modified or assembled in advance in the factory by the firms involved. Measurements

Preliminary planning period for trades

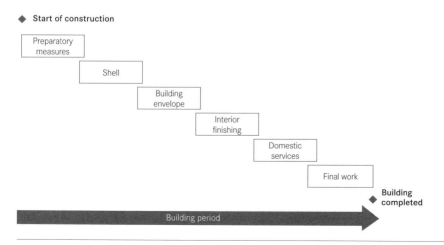

Fig. 13: Sequence of building work

for prefabrication may need to be made on site, which adds another factor for meeting completion deadlines, for example if masonry with apertures has to be completed before fixing the dimensions of the windows that have to be prefabricated.

Time needed for realization

When timetabling tenders it is important to know how long it will take to complete a particular piece of work, given that a possible completion deadline has to be fixed. > Fig. 13 There is only limited scope for shortening such an individual completion time. The length of time needed can be affected by the number of people working on the job, working hours and the use of machines. There are natural restrictions on speeding up work, for example the time that certain building materials take to dry or harden (e.g. screed). Space on the building site may be at a premium, so increasing the workforce could mean people getting in each other's way while working.

TENDERING SEQUENCE AND NATURE OF TENDER

Time sequence
The order for drawing up invitations to tender is usually based on the order in which work is carried out on the building site. > Fig. 13 First bids are invited for preparatory measures for the actual building project, followed by bids for shell realization, exterior finish, interior finish and fittings, down to bids for the final work needed. Sometimes the preliminary preparation period makes it necessary to deviate from the on-site sequence when inviting to tender. For example, facade construction can

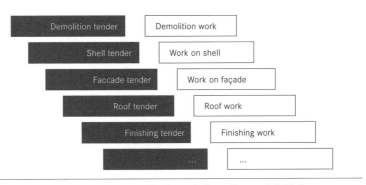

Fig. 14: Sequential planning when awarding by trade (award by specialist lot)

entail a preparatory period lasting several months, which must be taken into consideration when drawing up the invitation to tender.

The sequence described here relates to invitations to tender issued while building is in progress. > Fig. 14 For tendering in this way, all the services required are drawn up in sequence, and invitations to tender issued. For example, the interior is planned and invitations to tender are issued after the shell has already been completed. In comparison with a blanket invitation to tender > Chapter Organizing the tender, Fixing bid units, Package awards this approach offers the advantage that an appropriate response can be made to unexpected cost developments. > Introduction, Tendering requirements, Costs It is also possible to accommodate changes that have occurred during the completed building phases. For example, if the ceiling slab thicknesses have had to be changed for practical reasons, they can be compensated for in the finished floor height. However, it is impossible to be certain about costs until the last invitation to tender, because of the difficulty in predicting the effect market fluctuations and other eventualities could have on services offered.

Invitations to tender while building is in progress

Awarding to a main contractor offers greater cost security. > Chapter Organizing the tender, Fixing bid units, Package awards Here, all the services have to be identified in full, and submitted to the contractor with an invitation to tender. The planning period involved is correspondingly long. Planning previously undertaken in parallel with the building work now has to be

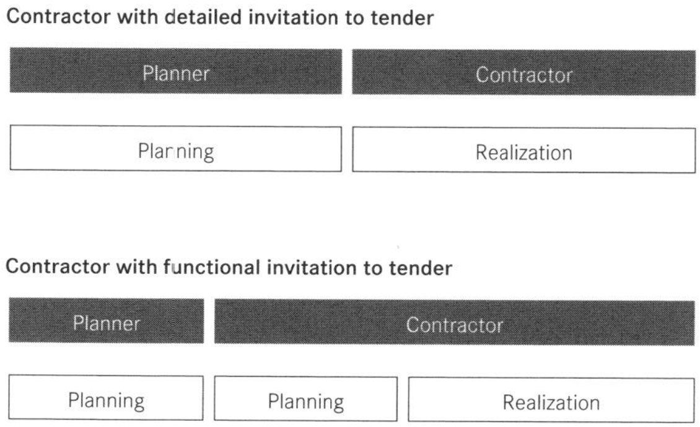

Blanket tendering

Contractor with detailed invitation to tender

Planner	Contractor
Planning	Realization

Contractor with functional invitation to tender

Planner	Contractor	
Planning	Planning	Realization

Fig. 15: Award procedure and time consumed

Total package award
All work awarded to one contractor

Award by lot
Whole package broken down into "lots"

Trade lot award	Part lot award
With specialist subdivision (award by trade lot)	With subdivision by rooms (award by building phases)

Fig. 16: Definition of the terms for award units

completed before the first ground is dug. > Fig. 15 If there is not enough time available for a detailed invitation to tender, planners must concentrate on requirements that are important to the client and describe only these in detail > Chapter Organizing the tender, Tender style, Detailed tendering and the rest merely functionally. > Chapter Organizing the tender, Tendering style, Tendering by function Sometimes the pressure of time can be so great that a purely functional invitation model has to be considered, giving no detail at all.

FIXING BID UNITS

Bid unit   A bid unit defines the range of service provision awarded to a particular contractor. Bid units can be itemized according to size for individual trades (trade lots), part lots and complete packages; it is also possible to include all the services in a total package award. > Fig. 16

Tendering by trade

Trade (specialist lots)   Subdivision by trades (trade or specialist lots) is based on craft and technical skills traditionally delivered by an individual or a firm (e.g. craft trades such as stonemason, carpenter or screed layer). This is generally the smallest bid unit. > Fig. 17

○   A trade can be broken down into even smaller units if a number of different services are provided. For example, a tender invitation for metalworkers could include all the services this trade offers. It is also possible to draw up several invitations to tender identifying individual items, such as a service described under facade construction in metal, and

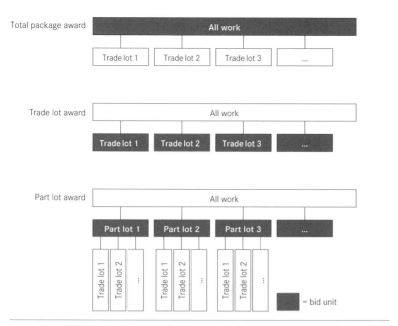

Total package award

All work

Trade lot 1 | Trade lot 2 | Trade lot 3 | ...

Trade lot award

All work

Trade lot 1 | Trade lot 2 | Trade lot 3 | ...

Part lot award

All work

Part lot 1 | Part lot 2 | Part lot 3 | ...

Trade lot 1 | Trade lot 2 | ... | Trade lot 1 | Trade lot 2 | ... | Trade lot 1 | Trade lot 2 | ...

= bid unit

Fig. 17: Bid units

another for steel staircases and banisters. The smallest possible bid unit is a single service. > Fig. 18

So tendering by trade may include all the services performed by that trade or just some of them. It makes sense to break a trade down into smaller units if particular firms' specialist fields are to be used.

○ **Note:** The term trade is also generally applied to less traditional work such as structural engineering, media planning or sign-making. Although these are not traditional trades, the important feature here is that the services form a unit.

● **Example:** A construction company that produces and assembles stairs every day can offer this service more professionally and possibly more cheaply than a metal-worker who specializes in facades but theoretically covers all aspects of that trade.

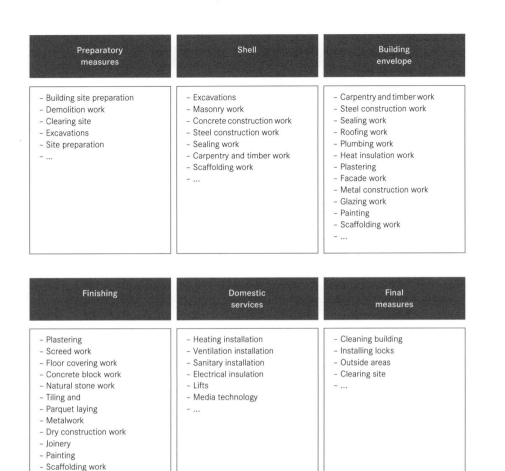

Preparatory measures	Shell	Building envelope
– Building site preparation – Demolition work – Clearing site – Excavations – Site preparation – ...	– Excavations – Masonry work – Concrete construction work – Steel construction work – Sealing work – Carpentry and timber work – Scaffolding work – ...	– Carpentry and timber work – Steel construction work – Sealing work – Roofing work – Plumbing work – Heat insulation work – Plastering – Facade work – Metal construction work – Glazing work – Painting – Scaffolding work – ...

Finishing	Domestic services	Final measures
– Plastering – Screed work – Floor covering work – Concrete block work – Natural stone work – Tiling and – Parquet laying – Metalwork – Dry construction work – Joinery – Painting – Scaffolding work – ...	– Heating installation – Ventilation installation – Sanitary installation – Electrical insulation – Lifts – Media technology – ...	– Cleaning building – Installing locks – Outside areas – Clearing site – ...

Fig. 18: Typical trade subdivisions

The disadvantage is that more time and effort have to be invested in coordination when commissioning several firms, and synergies (e.g. travel to the building site or larger delivery quantities at correspondingly more favorable prices) could be lost.

Bundling trades It can sometimes make sense to bundle a number of trades. It seems logical to commission a single firm to take on all the work relating to a roof, and avoid having to coordinate a number of firms. Thus, carpentry (constructing the roof truss), roof-covering work (roof construction from insulation to the pantiles), and some metal-fitting work (fitting gutters, protective leading) can all be done by the same firm. Many firms have adapted to the clients' desire to deal with a single contact person, and advertise as providing a complete service. Note here that some firms that seem quite large simply "buy in" services and often cannot offer them at particularly reasonable prices. The client is then buying convenience by paying an additional price for in-house subcontractor organization by the firm commissioned. > Chapter Organizing the tender, Fixing bid units, Invitation to tender ○ by part lot

Invitation to tender by part lot

The part lot is another bid unit. Here, services are not classified in terms of a specific trade, but structured in sections. These sections derive mainly from a desire to be able to award to several firms when a great deal of work is involved.

Part lot

In public commissions, this can take place with the intention of involving as many firms as possible in the bidding process, as the scope of services required will then be based on the capacities of essentially average companies.

Subdividing services

Another sensible reason for structuring in part lots is when planning work over a long period with possible interruptions. Building phases are often fixed for larger building projects so that some parts of the building can be used while others are completed at a later stage. > Fig. 19

Building phases

Package awards

Bundling several trades, with only one contact person on the realization side, as mentioned above, is pursued further in awards to a main contractor. > Chapter Organizing the tender, Fixing bid units, Invitation to tender by part lot

Main contractor tendering

○ **Note:** A subcontractor works for the firm with which the client has signed the building contract. The subcontractor has no official relationship with the client. The commissioned firm remains responsible for commissioning, finish, payment and guarantees.

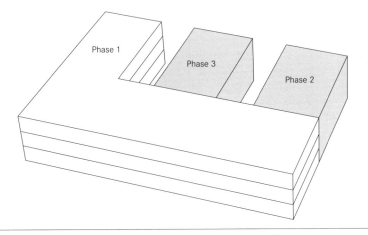

Fig. 19: Bidding for part lots is possible if buildings are constructed in various phases.

Here, the client commissions a single building firm to provide all the services needed to complete the building work. A single contract is agreed, rather than a large number of them.

Meeting deadlines   It is easier for a main contractor to fix completion dates because such a firm will be able to compensate for delays in parts of the project by pushing the work ahead in other areas, as part of the overall coordination process. It is more difficult to set binding deadlines when commissioning a number of individual firms because of the large number of mutual dependencies: individual building firms are not contractually obliged to each other.

Main contractor supplement   A main contractor is responsible for all this, and will generally exact payment for this often voluminous coordination work, and sometimes also risk coverage for guarantees undertaken, by building supplements into the bid. In practice there are few firms that can cover all the services required using in-house workers. In fact, they tend to tender the services out to other firms, which then – if they are commissioned – work as subcontractors. A main contractor's bid concludes in a guaranteed price for which the services must be delivered by a contractually fixed deadline.

TENDERING STYLE

A distinction is made between <u>functional</u> and <u>detailed</u> tendering, but these are rarely separated consistently in practice. Any detailed invitation to tender will always contain functional elements. For example, even a meticulously detailed description of a plasterboard stud wall will not contain precise information about fixing the plasterboard panels. It is assumed that the workmen will have the appropriate technical knowledge and will know the correct screws to use for fixing the panels to the frame. A functional invitation to tender can work without detailed elements, but here, too, there will in practice be areas where the requirements are formulated in greater detail. The more questions the planner asks the client about requirements, the longer the list of detailed requirements within the actual functional invitation will become.

Tendering by function

Functional tendering does not describe how the work is to be done or the precise building process, but focuses on the required outcome. The bidder takes responsibility for planning the work and thus also carries the risk of achieving the required result even if there were omissions in the original bid. As well as being responsible for possible planning errors, the contracted firm also carries the quantity surveying risks.

Bidders are able to determine how the work is done by choosing procedures in the light of their expertise and experience. They can optimize the entire range of services offered in terms of their own resources, as the contract offers room for manoeuvre.

The criteria for assessing bids include price, and the way the set requirements are addressed. The bidder will have spent time and effort on the bid, and the planner now has to assess it in some depth. Consequently, clients or planners have no further influence in principle on the subsequent execution of the process. This loss of control, which applies to detailed planning in particular, may lead to a loss of design quality. Assessing bids

Functional tendering is often chosen through lack of time. > Introduction, Tendering requirements, Deadlines It thus clearly reduces the extensive planning process that would have to precede award to a main contractor. Lower client demands on the realization details may lie behind a functional invitation to tender, especially as the firm to which the contract is awarded takes on a large number of risks as well. Another reason for choosing a functional style may be simply that the planner has no idea how to achieve the required aims by means of a detailed invitation to Choosing
functional
tendering tender. Thus, planners will not invite tenders for the individual components of an air-conditioning plant or the way they are assembled, but will simply describe cooling or ventilation rate requirements.

Detailed tendering

Detailed tendering requires every detail of the work required to have been planned in advance to the greatest possible extent. Planners do not simply describe the required result, but also how it is to be achieved. They thus accept the risk that the finished work will not meet demands, or that there will be errors and omissions in the tender invitation, or it will not be completely clear. This can lead to additional costs for additional work (services that are needed but were not included in the original invitation to tender).

Assessing the bids It is much simpler to assess a detailed invitation to tender, as the choice of procedure is fixed, and only the prices have to be compared.

Choosing a detailed invitation to tender It always makes sense to opt for a detailed invitation to tender if the client wishes to remain in control of the building process. This is the only way of checking every detail of the realization work, and avoids disagreeable surprises.

Depth of tender

It is fundamentally possible to mix functional and detailed tendering. This opens up considerable creative possibilities for planners. They will be able to submit detailed final working plans for all the areas that are important to clients, and to describe the realization process with equal precision. In areas that do not require so much detail they can confine themselves to describing requirements and choose the contractor who offers the best possible solution.

Detailed or functional? If planners put out detailed invitations to tender they must have the appropriate knowledge at their fingertips. They will be responsible for any mistakes in their description of the services they are offering. It is therefore advisable to tender on the basis of function, bearing the desired result in mind, for any elements about which they are not thoroughly informed.

Completeness of the bid Planners must always ask themselves whether the invitation to tender they have prepared is complete, in other words whether the information they have provided is unambiguous, and that there are no omissions. For example, if they ask for an "orderly and symmetrical" pattern of screws for securing the facade elements, they must add a diagram showing the pattern of screws, to avoid contentious interpretations of this requirement. As a rule, only detailed descriptions allow control of the way the work is ultimately done. This is very time-consuming, and cannot always be managed for every aspect of the building. Planners should always consider carefully what degree of detailing is necessary and appropriate. For example, requirements about formwork for an exposed concrete wall must be much more carefully formulated than those relating to formwork for foundations that will not be visible when the building is completed.

Structuring an invitation to tender

The invitation to tender – functional or detailed – is made up of several elements. > Figs. 20, 21 It includes all the documents required for awarding a building contract.

○

TEXTUAL ELEMENTS

Textual elements mean all the descriptions couched in words and figures that provide information about the sequence and execution of the planned building project. An invitation to tender is drawn up using these elements, and consists of the following components:

— General information about the project
— Contractual conditions
— Technical requirements
— Information about building site conditions
— Description of the work required

Textual elements usually make up a large proportion of a tender bid. Words enable planners to convey information that cannot be found in the plans.

General information about the building project

A complete tender package contains general information about the planned building project and the awarding procedures. This information is conveyed in a cover sheet or accompanying letter containing the invitation to tender and other details relevant to the award, as well as the names of the key participants and a short description of the building.

General description

○ **Note:** For an invitation to tender to be absolutely unambiguous it is important for individual elements not to contradict each other; this may be avoided by fixing a rank order for the individual elements. Thus, a precise description of the services required always ranks higher than the technical requirements.

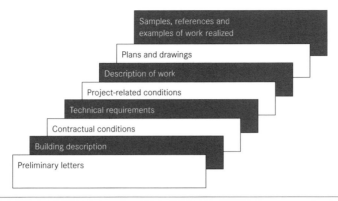

Fig. 20: The elements of an invitation to tender

Samples, references and examples of work realized

Plans and drawings

Description of work

Project-related conditions

Technical requirements

Contractual conditions

Building description

Preliminary letters

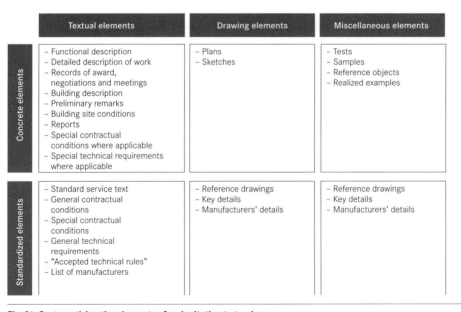

	Textual elements	Drawing elements	Miscellaneous elements
Concrete elements	– Functional description – Detailed description of work – Records of award, negotiations and meetings – Building description – Preliminary remarks – Building site conditions – Reports – Special contractual conditions where applicable – Special technical requirements where applicable	– Plans – Sketches	– Tests – Samples – Reference objects – Realized examples
Standardized elements	– Standard service text – General contractual conditions – Special contractual conditions – General technical requirements – "Accepted technical rules" – List of manufacturers	– Reference drawings – Key details – Manufacturers' details	– Reference drawings – Key details – Manufacturers' details

Fig. 21: Systematizing the elements of an invitation to tender

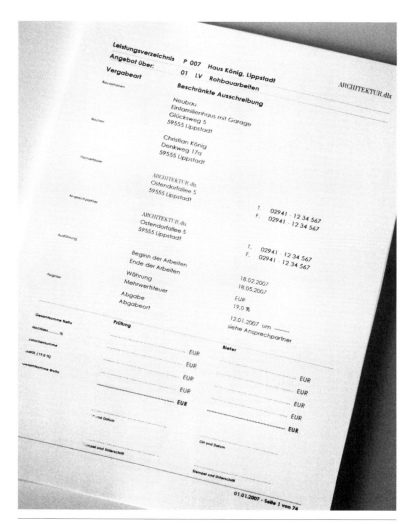

Fig. 22: Example of a cover sheet

The cover sheet is both an introduction to and a summary of the contents of the invitation to tender. It includes brief summary of all the information required for the building firm to process the tender, along with
the conditions of application. The cover sheet should contain the following information:

Cover sheet /
accompanying letter

243

- Details of the sender and recipient of the documents
- Date
- Definition of the building project
- Location, nature and scope of the work required
- General conditions relating to the building project (type of award, timescales, etc.)
- Express invitation to tender
- Conditions of application
- List of documents enclosed (contractual documents)

Description of the building project

Details about the location, nature and scope of the services required are needed, along with a definition of the building project, so that it can be clearly identified. These should be as succinct as possible. If more information about the project is required, this should be included in the building description. > Chapter Structuring service specifications, Approach to functional service specifications, Functional specification with designs

Information about the awarding procedure

The awarding procedure should be clearly defined in the cover sheet and must be given by public clients. > Chapter Organizing the tender, Timetabling the invitation to tender, Time invested by participants

Viewing dates

Identifying the location is also important in relation to possible viewing dates. Such dates should be identified on the cover sheet, giving location and date. The same applies to planned inspection dates in other documents not included in the tender package.

Tendering period/ submission

Details about the tendering period, the submission date and binding dates for the tender are equally important. > Chapter Organizing the tender, Timetabling the invitation to tender The tendering period identifies the date by which the bid must be submitted. The bidder will be committed to the offer made until the date given. Bidders should be informed about the essential award criteria (e.g. price) in the cover sheet for the tender documents.

Binding nature of the bid

To avoid misunderstanding, the cover sheet should include a formulation stating that the bidder will incur costs as a result of bidding. The formulation could be:

"We request your binding bid for this building project, at no cost to us or our client..."

Conditions of application/ admissibility criteria

Planners can influence potential applicants through the application conditions in the accompanying letter. Possible conditions can regulate the use of subcontractors, or admit or exclude group bidding for the award.

Planners can use a request for proof of suitability and admission criteria to check whether bidding companies are qualified to carry out the work. As well as an informed check on suitability, by reference to projects previously carried out, for example, it is also possible to call for information about a company's economic situation, to ensure that it is sufficiently liquid. It is also customary to ask for information about the building firm's capacities, its membership of professional organizations and its liability insurance, stating the minimum sum covered.

Proof of suitability

The building description contains other general information about the building project. It provides the company carrying out the work with a general summary of the building project, with no detailed information about individual services. Bidders should complete the picture for themselves with construction descriptions and information about the key conditions affecting costs for the building project.

Building description

For larger building projects it can make sense to include more precise information about the body of the building or the structure and organization of individual building sections in the building description, so that bidders can form a clearer picture of the possible building phases.

Contractual conditions

The invitation to tender aims to prepare the way for a contractual relationship between the client and one or more companies realizing the project. Against this backdrop, provisions governing contractual modalities for carrying out the building work are important, as well a description of the services required.

Planners prepare the way for the future contract appropriately in the invitation to tender, by stating general and particular contract conditions. General contract conditions are available in the form of complete sample contracts, but as a rule special contractual conditions must be formulated as business conditions laid down by the client.

General contractual conditions

General contractual conditions are based on national or international standards for managing building projects. They contain important information about:

- <u>Nature and scope of the work required</u> (details of contract elements and their ranking, and information about rights of change or extension relating to the building project)
- <u>Compensation</u> (provisions for dealing with claims for compensation in cases of deviation from the work as described)
- <u>Implementation</u> (provisions for supervision of the work by the client, for ensuring general order on the building site and the use of on-site facilities by the company carrying out the work; provisions governing rights of appeal if the company carrying out the work has complaints about a service required by the client or the planner)
- <u>Implementation documents</u> (information about handing over the documents relating to implementing the services required)
- <u>Timings</u> (general provision, for example ensuring that building work will begin within a stated period of time if no date was fixed contractually)
- <u>Impediments</u> (fixing procedures if impediments are in the offing. For example, obstructions should be notified to the client in advance and their effect described, so that counter-measures can be taken)
- <u>Cancellation</u> (provisions for cancellation by the client or the company carrying out the work)
- <u>Liability</u> (details of the contractual parties' responsibilities)
- <u>Contract penalties</u> (provisions governing modalities for contractual penalties not covering the penalty level)
- <u>Acceptance</u> (setting down timings for legal acceptance of building work)
- <u>Guarantee</u> (provisions for securing the client's claims after the building work has been accepted)

- <u>Settlement</u> (details about how and in what order settlement must take place after completion of work required, or parts of that work)
- <u>Work paid by the hour</u> (provisions for dealing with remuneration for services required that are not contained in the description of services, for example a commitment by the firm carrying out the work to inform the client before undertaking such work)
- <u>Payments</u> (general provisions governing instalments, part-final and final invoices, for example, timings are laid down for the duration of the final invoice check)
- <u>Security</u> (provisions governing mutual security for the contract partners, for example in the form of guarantees or security retentions)
- <u>Disputes</u> (provisions in case of dispute, such as fixing the client's location as the place of jurisdiction)

Special contractual conditions can relate to the same matters as the general contractual conditions and complement them in certain points. They serve as an addition to the general contractual conditions, and not as a substitute for them. Typically, special contractual conditions are included in the tendering documents if there is already a provision in principle in the general contractual conditions. The following areas are also addressed:

Special contractual conditions

- <u>Invoices</u> (invoices must be identified according to their purpose as instalment, part-final or final invoices, and always numbered continuously. Other formal requirements can deal with the sequence of the work carried out, identifying it according to the description of work required, for example.)
- <u>Special payment modalities</u> (provisions governing the client's payments to the company carrying out the work and the conditions to which the payments are linked. For example, a payment plan can be agreed, giving information about the level and date of payments. Payments are often agreed at particular times to cover the work carried out to this point.)
- <u>Basis for establishing the price</u> (the bidder's calculations used to determine the prices in the bid)
- <u>Flexible price clauses</u> for wages or materials (provisions allowing for contract prices to be modified if the agreed wage levels or building material prices change during the building phase)
- <u>Notification of additional costs</u> (provisions establishing that the client be informed at an early stage of any additional costs that may occur)

- Subcontractors (subcontractors are used to provide services that a company cannot itself cover. If the use of subcontractors is to be excluded or is permissible only under certain circumstances, this should be laid down in the special contractual conditions.)
- Competition restriction (inadmissible competition restrictions arise from prior agreements that are unfavorable to competition between bidders relating to the submission or non-submission of bids, to prices or profit supplements. Special contractual conditions lay down the consequences of behavior that is unfavorable to competition.)
- Price reductions (are regularly agreed as a percentage and deducted from all invoices appropriately)
- Environmental protection (Normally no concrete environmental protection measures are formulated. It is customary for the special contractual conditions to refer to reduction of environmental damage by the building measures.)
- Changes to the contract (Contract alteration modalities should be stipulated in the special contractual conditions. For example, it can be agreed that alterations to the contract must be in writing.)

Technical requirements

As a rule, planning a building project and describing the work required to realize it end when a certain degree of detail has been reached. Everything else is fixed by the agreement on technical requirements. This contains instructions about the way the work is to be carried out. For example, planners might provide a drawing of a reinforced concrete wall, and possibly supplement it in the text with description containing details about formwork, reinforcement and concrete. But they will not describe in detail how the formwork should be constructed, the reinforcing steel secured in position or the concrete compacted. Such information forms part of the specialist knowledge of the company carrying out the work, and will be conveyed by the planners to the building firm via the technical requirements laid down in the invitation to tender.

Technical requirements are available as a comprehensive package of provisions for most services provided by different trades. > Appendix They contain relevant stipulations for a large number of building jobs in the form of a minimum standard. Special technical requirements are formulated to define a higher standard.

General technical requirements

General technical requirements are standards that apply in terms of the generally acknowledged rules for a particular technology.

Regulations are usually arranged specifically to trades and contain information about the sphere of validity, the substances and materials used, implementation, additional services that form part of the service as a whole, and about financial settlement and hints for compiling a description of the services.

Special technical requirements are regulations that are used either to complement the general technical requirements or that apply to areas not previously regulated. For example, a special technical requirement can relate to a building process not covered by the general regulations, or can stipulate a higher dimension tolerance requirement to complement the existing minimum requirements.

Special technical contractual conditions

Special technical requirements are based on standards, as well as on other sets of technical regulations, manufacturer's guidelines or provisions, and instructions from interested parties.

It is also possible to agree on more demanding requirements taking account of the current state of technology and of science and technology for certain services; these requirements will be based on individual licences.

Furthermore, there are special technical requirements for intermediate acceptance: for example, when for technical reasons certain pieces of work have to be accepted during the building period as they will be inaccessible at a later stage because of building progress.

○ **Note:** If certain provisions apply to one particular building project, they should be addressed in the contractual conditions relating to the project, and not in the special contractual conditions, which are usually formulated to cover several building projects.

○ **Note:** The generally acknowledged rules of technology are a set of regulations based on technologies that have proved their worth over a long period of time. A higher standard is set by a level of technology that represents the latest technical progress, but need not be tried and tested. A further step upwards is offered by a level of science and technology that takes the most recent scientific insights into account.

Project-related contractual conditions

Project-related information covers the general conditions of the building project. They cover all the regulations of a contractual and technical nature affecting the building project as such.

Information about the building site These particular contractual conditions have to be compiled specially for every project. They should contain the following information about the building site:

— <u>Location</u> (address and description of where the building site is situated)
— <u>Access</u> (how to reach the building site)
— <u>Storage space</u> (areas that will be at the contractor's disposal for work on the building program)
— <u>Lifting equipment</u> (lifting equipment such as cranes or hoists are often in place on building sites and can be used by various firms to transport their building materials)
— <u>Scaffolding</u> (scaffolding may be placed at the disposal of other firms)
— <u>Connections for electricity, water and sewage</u> (the appropriate supply points are fixed before building starts as part of the site equipment)
— <u>Sanitary facilities</u> (if available)
— <u>Waste disposal</u>
— <u>Telephone connections</u>

Apportioning general building site costs The general building site costs can be contractually apportioned to all the contractors involved. Costs for setting up site signs, using on-site equipment and waste disposal can also be apportioned in the project-related contractual conditions.

Implementation period/contract deadlines Stipulations about the time available for the work are particularly important. All statements relating to this are fixed in relation to the project. They include statements about the beginning and end of the building work. These periods are binding for later implementation of the building commission, and if not observed they represent a breach of contract with the possible consequence of claims for damages, or a contract penalty. Only contractual periods that the company undertaking the work has acknowledged in the project-related contract conditions are legally binding. If intermediate deadlines other than the starting and finishing deadlines are agreed contractually with the company undertaking the work, these must be identified as individual fixed periods in the project-related contract conditions.

If contract deadlines are not met, this usually means claims for dam- ages by the client against the company undertaking the work. Here, only loses that have actually resulted can be considered. If other provisions are also made for handling breach of contract, these must be indicated appropriately in the project-related contract conditions with reference to a contract penalty.

It is also possible to agree on other project-related contractual conditions if required, for example stipulations about parallel services by other contractors, or provisions for clearing and cleaning the building site.

Tender specification

The tender specification is the key element in an invitation to tender. The distinction between functional and detailed tendering is based solely on the nature of the tender specification. A directory of services is used for a detailed tender specification, and a program of services is drawn up for a functional tender specification. In exceptional cases, building descriptions are used as functional tender specifications. > Fig. 23

The procedure for drawing up a detailed or functional tender speci- fication is discussed in detail in the final chapter.

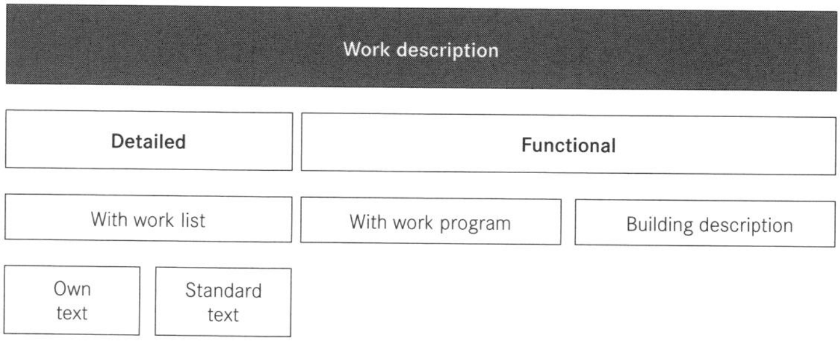

Fig. 23: **Tender specification types**

DRAWING ELEMENTS

The plans, drawings or sketches appended to an invitation to tender should make it easer for the contractors to compile their bid in terms of the services to be calculated. They will therefore need all the planning documents necessary for general geometrical orientation, and for understanding the services required.

Range of drawn descriptive elements
The spectrum of drawn descriptive elements extends from simple hand-drawn sketches to technical drawings, with plan content varying from site plans to scaled implementation details. > Figs. 24, 25

References
The architect can use references to particular planning details in the tender specification to identify particular points that do not emerge directly from the descriptive text or that are more easily conveyed by a drawing.

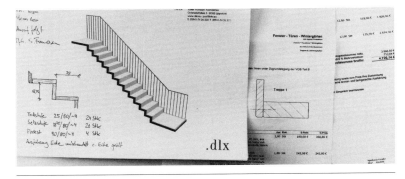

Fig. 24: Sketch by hand

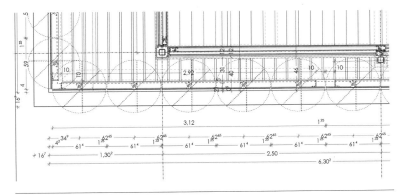

Fig. 25: Representing complex spatial connections

OTHER DESCRIPTIVE ELEMENTS

If texts and drawings cannot define the services required adequately, specimens can be used. For example, if the reinforced concrete requires a particular surface structure that is not covered by the general regulations and definitions for surface quality in exposed concrete, it makes sense to construct a specimen surface and make this accessible to bidders or even enclose it with the invitation to tender (e.g. a related wood veneer that is already in the building).

Specimens

If a specimen is available, the invitation to tender text need not embark on a full description, but concludes with the formulation *"Finish as per specimen ..."*

Markings can also be addressed in the invitation to tender. Markings need to be considered in the case of materials such as natural stone, as the appearance of stone can vary considerably. Here, verbal descriptions and drawings are almost impossible. The company carrying out the work should be required to lay a representative area of the material, so that the crucial criteria such as color, shade and the nature and distribution of inclusions can be fixed according to the sample.

Markings

It is also possible to set up show rooms in which the client can see and assess the effect made, from surface materials to individual pieces of furniture and fittings in context.

Reference items are particularly important when building in existing stock, or in the case of ensembles. For example, when designing the exterior of a building, the choice of brick can be specified to be the same as the existing buildings, with the same pattern of joints, without the planner needing to explain format, coloring or bond. Reference to buildings that are already in existence and the quality achieved there can also form the basis for describing building work.

Reference items, examples of finish

Structuring service specifications

We distinguish between three basic starting situations for functional or detailed service specifications. > Fig. 26

1. No design is supplied
2. Plans or planning permission are available
3. The final planning stage has been reached

APPROACH TO FUNCTIONAL SERVICE SPECIFICATIONS

The aim of functional tender specifications is to bring all the necessary requirements for a building together. Aims

Drawing up a functional tender specification can be considerably facilitated by recourse to various descriptive instruments. They include: Functional specification instruments

— Building descriptions
— Building programs
— Room programs
— List specifying all the work required

Construction and fittings and furnishings manuals are a further step in relation to detail in tender specifications. Their language is not essentially functional. It contains too many concrete requirements, and thus runs counter to the open concept principle of a functional invitation to tender. But such manuals can be used as part of a functional invitation

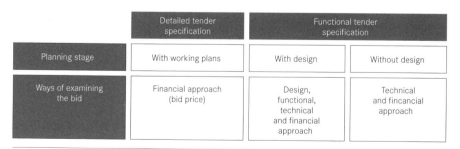

	Detailed tender specification	Functional tender specification	
Planning stage	With working plans	With design	Without design
Ways of examining the bid	Financial approach (bid price)	Design, functional, technical and financial approach	Technical and fincancial approach

Fig. 26: Service specification characteristics

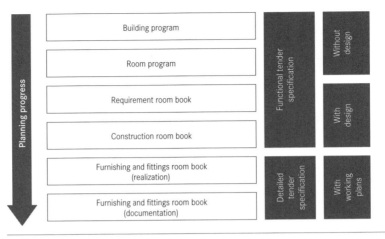

Fig. 27: Instruments for functional tender specification

to tender if a quality requirement is fixed beyond further discussion and is to be implemented when furnishing or decorating certain rooms, for example. > Fig. 27

The instruments listed either serve as a basis for drawing up a functional tender specification, or become part of the specification themselves. Without a design, only a building or room allocation program can be drawn up; a design must be made available if a book listing all the work required for the rooms ("room book") is to be compiled.

Whether a design is available or not, nothing changes the basic principles of functional tender specification. The aim is to define everything the client requires, although more creative input is required from the bidder if no design is provided.

○ **Note:** Building program and room allocation program can be used for functional tender specification even when a design is provided, as long as they do not contradict it. But it is customary to provide a more detailed description of services required in terms of rooms, structural elements and construction products.

Functional tender specifications without a design

A building program and a room allocation program, offered without a design, simply describe requirements for the building as a whole, for individual parts of a building or for areas intended for a particular use. The bidder is responsible for design, technical, use-oriented and economic planning.

○

A building program makes basic statements about a building. It first gives details of the property, for example covering use, office size, office type, the number of floors, number of offices per floor, or cellarage.

Building
program

No.	Field	Requirement
I	Area	Sample street 12, 00001 Sample town
II	Requirement (description)	Inner-city office complex
III	Nature of project	Conversions
IV	Use	Office, canteen
V	Plot size	10,000 m²
VI	Number of floors	3
VII	Cellars	yes (1 floor)
VIII	Building structure	2 Main building office 1 Ancillary building, canteen
IX	Office space	from ... m² to ... m²
X	Canteen space	from ... m² to ... m²
XI	Office type	Individual offices and open-plan office
XII	Individual offices	from ... m² to ... m²
XIII	Open-plan office	from ... m² to ... m²
XIV	Access	The building is to be connected to public utilities and transport
XV	Parking	Underground car park in cellar, parking spaces on the north side of the building, 1 parking space per workspace
XVI	Waste	Central waste disposal
XVII	Open spaces	Park with pond
XVIII	Rules and regulations	Development plan, local building requirements

Fig. 28: Sample structure for a building program

Building programs contain information about the building project in general, supplying additional information about connections to public services (sewerage, water, gas, electricity and telecommunications), the transport system and access to outside areas.

Building programs must specify requirements for the prescribed areas of use. These requirements can be differentiated and concretized in part. For example, it is possible even at this stage to fix sound insulation requirements for an area with individual offices. > Fig. 28

Room allocation program

A room allocation program provides a more refined definition of the requirements. It will give information about rooms and use areas, and also about how they are placed and linked together. The bandwidth of possible information in a room allocation program depends on the planning stage reached. Sensible subdivision of the areas according to the following criteria forms a good basis for a description system:

— Use
— Number
— Size
— Position and orientation > Fig. 29

Function scheme

A function scheme shows how individual areas relate to each other without illustrating the areas required. Essential links between individual areas are indicated in order to clarify the sequence of events arising from a particular use. > Fig. 30

Graphic room allocation program

Information from a tabular room program and function scheme can be summarized in a graphic room allocation program. This can contain basic elements of the architectural design that have already been determined: formal statements are presented, taking the areas and rooms

■ required and the way they relate to each other into account. > Fig. 31

Use	Number	Size	Position and orientation
Reception foyer	1	150 m²	Ground floor north side / west side
Canteen	1	200 m²	Ground floor north side / east side
Kitchen	1	80 m²	Ground floor center / east side
Office	4	each 25 m²	Ground floor south side / west side
Events room	3	1 × 200 m²	Ground floor south side / east side
		2 × 50 m²	

Fig. 29: Example of a tabular room allocation program

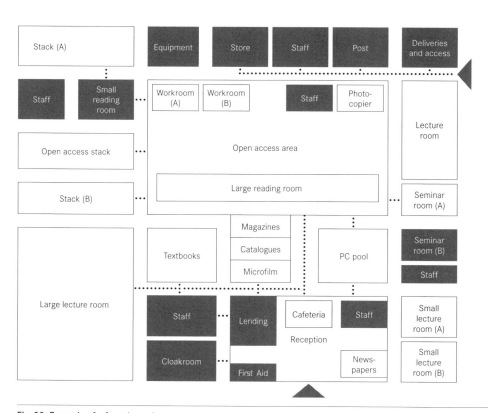

Fig. 30: Example of a function scheme

Other means of description are suitable as well as building and room allocation programs. A building description for drawing up a functional tender specification without a design is one of these.

The building description essentially provides a rough idea of the building project as a whole, but can also convey functional details. > Chapter Structuring an invitation to tender, Textual elements, General information about the building project Unlike the room allocation program, which is based on spatial organization, a building description is structured in terms of construction or trades. This is also why it is only very roughly suitable as a basis for functional tender specification. Saying "reinforced concrete hall, area 2,000 m^2" is a very rough description, but it is perfectly appropriate for use as an element in a functional description. Specifying "reinforced concrete" rules out alternative construction elements, such as steel girders.

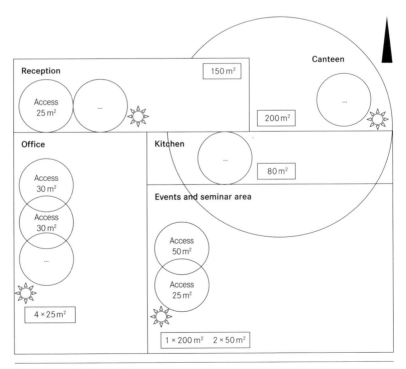

Fig. 31: Example of a graphic room program

The more specifically the building description addresses a particular construction method, the more effectively unwanted elements will be ruled out as alternatives for bidders.

Functional specification with design

If a design is available, definite requirements for the building project are already in place, and these are shown in plans. But the functional character of a tender specification with design supplied is still guaranteed, as it remains possible to define the quality of individual construction systems, structural components or construction products. In this context, using a room book – a set list of all the services required to complete a particular room – is a helpful device for systematizing requirements.

A room allocation program can be addressed in greater detail by introducing room books at an appropriate point in the planning phase. This is a system that makes it possible to supply information about any planned room. A room book sums up the space required systematically and defines use requirements. Each room book should contain the following information to ensure unambiguous identification and simplify further use of the information provided:

Room book

— Room number, following a defined system for structuring
  the building project
— Definition of the room
— Information about the nature of the area
— Information about requirement or furnishing characteristics   ○

○ **Note:** Room books can be used for different purposes: identifying planning needs for a design; forming the basis of a function tender specification; as sales documents for marketing buildings; supporting the site management teams during the construction phase; recording the state of affairs when work is completed to provide a guarantee; or in relation to running the building. They also provide a useful basis for planning as a stocktaking device for future extension or conversion measures.

There are three different kinds of room book, fulfilling different purposes and so requiring different planning levels:

— Requirement room books
— Construction room books
— Furnishing and fittings room books

Room book

	Requirement room book	**Sheet:**	05

Building project:	Weinreich Versicherungen, Musterstadt South (P45/145)
Building type:	Office complex

Date:	05.03.2007	**Prepared by:**	Mr Müller
		Approved:	Ms Sanders

Room description:	Office	**Floor:**	1st floor
Room number:	1.304		

Technical requirements		
Area	**Requirement**	**Statistics**
Statics ...	Maximum deflection ...	f = l/300
Building science ...	Fire prevention as per DIN 4102 ...	Structural component at least F30 ...

Requirements by function		
Area	**Requirement**	**Statistics**
...	...	...

Design requirements		
Area	**Requirement**	**Statistics**
...	...	...

Financial requirements		
Area	**Requirement**	**Statistics**
...	...	...

Ecological requirements		
Area	**Requirement**	**Statistics**
...	...	...

Fig. 32: Example of a requirement room book

A requirement room book plays a key part for a functional tender specification with design supplied. A sheet with a table of all the known requirements is drawn up for every room or area. > Fig. 32

Requirement room book

A construction room book offers another form of description, providing a detailed description of the construction, but not the fittings and furnishings in a particular room. > Fig. 33

Construction room book

Room book

		Page:	05

☐ Construction room book
☒ Furniture and fittings room book

Building project: Oberstrasse 1
12345 Dorla

Building type:

Date: 05.03.2007

Prepared by: Mr Müller

Approved: Ms Sanders

Room description: Office — Room height: 3.00 m

Room number: 1.304 — Area: 20.60 m²

Floor: 1st floor — Type: Use

No.	Element	Fixtures/Structure	Properties	Quantity
1	Floor	Reinforced concrete slab in site-poured concrete Impact sound insulation Separating layer Screed, carpet	C20/25 PE sheet ZE 20, d = 50 mm	1
2	Ceiling	Reinforced concrete slab in site-poured concrete False plasterboard ceiling Grouted joints Paint ...	C20/25	...
3	Wall	...	...	...
4	Window	...	...	...
5	Doors	...	...	...
6	Lighting	...	...	...
7	Power supply	...	...	...
8	Heating	...	...	...
9	Ventilation	...	...	...

Fig. 33: Example of a furnishing and fitting and construction room book

Furnishing and fittings room book

A furnishing and fittings room book simply provides a complete description of the furniture and fittings for every room. It lays down which elements are to be fitted in each room, and in what quality and quantity. Each element is listed by number and manufacturer's description, or in

○ comparable detail.

Structuring a functional tender specification

Building breakdown

The building should be broken down in order to systematize a tender specification by function offering a general program of services – in contrast with a trade-oriented tender specification with a complete list of services. Rooms are recorded clearly and systematically, and numbered consecutively, following their position in a part of the building and a storey.

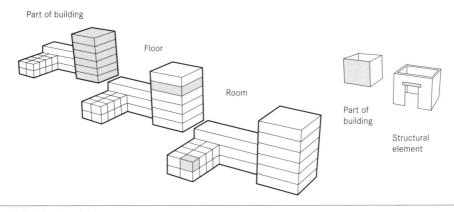

Part of building

Floor

Room

Part of building

Structural element

Fig. 34: Building breakdown

For further breakdown, a list of use or function areas should be drawn up. At this level, it is already appropriate to provide information about individual supply and technology elements, foundations, the loadbearing structure, the facade and the roof. If individual uses are known or intended, requirements can even be defined on the basis of structural components, such as a non-loadbearing wall between two offices. > Fig. 34

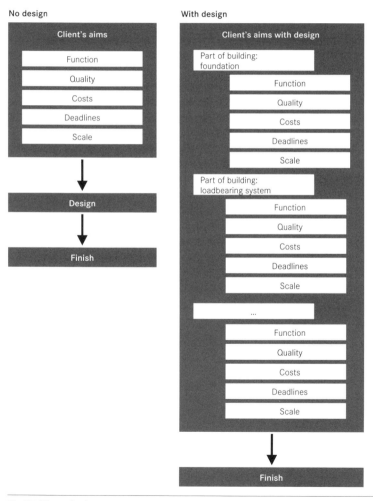

Fig. 35: Plane of reference

A building project needs to be broken down only to a certain extent: it must be possible to define different requirements on the basis of the client's intentions and the known general conditions. If the client prescribes a function specifically, it does not make sense, and it is usually not possible, to break such a function down into its individual components. ● > Fig. 35

Breakdown by building or room allocation program and by room book

The above-mentioned building program, room allocation program and room book are structured to provide a breakdown. They can be used in relation to the different breakdown levels as a function tendering specification with program of services, by allocating requirements. They do not have to be used, however. All that is fundamentally necessary is to establish a plane of reference for defining requirements. This could be a part of the building, or a construction component.

Drawing up a requirement profile

After establishing a breakdown system the use profile (client's aims and general conditions) can be applied successively to the smallest unit selected (a room or a construction component).

Rough description of the function of a building

It is recommended that the first step should be to allocate the planned building project to a function group:

— Housing construction
— Office building
— Department store
— School, college
— Factory
— Hospital

Requirement categories and aspects

The use profile can be differentiated further by identifying design (social and aesthetic), technical, functional, financial, and other categories if required. Each category will contain coherent requirement aspects. For example, building science and construction are both requirement aspects within the technical requirement category.

Individual requirements and ratings

Further subdivision is also possible on the basis of individual aspects. These again refer to certain subsections of the requirement aspects, and can be fixed more precisely in terms of ratings. Individual requirements regularly contain references to standards and regulations laying down certain minimum values. One possible individual requirement in terms of building science is fire protection for a door that can be fixed at a minimum rating of F30. ○

266

Requirement category	Requirement aspect	Individual requirement	Statistics
e.g. Technical requirements	e.g. Building science	e.g. Fire prevention	e.g. F60
			...
		...	...
			...
	e.g. Statics	...	...
			...
		...	...
			...
e.g. Aesthetic requirements	...	...	...
...	...	...	...

Fig. 36: Example of a system for recording service program requirements

The individual requirements and the ratings that lie behind them can be compiled clearly using the breakdown system shown in Fig. 36.

However, summing up requirements in a service program is not the only descriptive language available. Requirements can also be defined in continuous prose, so long as this retains concrete allocation of the requirement to a particular element (e.g. a part of the building or a room).

Possible ways of presenting a functional tender specification

Requirements should be defined in full and unambiguously with a view to the client's wishes and the general conditions of the building project. Possible requirements are explained in greater detail with reference to this below, following the categories identified above.

Defining requirements

● **Important:** Considerable variations are possible in the depth of analysis required to describe a client's intentions. It is possible that a client will simply identify an output value for a production plant. It is then up to the bidder to investigate all other criteria within the general conditions, which cannot be changed. If this procedure is being followed, it is neither possible nor appropriate to break the building project down.

○ **Note:** Ratings provide a clear, measurable basis for individual requirements. If no ratings are given, or if they are defined only qualitatively (e.g. enhanced sound insulation), this may give undesirable scope for the bidder's interpretation.

Design requirements The design requirement category includes both aesthetic and social aspects. The content of this category is largely a matter of the client's sensibilities, and includes aspects like convenience, privacy and comfort in the social sphere, and architectural quality, elegance and prestige in the aesthetic sphere.

These subjective requirements might include specifying high quality building materials or imposing public areas (for example a spacious atrium).

Function-oriented requirements Functional requirements are also determined by the client's aims. Mere allocation to a general function group (e.g. school) identifies key features of the intended function. The requirement aspects within this category provide information about the function grid, ceiling spans, the number of floors, floor area, usable area, variability for the ground plan, or possible changes of use for the building. Various requirements of a technical nature also follow from the building's function.

Technical requirements Technical requirements are derived directly from the function, from standards and regulations, or from the client's express wishes. Essentially, all the areas relating to loadbearing capacity, stability and building science (e.g. heat and sound insulation, fire protection and waterproofing) are defined more fully by requirements.

For example, a technical requirement may follow from a client's wish for air-conditioned office spaces, and would have to be accounted for in the functional specifications.

Financial requirements Financial aspects applying to a building are also largely determined by the client's aims. Aspects such as investment costs, building maintenance costs, running costs or yields from use are directly linked to the client's intentions and the function and technology of the planned building. One of the client's strategic aims could be to use alternative rather than fossil fuels in his or her building, which could mean higher investment costs, but lead to savings in the long run.

Ecological requirements Themes like recycling potential, environmental soundness of the building materials used or implementation of an environmentally friendly energy concept are covered in the ecological requirement category. The general conditions for this category are primarily of a legal nature, but they can also be determined by the client's aims. The client may view state subsidies for environmentally friendly technologies as a reason for using them. However, the client may ask for a low-energy building without going into any further detail. Other examples of ecological require-

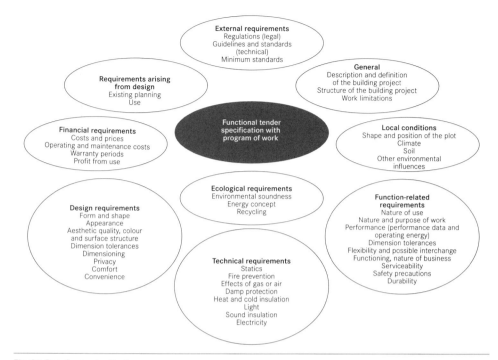

Fig. 37: Requirement criteria

ments arise from long-term considerations in terms of pollution-free conversion or demolition of the planned building.

Other information not contained in the program of services is important for a functional tender specification over and above the requirements that have already been mentioned. It includes details of legal and technical regulations, a rough description of the building, from which it should be possible to discover the local conditions for the project, and establish which works do not have to be included in the tender bid.

Other information for a functional tender specification

Figure 37 sums up the most important points to illustrate the possible requirements.

Requirements must be clearly presented in the program of works. The presentation can be in the form of continuous prose, lists or tables. This largely depends on the way the program of works is broken down. If the program runs from the building as a whole to the individual room, a table of requirements can be systematized as follows:

Requirements for the building as a whole:
— Two storeys
— Solid construction
— Minimum requirement low-energy building in accordance with current regulations

Requirements for individual parts of the building:
— Conservatory finish with overhead glazing
— Natural ventilation
— Maximum summer temperature in rooms: 29 °C

Requirements for individual rooms:
— Study facing the garden
— Staircase with natural lighting
— Bathroom with separate toilet

Systematic listing of this kind quickly produces a program of works that is very highly differentiated in individual areas. Individual requirements can be formulated down to a particular rating, but design requirements are difficult to formulate precisely. It is perfectly clear to stipulate that all the rooms in a hotel must have a sea view, but descriptions like "comfortable atmosphere" or "lounge style" are very much governed by individual ideas and experience, and serve little purpose unless they are not made more specific.

PROCEDURES FOR A DETAILED DESCRIPTION OF WORKS

Aims   The most economical bid for required work can be compiled with a detailed description of works. The tendering pathway must be described to bidders in detail, and in full, on the basis of the completed working plans. A tried-and-tested system is available to planners.

Structure   The tender specification is a general structural system that makes it possible to record individual works coherently. The individual works are itemized in tables, giving quantities by batch, trade and title. In practice, the tender specification breakdown shows the work to be done expressed by location and specialist fields. > Fig. 38

Tender specification with list of work								
Lot 1	Trade 1	Phase 1	Item 1	Item 2	Item 3	Item 4	...	
		Phase 2						
		...						
	Trade 2							
	...							
Lot 2								
...								

Fig. 38: Breakdown system for a tender specification

Subdivision by location or room is familiar from the procedure for a function tender specification. Subdivision by trades is another possible way of systematizing the work required.

The principle behind the tender specification is that it aims to make a direct enquiry about prices for the smallest descriptive elements, item by item. Bidders should provide unit prices for the items, which are described precisely by nature, quantity and quality.

Tender specification and unit price contract

○

The total price for an item is arrived at by multiplying the planned quantities by the unit price in each case. The sum of all the totals is the net total for the bid. When invoicing work after it has been carried out, the unit prices are quoted, but not the planned quantities. A unit price contract of this type is usually billed in terms of the quantities actually used.

○ **Note:** Unit prices are prices based on a unit, for example EUR $10/m^2$.

If a description of the work required is needed with a tender specification, the information has to be systematically converted from the plans into individual subjobs arranged by trade, as plans are, by their very nature, structured according to construction components.

If individual subjobs are to be listed with absolute clarity, it is first necessary to consider the sequence of work and the construction method. Adopting this approach makes it easier to identify subjobs of the same nature in more detail, and allot them to a trade. Identifying the subjobs, allocating them to individual traces and also actually describing the work required can be based on answering the following simple questions:

— What are the construction elements for which subjobs have to be described?
  Ceiling; wall; foundations ...
— What are the construction types for which subjobs have to be described?
  Masonry; reinforced concrete ...
— What are the processes for which subjobs have to be described
  Earth moving; reinforced concrete work ...
— What connections are there between the building phases and the trades?
  Excavations = earth moving; foundations = reinforced concrete work ...
— What subjobs can be allocated to particular trades and construction components?
  ■ Reinforced concrete ceiling = formwork, reinforcement, concrete ...

The next step is to record more detail about the individual subjobs. Here we recommend that the relevant standards, guidelines and regulations are summed up, to provide a frame of reference for describing

---

■ **Tip:** A useful instrument for compiling a tender specification with list of works is a room book detailing furnishings and fittings. This gives the number of rooms with a detailed description, as well as information about areas. Certain jobs can thus be recorded quickly and systematically in terms of quality and quantity for further description in the tender specification.

○ **Note:** Information about professional execution of building work can be found in the trading standards. These standards also contain information about classifying the work, the building materials and construction components used, the units to be used as a basis, the appropriate subjobs, and for invoicing and drawing up the tender specification (see Appendix).

each subjob in detail in terms of a sound, expert source of information
about building materials, construction components for listing the works ○
required.

The tender specification for all jobs can be drawn up stage by stage
on this basis.

Lot
The lot is a complete award unit allocated to a company. Lots are to
be seen as independent subprojects that can be defined equally on the
basis of criteria relating to spaces (part lot) or to expert services (specialist lot, trade).

Subdivision into lots by area usually only takes place for large build- Part lot
ing projects, and would allow for dividing a road-building project up into
several phases or street construction contract sections. If the client perhaps intends to commission only part of the building work and allocate
subsequent work to other firms, he or she must draw up appropriate lots.

If the client is awarding the contract by breaking down trades, the Specialist lot
term specialist lot is used. > Chapter Structuring an invitation to tender A trade can
be split up into several specialist lots. For example, one metalworker can
be commissioned to make railings and another to work on the facade. ○

Title and subtitle
Titles are a further way of breaking down the building project below Title
the level of the project as a whole. A title describes a part of a building
or a particular trade within a lot or an overall building project. It can
describe a subjob within a trade, without representing a unit that is complete in itself with its own price within the bid. The function of the title,
as opposed to the lot, is to sum individual job items up in coherent
sections. Bundling individual jobs (items) that belong together in terms

○ **Note:** Just like an independent building project, lots
can also be further broken down in terms of areas and
expertise to relate to parts of a building or individual
trades. Lots can also be defined on the plane of individual trades or titles, and are then awarded as a complete
package of works.

of speciality or physical area provides a suitable basis for establishing prices by placing an item within the overall context.

For example, the "metalwork" tender specification may contain titles such as "stairs and banisters," "doors and frames," and "fencing," in order to break the work down into coherent sections. Further differentiation can then be done in subtitles, such as "outdoor stairs and banisters" and "indoor stairs and banisters." Work can also be divided up according to individual structural elements. The tender specification for "shell construction work" can be broken down into titles such as "foundations," "floor slab," "exterior masonry," "interior masonry," "ceilings" etc., or even more fully in relation to the place where the work is to be done, as in "kitchen tiles," "toilet tiles" and then again into "floor tiles" and "wall tiles."

The number of breakdown levels is up to planners. They should break the tender down only to the extent that the complexity of the project requires. Breakdown by title and subtitle should always aim to form coherent units. As well as better understanding by making it easier to allocate the individual job items, this means that when comparing bids it is possible to compare something other than just individual items within the total price. In addition, planners can compare the bids in terms of the titles. For the above-mentioned example of metalwork, it could turn out when comparing the individual titles that one metalworker is offering the best prices for stairs and doors, but is bidding well above the average for
■ fencing work.

Subtitle   Individual titles can be further broken down by the use of subtitles. For example, the reinforced concrete work required for a particular job can be summed up under a title, and the formwork and reinforcing material it requires in subtitles.

The extent to which there is differentiation between titles and subtitles or other breakdown levels (main titles where appropriate), and the sequence in which subdivisions are made in terms of working area and

> ■ **Tip:** Listing by title makes it easier to evaluate bids for individual sections or trades. To do this, the total prices for items under a particular title are summed up and presented in a list of the individual titles.

- Earthworks
- Drilling
- Preparatory work
- Ramming, sieving, compressing
- Waterpipes
- Sewerage drains
- Draining
- Spray concrete
- Road and path construction
- Landscaping
- Injection spraying
- Underground cabling
- Rail construction work
- Masonry
- Concreting
- Natural stonework
- Artificial stonework
- Carpentry and woodwork
- Steel construction
- Sealing
- Roof covering and roof sealing
- Plumbing
- Dry construction work

- Plastering and stucco
- Ventilated curtain facades
- Tiling and slab installation
- Screed work
- Poured asphalt work
- Joinery
- Parquet work
- Metal fittings
- Blinds
- Metalwork
- Glazing
- Painting, varnishing, coating
- Corrosion prevention for steel
- Floor coverings
- Wallpapering
- Timber flooring
- Ventilation installations
- Heating and central water-heating facilities
- Gas, water and drainage facilities
- Low- and medium-frequency equipment
- Lightning protection
- Conveyor systems, lifts, escalators
- Building automation

Fig. 39: List of different trades

expert fields depends on the size and complexity of the individual building project and the nature of the contract relating to it. Figure 39 shows possibilities of breakdown that are already available on the basis of specialist allocation of individual services.

Items

A single item within a tender specification is the smallest tender unit and represents a subjob within the building work. It is made up of individual descriptive elements defining the work to be done and the particular service required clearly and unambiguously. The descriptive elements can be formulated as required or put together from standard catalogues.

It is possible to include more than one activity within a particular item, as long as they can be seen to be the same in their technical nature, and for price calculation.

No.	Text	Item	Quantity	Unit	UP	TP
01.02.02.0001	... Formwork Floor slab ...		50	m		

Fig. 40: Components of a tender item

Components of
a tender item

Against this backdrop we recommend describing all the items systematically in a tender specification. In this context, the typical components of a tender item are grouped within the following categories:

— No.   number
— Text   descriptive text (short and long text)
— ITy   item type
— Quantity   the quantity worked out from the plans in terms of UQ
— UQ   unit of quantity
— UP   unit price (price for a unit)
— TP   total price per item (unit price × planned quantity)

These categories are applied to every item, thus producing a specification arranged by lots, trades and titles or subtitles. The bidder enters the unit and total prices. > Fig. 40

The following information should be given in the individual categories for a tender position:

Number

The number helps to make it easier to find one's way around a tender specification. Each piece of work (subjob) in the same category in terms of techniques and pricing is identified by a particular number according to a defined breakdown key. This number relates directly to the way in which the project is broken down, and reflects this in the tender specification. In a relatively simple project a subjob can be identified by number as follows.

Lot	Trade	Title	Item	Index
01	01	01	0001	a

Index

The index can be used to show the relationship between a basic and an alternative item in the numbered list.

Numbering is consecutive at every level. > Fig. 41

Tender specification
text

The tender specification text should be drawn up in long and short form by the planner inviting tenders.

01.02.01.0001	Activity 1 of title 1 in trade 2 des Loses 1
01.02.01.0002	Activity 2 of title 1 in trade 2 des Loses 1
01.02.01.0003	Activity 3 of title 1 in trade 2 des Loses 1
01.02.02.0001	Activity 1 of **title 2** in trade 2 des Loses 1
01.02.02.0002	Activity 2 of **title 2** in trade 2 des Loses 1
01.02.02.0003	Activity 3 of **title 2** in trade 2 des Loses 1
01.02.02.0004	Activity 4 of **title 2** in trade 2 des Loses 1
01.03.01.0001	Activity 1 of title 1 in **trade 3** des Loses 1
01.03.01.0002	Activity 2 of title 1 in **trade 3** des Loses 1
01.03.01.0003	Activity 3 of title 1 in **trade 3** des Loses 1
01.03.02.0001	Activity 1 of **title 2** in trade 3 des Loses 1
01.03.02.0002	Activity 2 of **title 2** in trade 3 des Loses 1
01.03.02.0003	Activity 3 of **title 2** in trade 3 des Loses 1

Fig. 41: Example of the use of numbering

The short text is used essentially as a short textual summary of the service required for further use in drawing up the bid and raising the invoice. The short form must not lead to possible confusion between items, each item should be identified unambiguously: "masonry 36.5 cm, cellar," "masonry 36.5 cm ground floor," "masonry 17.5 cm ground floor" etc.

Short text

In contrast, the long text should describe the work required unambiguously and exhaustively, so that all the bidders understand exactly the same thing.

Long text

In principle, texts can be freely formulated, taking legal and technical regulations into consideration. But to simplify this process, planners can make use of standardized sample texts, which are generally available.

Freely formulated or standard texts

Such standard works catalogues are collections of texts that can be used to described work required or subcategories of it. These are structured according to predefined patterns and contain a range of information about building work, building materials, dimensions and units of quantity for various works. ∎

Standard texts

The great advantage of standardized specification texts is that they mean the same to all bidders, and so no there is no unnecessary effort or additional risk when fixing prices. Furthermore, the usually modular compilation of the standard text collections and the hierarchical structure imposed facilitate the exchange of data between the compiler and the recipient of the tender specification, because of good IT compatibility. All that remains for planners is to check the accuracy of the content.

It is possible to ensure that a description is complete to the greatest possible extent on the basis of the prescribed system using standard texts. But it should be noted that appropriate pattern texts are not available for all special solutions.

Building product manufacturers in particular usually offer appropriate pattern texts, which can be taken over into the tender specification very easily. Planners should remember that manufacturers do not see this as an altruistic service, but use drawing up a tender specification as a way of placing their own product. They are also keen to establish unique selling points to exclude rival products from the competition. So information can be supplied with the tender specifications containing production-related information about the thickness of layers or alloys for a particular product that are unique to one manufacturer, but irrelevant in terms of the product's suitability for use and durability. This often sets the hurdle for finding a possibly more reasonably priced alternative unreasonably high for the tendering firm.

In any case, planners are advised to be careful when adopting a manufacturer's product descriptions. If they are not sure what a particular formulation implies, they should consult the manufacturer or more neutral institutions.

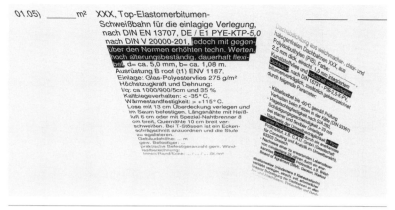

Fig. 42: Biased manufacturer's description

Freely formulated texts

Formulating the text freely requires a high level of expert knowledge of the work to be described. This approach is also used to distinguish important from less important information. A range of manufacturers, the appropriate associations or other competent partners should be consulted in order to obtain the information relevant to particular requirements. Planners must apply requirements arising from standards and directives responsibly. The same applies to checking for completeness. To ensure this, the description should cover the following points:

— Description of the work required
— Description of the type of work required
— Spatial frame of reference for the work required (information about the part of the building, but also its location in the building, if this is not clear from the numbering)
— Information about quality (material, surfaces, etc.)
— Information about dimensions falling outside the reference unit o

○ **Note:** A tender specification can be based on a reference object without excluding alternatives (e.g. "door handle stainless steel 1076 brand FSB or of equal standard"). Equality of standard can be checked by requesting data sheets or samples accompanying an alternative suggestion in the bid.

The following scheme systematizes the textual description of work, and can be applied to any subsection of the work in this form. Modular standard texts are based on similar patterns.

- Building method, building type (production by fitting building materials and components together)
- Structural element (part of the building forming a room or system)
- Building materials (required or desired building materials)
- Dimension 1 (element dimensions, such as the thickness of a wall)
- Dimension 2 (general dimensions, such as the installation height
- for a particular piece of work)

It would also be possible to place other information about the purpose of the work on hints on invoicing or realization techniques in the descriptive text. For example, if a building is to be in reinforced concrete, the building method is directly influenced by the requirement to use prefabricated elements. Equally, legal requirements can form part of a tender specification, for example if material removed is to become the contractor's property when the work in completed.

It is customary when using texts to describe work required to make reference to other documents, such as statical calculations, plans, samples or reports. For example, a tender specification text could contain the formulation *"reinforcement as per reinforcement plan."*

Reference to a drawing is particularly useful in the case of spatially complex situations or complex building sections. For example, if an item describes the construction of stairs with a banister, a drawing will help to identify individual elements mentioned in the text and to understand

● **Example:**

Building method:	masonry according to the standard xxxx	This subservice can be further explained by complementing the above description with information on quality relating to the structural element (e.g. finished as exposed masonry on both sides) or the building material (e.g. salt-water-resistant finish) or on the building method (e.g. build with prefabricated wall elements).
Structural element:	for the interior wall in section EG XX/YY	
Building material:	with calcareous sandstone blocks yyy standard	
Dimension of element:	with a thickness of 17.5 cm	
General dimension:	built to a height of 3.00 m	

unambiguously the way they fit together. This means that the bidding firm can check the completeness of the service description, and it is easier to estimate the assembly time required.

Reference to reports makes sense in the case of special sound insulation requirements, for example. In this case the relevant requirements laid down in the report do not have to be described in the individual items, but are defined in an appropriate reference: *"Higher than usual demands will be made on the completed building element according to the appended sound insulation report. These requirements must be met, and considered in the bid price."* In this way, planners avoid possible sources of error when transferring individual requirements into the tender specification.

Different types of works positions can be used in a tender specification. Planners identify a particular item appropriately in the "Item type (ITy) column." *Item type (ITy)*

Distinguishing between different item types makes it possible for planners inviting tenders to test the market with a view to optional and alternative services. For example, not all decisions will necessarily have become final at the time the work is put out to tender (e.g. the choice of floor coverings), or the requirements for a particular service will not have been fixed (e.g. installing drainage). Subsequent changes can then be addressed through contingent items. If these works are not ordered until after the contract has been completed, the bidder's prices given as per tender specification are binding.

Standard items are always realized. Bidders will provide a unit price and a total price for these in the tender specification. *Standard item*

○ **Note:** If identical descriptions occur in different items, there are two ways of avoiding unnecessary repetitions. Planners can describe the work in full in one item and then refer back to this in subsequent items (e.g. plasterboard stud wall, finish as in previous item, but with double boarding). If identical descriptions apply to a number of items, planners can sum them up and identify them in their preliminary notes (e.g. finish plasterboard stud wall as in preliminary note type A). Preliminary remarks always relate to particular pieces of work and are used exclusively in the context of tender specifications listing the works in full. Fundamentally they are the same as texts with lists of works and should therefore match them in terms of content. There is no conflict with general or special contract conditions.

No.	Text	Item	Quantity	Unit	UP	TP
01.02.02.0001	... Textile floor covering ...	BI	30	m^2		
01.02.02.0001a	... Parkett ...	AI	30	m^2		

Fig. 43: Example of alternative items

Contingency items

Contingency items make it possible for planners to test the market in relation to services they may wish to use additionally.

If it is not certain that an item of this type will be realized, it is not provided with a total price in the tender specification and thus not in the final bid price either. If the client orders a contingency item after the contract is concluded, its price will be calculated on the basis of the unit price entered by the bidder. If they are not commissioned, contingency items are omitted without claim to remuneration.

Basic and alternative items

Basic items are items that are fixed for realization. Enquiries can also be made about alternative items. Thus, a basic item is considered to be a component of this service to be carried out, and must be provided with a unit and a total price.

Alternative items can replace basic items if the service described is to be realized in an alternative way. As for a contingency item, an alternative item must also be identified appropriately and provided with a unit price only by the bidder. > Fig. 43 Planners can use such items to make the best financial decision about a service. The basic item is always realized unless the client expressly orders the use of the alternative item.

○ **Note:** Contingency items should be used only for subsidiary works that are not essential to the overall success of the building project. It would make sense to use contingency items if certain items have not been fixed before building starts because of insufficient information about the soil conditions on the building site.

■ **Tip:** Contingency items are often not checked carefully enough when examining the bid, as they are not included in the bid total. This can lead to accepting inflated unit prices that have to be kept to when ordering the realization of contingency items.

No.	Text	Item	Quantity	Unit	UP	TP
01.02.02.0001	... Excavation soil class 3–5 ...		1000	m²		
01.02.02.0001a	... Excavation soil class 6 ...	SI	200	m²		

Fig. 44: Supplementary item

Supplementary items are a different item type. They identify poten- Supplementary item
tial impediments or additional work needed in relation to a standard item.
Bidders provide a unit price and a total price for supplementary items in
the tender specification. The corresponding standard item then covers
something like a basic finish for the item, and the supplementary item
describes a higher standard or a special installation situation. The price
for a supplementary item is calculated from the difference between the
price for a higher standard and the basic finish.

An example shows the possibilities arising from using a supplementary item. Figure 45 presents two variants for describing the same work
for applying exterior rendering.

The first variant shows the rendering in two standard items, separated for the high and the low building. The other provides a tender specification with a standard item for the whole building project and a
supplement for the higher areas, for which scaffolding costs may have
to be quoted. The second variant has the advantage that a bid will not be
made for the ground floor of the high-rise building at a higher price because of additional scaffolding costs.

○ **Note:** An alternative item offers the possibility for contractors to propose their own solution for implementing a basic item (e.g. "Masonry to be produced according to previous item, but realized according to the bidder's choice.") A description of the proposed finish must be appended.

● **Example:** The example in Figure 44 clarifies the principle behind a supplementary item. The work described in item 01.02.02.0001 covers excavating 1000 m³ of soil in classes 3–5. The appropriate supplementary item enquires about the price if the problem arises from "excavating class 6 soil" to the extent of 200 m³. Thus the price contains only the proportion (supplementary price) for dealing with the problem, and does not represent a price in its own right for excavating class 6 soil. Hence the areas (200 m²) are already included in the standard item.

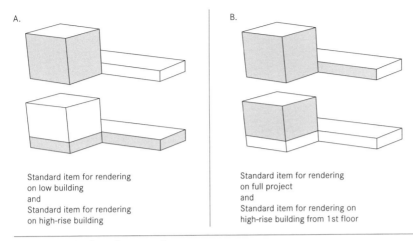

A.

Standard item for rendering
on low building
and
Standard item for rendering
on high-rise building

B.

Standard item for rendering
on full project
and
Standard item for rendering on
high-rise building from 1st floor

Fig. 45: Example of supplementary item

Quantities can be expressed in various units. But the unit of quantity (UQ) should always relate meaningfully to a particular subservice. Thus, it is possible to calculate reinforcement in cubic meters (m^3), although this is a disadvantage in terms of the form reinforcement bars will take and the industry standard of calculating in tones to determine prices. Sensible units are tones, or where applicable square meters (m^2) for steel mats and meters for steel bars.

The unit of quantity fixed for an item forms the basis for quantity surveying and is the reference value for bidders when fixing prices for subsections of the work.

■ **Tip:** Supplementary items often differ only very slightly from the corresponding standard positions. In such cases the descriptive text can be reduced to the essential changes, there is no need to repeat textual elements that remain unchanged. It is sufficient to write "supplement to item xxx for double boarding."

○ **Note:** The general and special requirements contain guidelines for the use of units of quantity. For example, wall areas are calculated by area (m^2) for rendering work and soffits by length (m).

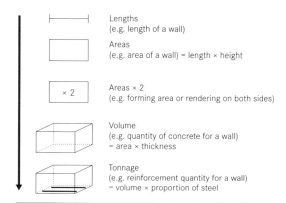

Fig. 46: Quantity surveying procedures

Quantities relate to the quantities required for completing a piece of work on the scale required. The quantity is given as a preliminary estimate representing the quantities required for completing the work according to plan. They are derived directly from the working plans, or in the case of refurbishment work also by on-site estimates, and built into the tender specification by the planner inviting tenders. It is fundamentally advisable to record the quantities for a work item within a particular frame of reference (total building project, part of building, floor, etc.) and to color code the corresponding structural elements in the plan appropriately to avoid redundancies. Quantities can also be worked out by using appropriate construction software (e.g. CAD). The degree of automatic quantity calculation extends from simply working out area to a complete component-oriented list of quantities using a 3D model.

Conscientious quantity surveying also makes it easier to account for building works at a later stage.

The unit price (UP) is calculated by unit quantity by the bidder on the basis of the description of the subservice and built into the tender specification. As a rule the unit price is fixed and usually forms the basis for later invoicing for the work. Unit prices are changed only if quantities vary considerably or content deviates from the work as described.

Unit price (UP)

Total price (TP)   The total price is arrived at primarily from the product of unit price and preliminary estimate (planned quantity). Bidders should work it out for all items basic and supplementary items intended for realization and include it in the tender specification in the appropriate place. The sum of all the intermediate totals for a building project is the net final tender price. Adding VAT at the statutory rate gives the gross price the bidder is offering for the commission to provide the services described in the various lists. Total prices are not stated for alternative and contingent items, as it is not clear at the point the bid is being made whether these items will be realized or not.

Subservices are invoiced on the basis of the total prices for the individual items and the quantities actually realized.

In conclusion

Tendering is not usually one of the activities planners find themselves looking forward to with particular glee. This is understandable, as the charms of a beautiful design, a magnificent view and even carefully planned details seem incomparably greater. The large proportion of text alone often detracts from the allure of the tendering process.

But planners who take the trouble to tender carefully for the ideas in a design will gain some very sound insights into their own planning and the necessary sequences of events needed to realize it.

It is only the invitation to tender that will ensure a high standard of planning is also reflected in outstanding realization.

So this volume is intended to spur planners on to formulate their own invitations to tender comprehensibly, and to structure them meaningfully. If the contractors understand the invitation to tender, the planners have not let themselves down.

Lars-Phillip Rusch

Site management

Site management begins when the time comes to translate abstract plans and texts into their precise physical counterparts on the building site. Experiencing the process by which the planned building first takes on form as a shell, and then is progressively turned into something that previously only existed on paper or as a model, is often laborious but always instructive.

Successful site management is measured in terms of its capacity to meet targets in the three most important categories: costs, schedules, and quality. If costs remain within the agreed limits, if the building is finished within the agreed time frame, and if the quality of the building meets the client's requirements, the site manager will have successfully completed the project. > Fig. 1

During the building process, the site manager therefore has to control factors that influence costs, schedules and quality such that deviations remain within agreed limits, can be offset as the project progresses or can be agreed with the client.

Once the design, planning submissions and working plans have been completed, the results of initial invitations to tender need to be considered and the various contractors selected. For the architect and the client the phase of implementation now begins. Depending on the particular project structure, it is possible for the planning and tendering phases to overlap with the implementation phase. While details of the final structure and building services equipment are still being honed in the architectural office, the building shell is already taking shape on the site. > Fig. 2

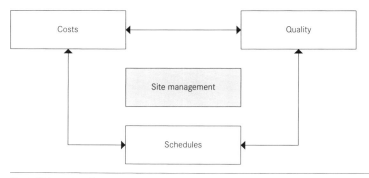

Fig. 1: Main tasks of site management

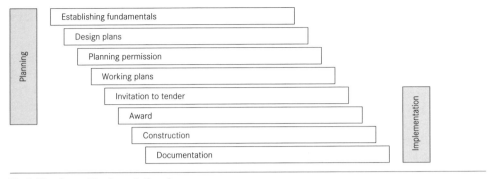

Fig. 2: Planning and implementation phases

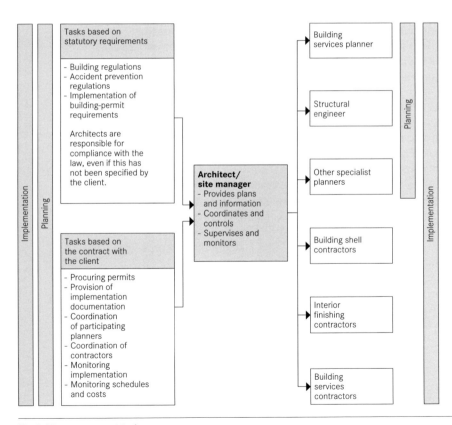

Fig. 3: Site management tasks

Fundamentals of site management

PREPARING SITE MANAGEMENT

The terms site management and site manager are often understood in the practical context as relating to different functions. On the one hand, the site manager is contractually responsible for monitoring the construction process, for checking that the wishes of the client are being professionally and properly implemented (i.e. according to the agreed plans) by the various contractors. Apart from the actual architectural design, this process includes a range of other agreements made during the planning phase, for example with regard to construction costs and schedules, which must be implemented by the site manager in the course of building.

Monitoring construction for the client

On the other hand, the site manager also has to ensure that the statutory provisions set down by building authorities are adhered to. The site manager is responsible for plans being realized in the form that has been given official approval. In addition, the site manager is responsible for ensuring safety standards are maintained in the construction process, and that the site does not pose any threat to the safety of those working on the project or anyone else. > Fig. 3

Monitoring statutory provisions

THE MOMENT OF TRUTH

The implementation of architectural plans is the real "moment of truth." At this point it becomes clear whether the envisaged construction can actually be built. Every architect should take the opportunity to experience this process, because the actual construction process can be an invaluable source of ideas for the development of other projects. As already stated, the tasks of the site manager include monitoring costs, schedules and quality. As a rule, the work required here is detailed in the fee structure for planning services. The architect's task is not an arbitrary one; it is the "bringing into being" of a building that accords with planning and is technically and functionally free of faults.

It is particularly important to bear in mind that construction always involves the production of varying objects under varying conditions. In contrast to factory-based forms of production such as automobile manufacturing, building projects are characterized by a range of features:

— The scope of the project, the available time and the required quality differ from case to case.
— The project comprises activities that are limited in terms of space and time.

- The location of the project is different in each case, and each has its own features.
- The cooperation of a large number of people/firms is required who have (often) not worked together before and who will (probably) not work together again.
- As a rule, the participants have contradictory interests (managing the client's money as best as possible while making a profit on the contract).
- Success needs to be achieved directly. There is no scope for "practice" prior to carrying out the project. Although some projects may be based on prototypes, there is no such thing as a "pilot run."
- Targets and results cannot usually be negotiated in retrospect (particularly deadlines).

QUALITY SPECIFICATIONS

Since site management is primarily concerned with realizing the client's wishes as set out in the tender specifications, it is these specifications that form the basis of all activities falling within the site manager's area of responsibility.

Tender specifications
Depending on the type of tender, tender specifications can describe all required work in detail (detailed tender) or the targeted performance of the end result (functional tender).

If the award, i.e. the commissioning of contractors, has been made on the basis of detailed tender specifications, the site manager can usually rely on the details regarding building quality and quantities that have been agreed and defined in these specifications. Nevertheless, he or she should – as with all other relevant documentation – check that these details are correct and complete.

■ The scope of services is precisely defined in the course of implementation planning and tendering specification. If the tender is based on a functional tender, i.e. the desired result is functionally defined by the tender specifications, the contracted firm is free to choose the building procedure and the details of its implementation. In this case, site management is limited to checking the quality of work as specified in the functional specification.

Agency site management
Since in the case of functional tender specifications a contract is usually awarded to the relevant building firm early in the planning process, the firm in question assumes responsibility for further detailed planning and the supervision of implementation. However, clients still require site managers who can act as their advocates and monitor the work of

the contracted firm. Even if the building firm is coordinating itself in this situation, it must adhere to the prevailing regulations and standards. The supervising role of the architect is therefore often referred to as "agency site management" in this context.

SCHEDULE SPECIFICATIONS

Apart from ensuring that the required quality is achieved and that costs remain within the framework set by the client > Chapter Cost specifications the site manager is responsible for the completion of the project on schedule. As a rule, the completion date is set at an early stage of planning and is no longer negotiable once building and the task of site management have commenced. For the client, meeting the deadline for completion can be extremely important. For example, failure to meet completion deadlines can mean enormous costs in unpaid rents on large commercial properties.

The basis of site-management deadline planning is the framework time scheduling carried out by the architect, the client or the project manager. The framework time schedule covers not only the planning phase (at what point do particular plans and tenders need to be completed?) and the implementation phase from commencement to completion, but also a number of intermediate deadlines relevant for the client, such as the laying of the foundation stone, the topping-out ceremony and the date of occupation. These dates are often fixed and linked with other schedules and thus cannot be renegotiated. The planning of the construction process and the way site management can influence it are discussed in detail below. > Chapter Scheduling and implementation planning

Framework time schedule

> ■ **Tip:** If the responsible site manager has been only partly involved in the production of the relevant tendering documentation or not at all, it is essential that he or she make a thorough study of the commissioned offers by the contracted firms. Only in this way is it possible to gain an overview of which firm is supposed to provide which services and the quality and quantities involved as well as where there are interfaces with other specifications and contractors.

COST SPECIFICATIONS

Apart from specifications applying to the quality of and schedule for implementation, another aspect that is particularly significant for site management is the budget prescribed by the client, i.e. the cost framework. As a rule, costs associated with the project are covered by the budget designated by the client. One consideration influencing the awarding of contracts is thus ensuring that adequate funds will be available during the actual building process. Budget planning should also normally include a certain buffer to cover any unforeseen contingencies arising in the course of building. Nevertheless, a particularly important task of site management is ensuring the prescribed cost framework is adhered to. The site manager is not entitled to enter into agreements that can be disadvantageous for the client. This particularly applies to undertakings to contractors that will result in cost overruns. As one slogan puts it: "The architect's mandate ends where the client's purse begins."

As shown in Figure 4, in the course of construction, the site manager gains an increasingly precise overview of what the building will ultimately cost. It is imperative that the client is kept informed about the development of project costs. > Chapter Cost management

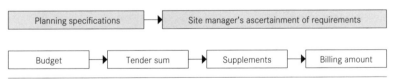

Fig. 4: Budget/tender sum/prognosis/billing amount

Organizing the building site

In addition to safeguarding the client's interests, site managers are also responsible for the overall structure of operations on the building site. This involves exercising a certain amount of control over the activities of all those participating in the construction process, for example by ensuring that the necessary safety measures are put in place and are maintained, that workers are using the required protective equipment, and that the building site is kept free of clutter. The responsibility for industrial safety plays a particularly important role in the organization of building sites.

BUILDING SITE FACILITIES

The type and size of the building project involved determines the type of facilities needed in terms of cranes, storage space, accommodation, and entrances and exits. In addition to various types of large and small machinery, site facilities need to include a well planned infrastructure with access points, internal roads and storage spaces.

Equipment
— Cranes, hoists, scaffolding
— Barriers and safety facilities
— Site illumination

Infrastructure
— Storage areas for materials and components
— Site offices, accommodation and toilets/washrooms
— Building site paths and roads with entrances and exits
— Connections for electricity, water, sewage and, where required, heating
— Measures designed to protect the environment and immediate surroundings, e.g. adjacent buildings

The question of which building site facilities and equipment are to be provided by the client and which by the contractors should be covered by the tender specifications and already settled at the time contracts are agreed. In the case of large building projects, the provision of site facilities and equipment is usually detailed and commissioned as a separate service in a tendering agreement. The division of costs for facilities used by all contractors, such as washroom containers, scaffolding, electricity and water, must be contractually established and itemized in the relevant contracts.

Contractual agreements regarding building site facilities

The type of facilities and equipment used on a building site will also be influenced by the following factors:

— Surroundings (inner city, open countryside, construction zone including other building sites, etc.)
— Type and size of the construction project
— Construction period
— Time of year in which construction is taking place
— Construction method, e.g. precast concrete sections, site-mixed concrete, prefabricated construction

The individual elements making up building site facilities and equipment are sketched in a site plan. > Fig. 5 The way in which facilities, storage and transit areas, and the building area are arranged needs to allow delivery vehicles to move within the pivot range of cranes and cranes to reach storage areas for building materials such as scaffolding, shuttering and armoring for reinforced concrete, prefabricated components, and facade elements. However, break rooms and site containers should be located outside this radius.

The fitness for traffic and stability of surrounding streets and open areas also need to be checked prior to beginning construction. It is often the case that temporary roads have to be built in the course of establishing a building site, and particular crane locations reinforced due to heavy loads.

○ **Hint:** Decisive factors for determining the appropriate size of cranes include the greatest load e.g. the weight of the largest prefabricated element in relation to the location of the crane, the required boom length, and the height of the building under construction and of the surrounding buildings. Particular attention should be paid to the necessary distance from the excavation pit, since the crane's loads exert a force on the ground around it. The stability of this ground can be significantly influenced by proximity to an excavation pit.

■ **Tip:** Particular consultation is required with permit authorities when building site facilities affect the flow of public traffic. It may be the case, for example, that access and evacuation routes used by the fire department have to be altered.

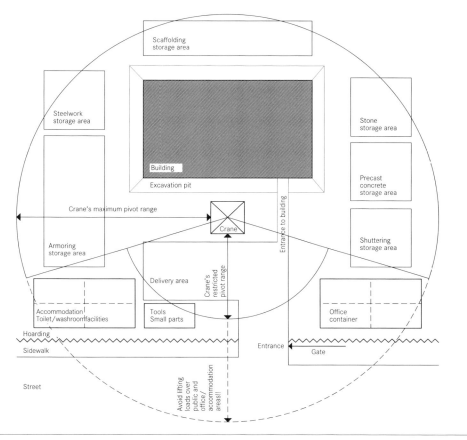

Fig. 5: Diagram of building site facilities

Where conditions on a building site are cramped, it may be necessary to adapt site facilities several times in the course of the project. Furthermore, adapting site facilities to the various phases of construction is also a part of good economic management. For example, once the building shell and the roof have been completed, it is usually no longer necessary to have a construction crane on site. All further transport needs can be met by hoists and mobile cranes.

Adapting building site facilities

Building in winter requires a number of additional provisions. These include:

— Road grit for paths and roads
— Additional lighting for roads and walkways
— Frost protection for water pipes
— Heating technology to achieve the temperatures required for particular building components
— Coverings for components (frost and general weather protection)
— Protective housing for project sections
— Coverings (and, where required, pre-heating technology) for building materials

In addition, site managers need to be aware of the limitations on outside work during periods of cold weather. Assessing whether work can be carried out or not requires consultation with the site managers for each of the contractors involved in the project, and safety must be the highest priority.

THE SAFENESS OF BUILDING SITES

Building sites located in urban areas present a number of dangers. Every building site must be signposted in a way that is visible by day and night and that clearly and simply indicates these dangers. > Figs. 6, 7 and 8
● Particularly dangerous areas must be cordoned off to prevent unauthorized entry.

Public authorities require that signage and barriers on public streets and walkways are supplemented by additional traffic signs. Moreover, optical barriers such as

— Barrier boards
— Warning tape
— Cones
— Warning beacons

must be arranged such that dangerous areas are clearly demarcated.

> ● Important: The site manager is responsible for ensuring these safety features are well maintained. When work finishes for the day, managers should tour the site to check all hoardings, doors and gates.

Fig. 6: Building site signage

Fig. 7: Examples of mandatory signs (white on blue, from left to right: helmets must be worn, hearing protection must be used, safety shoes must be worn)

Fig. 8: Examples of prohibition signs (black/red on white: no naked flames, do not set down loads, no entry)

Fig. 9: Building site facilities in London

Walkways on the building site should be constructed with safety in mind and, where applicable, equipped with railings. Public walkways adjacent to the building site must be protected in such a way that the site cannot present any threat whatsoever. This may involve completely
■ covering walkways or blocking and rerouting them. > Fig. 9

Industrial safety on the building site

Industrial safety covers not only accident prevention but also protection from occupational illnesses and other damage to health. The intensity of physical work on a building site and the use of dangerous materials, machines and tools mean that a well-organized occupational health and safety regime is essential. Due to their importance, the principles and organization of occupational health and safety are regulated by a range of laws and ordinances. These regulations deal with

— The internal organization of and responsibility for occupational
  health and safety within building firms
— The involvement of other organizations in occupational health
  and safety
— The client's responsibilities

Responsibility on the building site

The client is obligated to institute and implement occupational health and safety measures both during the planning of a building project and in the context of construction itself. Since very few clients are in a position to meet this obligation, the task is usually passed to the site manager. Where required, site managers will engage an occupational health and safety coordinator, or HSC, to assist in this task. In Europe, for example, EU guidelines require the involvement of an HSC in all large-scale building sites. The responsibilities involved, whether carried out by the site manager or HSC, include:

Occupational
health and safety
coordinator

— Adhering to the principles of occupational health and safety
  in implementation planning
— Notifying authorities about the project
— Drawing up a health and safety plan in the case of large building
  sites and/or particularly dangerous work
— Compiling health and safety documentation for later work
  on the completed building

■ **Tip:** In cases where walkways and/or streets near the building site have to be blocked for several hours or even days to allow for the delivery and assembly of large building components, approval must be obtained from local authorities. Adequate information regarding such occurrences should also be displayed for local residents and pedestrians several days in advance.

As a rule, the site manager and the HSC also draw up instructions regarding the specificities of the building site. These contain information on access roads, building electricity and water, safety regulations, areas of work, etc., and should be documented in reports.

Breach of duty   Maintaining and enforcing safety regulations on building sites is particularly important to the site manager. If contravention of these regulations results in an accident, the site manager is personally liable. Such cases involve what is known as breach of duty, an offence also committed by anyone who:

— Fails to give requisite instructions
— Fails to carry out checks
— Fails to stop wrong conduct despite the possibility of doing so
— Fails to report shortcomings they are unable to handle
— Fails to use provided safety equipment

Breaches of duty give rise to liability claims when:

— The result is damage to persons or property
— Such breaches contravene prevailing laws
— Personal fault is proved
— The task involved is within the field of personal responsibility
— The breach involves an individual acting or failing to act in a way that has caused the damage.

Safety and health plan   The safety and health plan (SHP) is one of the most important documents relating to occupational health and safety on the building site. It must be readable and understandable by all people working on the site. The plan describes the dangers that can arise during the building process and the ways of countering them, e.g. using the required safety equipment. This information is categorized by trade. Dangers arising as a result of the need to coordinate different types of work within the same time frame are also listed. The health and safety plan is based on the scheduling and implementation plan.

Organization of first aid   Should an accident occur on a building site, the provision of first aid must be guaranteed. Organizing the first aid system should cover the following aspects:

— First aid facilities and resources, i.e. first aid kits, stretchers and, where appropriate, a first aid room
— Identification of the site's first aider by name and location

— Visible display of "first aid instructions" including telephone numbers and addresses of emergency medical services, the local hospital and the local emergency doctor

The scope of the required facilities and resources will depend on the size of the building site.

Contractors' responsibilities

Contracted firms are required by law to protect their employees from dangers to life and health. Responsibility for ensuring that this obligation is met is usually assumed by someone with a supervisory role on the building site, and adherence to statutory requirements is also monitored by the client's site manager.

An effective occupational health and safety regime can only be established on building sites if all participants cooperate and a range of measures are coordinated. These include arranging work stations, machinery and tools so that they are completely safe or risk is minor. If this is not possible, personal protective measures should also be taken. All risk factors should be pointed out on easily comprehensible signs. > Figs. 7 and 8 Where several firms are working simultaneously on a building site, additional measures are required. For instance, firms need to inform each other about work that presents a risk for all parties and coordinate appropriate safety measures. This information exchange should take place in site meetings and also on the site itself. > Chapter Organizing the building site, Site meeting

COOPERATION ON THE BUILDING SITE

Site management means dealing with people with different interests, different levels and types of education and, in some cases, from different countries. The site manager not only represents the client but is also responsible for the coordination of the building site. For this reason the site manager often has to act as a moderator on the site and make clear and responsible decisions regarding questions that arise, for instance, between specialist planners or contractors. In this function the site manager is able to issue directives and has authority over contractors. The contractual relationships between the client, the site manager and the contracted firms are shown schematically in Figure 10.

As already indicated, depending on the type of building project and contract, other planners and specialists may also be involved in supervising firms contracted by the client and, where required, coordinating their different areas of work. > Chapter Quality management, Monitoring and safeguard-

Other site managers

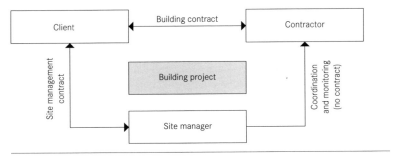

Fig. 10: Organization of participants in the construction phase

ing quality However, responsibility for overall coordination lies with the supervising architect. The other "site managers" working on the site are designated in terms of their function. Unfortunately these titles are not always used uniformly:

— Site architect/site manager: an architect or construction engineer commissioned by the client to manage a construction project (this is the person referred to in this book as the site manager)
— Specialist engineer: specialized planner commissioned by the client to manage construction in a particular trade area, e.g. building services
— Company site manager: staff member of contracting firm with a supervisory role. In situations involving several site supervisors there is usually also a senior site manager with overall responsibility.

Figure 11 shows a possible organizational structure for participants in the building phase.

Building contracts   In addition to safety, the basis of cooperation on the building site is provided by the building contracts. As a rule, tender specifications provide a basis for building implementation in the form of the regulations, guidelines and standards applying to the respective trades, which are described and contractually agreed. Building contracts can include further details relating to the construction process, particularly concerning schedules, methods of payment, and possible contractual penalties if deadlines are exceeded. In addition, contractors are generally expected to:

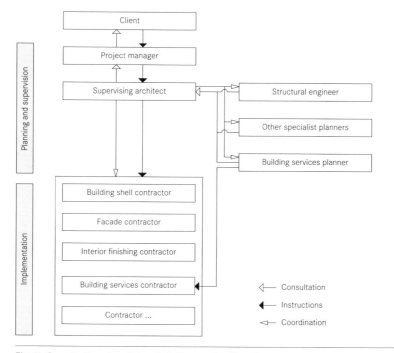

Fig. 11: Organization of participants in the construction phase

— Carry out their work as contractually specified on their own
   responsibility and on their own account
— Adhere to statutory provisions
— Fulfill obligations to the client imposed by law, government
   authorities and trade organizations
— Provide for order in the workplace
— Communicate in writing any misgivings they may have concerning
   the proposed form of implementation, materials or components
   provided by the client or work by other contractors
— Protect their work from damage and theft up until final inspection
— Remedy any defects in their work detected by the client prior to
   and during final inspection
— Comply with scheduled deadlines.

Of course, contractual agreements also give contractors rights in relation to the client. For instance, the contractor has the right to demand sufficient security for advance risk. If the contractor's services require financial investment in building materials, for example, he or she is entitled to demand proof that the client is able to pay the contractually agreed costs.

The organization or hierarchy of contractors is basically similar for all trades. The company site manager and the technical supervisor are the contact persons for the site manager. They are present at site meetings and are responsible for coordinating their company's employees and subcontractors, and to their own firm's management for the economical implementation of planning. In turn, the foremen are responsible for their respective crews.

On almost all building sites it is common practice for contractors to commission other firms, called subcontractors, to carry out work they cannot or do not want to do themselves. There is no contractual relationship between the client and subcontractors, and the respective contractor is responsible for all commissioning, implementation, payment, and warranties relating to its subcontractors. However, the engagement of such subcontractors does require the client's approval.

Systematizing site management documents

It is important to have all site management documents ready to hand. The content of this documentation will depend on the nature of the building project and how far it has progressed. In order to maintain an overview of the flood of correspondence, reports, plans and notes, a system of folders should be used. This system can be structured as follows:

— Folder 0: Current planning documents with plan list and plan receipt and delivery
— Folder 1: Building permit documents and related correspondence
— Folder 2: Correspondence with client
— Folder 3: Correspondence with specialist planners
    — Folder 3.1: Structural engineering
    — Folder 3.2: Building services planning
    — Folder 3.3: Fire security
    — Folder 3.4: ...
— Folder 4: Project manager
— Folder 5: Contractors with respective tender specification, building contract, correspondence, invoices, planning documents, bill of quantities, etc.

- Folder 5.1: Building shell
- Folder 5.2: Building services (BS)
- Folder 5.3: Plastering
- Folder 5.4: Screed work
- Folder 5.5: ...
- Folder 6: Site meeting/project meeting reports
- Folder 7: Delivery notes, certification reports, supporting documents
- Folder 8: Construction diary – site management
- Folder 9: Construction diary – contractors
- Folder 10: ...

Construction diary

In order to be able to comprehend which work has been carried out and when, which contractors were on the building site with how many workers, or whether there have been any notable incidents, the site manager must keep a construction diary. > Fig. 12 The construction diary should be updated daily and as well as structural descriptions should contain the following information:

- Date
- Weather (temperature, cloud cover, rainfall)
- Trades represented on the building site (carpenters, masons, ...)
- Number of workers present from each firm; if applicable, supervising foremen
- Notes describing work carried out
- Tools/machinery utilized
- Particular materials used (e.g. paints, primers)
- Particular components installed
- Installation and operating instructions for installed devices – as appendix
- Documentation of actual or suspected defects and damage
- Progress of construction work in general (overview) and in detail
- Working plans given to contractors
- If applicable, missing plans
- Agreed changes to plans

A range of forms are available for contractors to use for their construction diaries. > Fig. 13 Where possible, the site manager should also have forms made up that are tailored to the particular construction site. Contractors are usually contractually obliged to keep a construction diary, which must be handed to the site manager at agreed intervals.

Construction diary building 55		Mo	Tu	We	Th	Fr	Sa	Su
Date	05.06.2006							
Weather	Sunny				x			
Min°C	20							
Max°C	30							

Firms present:

		Workers
1	R&P	11
2	Acoustics firm	8
3	Miller, sanitary installation	15
4	Smith, electrical installation	4
5	Facade	8
6	Walthers metalwork	5
7	Roofing	3
8	BMA	4
9	Painting	3
10	Screed	2

Work performed:

1	Kitchen, toilet cores walled off, preparation for screed in kitchen
2	Plasterboard floors 4–6, kitchen ceiling
3	Kitchen installations, heating circuits, heaters 4th/5th floors
4	Electrical installations kitchen, core 10–11, office areas
5	Office facade floors 4–6, glazing floors 4–5, Office facade attachments
6	Canteen handrail, stairways 5–7, brackets stairways 5–7
7	Canteen roof sealed, remaining work on office roof
8	Kitchen installations area
9	Painting technical rooms, office balustrades, stairwells 10–11
10	Screed work basement

Visits to building site:

Directives:

Mr. Miller, fire prevention measures: removal of all fire loads (packaging, palettes, topping out wreath, etc.) from the building site. Hire fire risk from welding work.

Repair emergency drainage (R&P)

To be noted:

Heavy rain over night

Roof of 2nd construction section leaky

Emergency drainage damaged

Fig. 12: Page from site manager's construction diary

Construction diary

Construction diary Day: 05.06.06	Building site: Building 55	Page number: 34862	
Supervisor: Walthers / Miller Foreman: Galbraith / Smith	Weather: sunny	max.: 20 °C min.: 30 °C	

Labor deployment | Machinery deployment

	Number	Total hours	Machinery deployment
Supervisors	2	11	
Foremen			
Skilled craftsmen	7	60	
Machine operators			
Metal workers			
Laborers	2	17	
Total	11	88	

Contractual services

Job no.	Quantity	Text	Costs
		Brickwork done in bathrooms axis 4–6 d=9.5cm in pumice on 2nd floor	
		F90 brick walls done axis 9–10 on 6th floor d=11.5cm in limestone	
		Installation walls done on 5th and 6th floors axis 4–6 in aerated concrete	
		Toilet tanks and piping embedded in wall	

Non-contractual services

Forms stripped on foundation for installation walls in bathrooms axis 4–6 3rd–5th floor.

Doorway in wall on 3rd floor axis 9 chiseled out and rubble removed

Other + checks

Emergency drainage checked and repaired

Rennemann	Rusch
Signature R&P	for the client

Fig. 13: Page from contractor's construction diary

PROJECT MEETING/SITE MEETING

Complex building projects require the cooperation of all those involved. Depending on the task at hand, the site manager can make use of different tools to facilitate such cooperation. These tools include:

— Project meetings
— Site meetings
— Reports
— Face-to-face discussions
— Letter, fax, e-mail
— Telephone consultation
— Photographic documentation
— Sketches and drawings
— Workflow and cost charts
— Construction site inspection/site survey

Although all relevant agreements have been formally established in the building contracts, it may well be necessary to reach further agreements during the construction process itself. Since such agreements often involve detailed coordination between the different trades, they are made in the context of project and site meetings. > Figs. 14 and 15 Agreements detailed in meeting reports are binding and, depending on the specific agreement, have contractual status regarding subsequent work. Table 1 provides an overview of how such meetings can be productively organized.

Project meeting   Project and site meetings should be held at regular intervals. Along with the site manager, project meetings involve the project manager (if this is not the same person as the site manager), the client, the project supervisor, and, if required, the project and site managers attached to other specialist planners working on the project. In the project meeting the client is informed about the current situation on the building site regarding the progress of planning and construction, cost developments and schedules. If required, the meeting is also used to make decisions on changes relating to schedules, costs or quality. If decisions are required that can only be made by the client, the relevant information must be compiled and presented by the site manager in a way that facilitates quick and clear decision-making.

Site meeting   At the request of the contracted firms, the site manager must organize a regular site meeting. Site meetings involve the specialist engineers engaged on the site and the site managers representing the different contractors. In the early and latter stages of the building phase, meetings often only take place once a fortnight but may be required weekly during the main building period. One element of the site meeting is a collective

Project: new building, Swiss Re Headquarters, London				Participation required / Invitation	present	from – to	Ref.
Site meeting no. 12: Invitation/Report							
Date: 03.07.2007			Client	x			
			Architect	x			
Location: Building site, site management container			Site manager BS	x			
			Site manager GC	x			
Begins: 9 a.m.			SC building shell	x			
			SC interior finishing	x			
Ends: midday			SC sanitary facilities	x			
			SC ventilation				
Distribution list: as per participant list			SC electrical	x			
Additional: ☒							

Invitation			Report		
Agenda item	Prepared by	Goal		Execution	
Check correspondence since 18.06.07	GC	Identical documents			
Effect of flood damage on schedule	GC SC interior finishing	Assessment delay/speedup			
Inspect interior finishing quality	GC SC interior finishing SC sanitary facilities	Assessment execution			
etc.					

Fig. 14: Example of site meeting invitation

Project: new building, Swiss Re Headquarters, London				Participation required / Invitation	present	from – to	Ref.
Site meeting no. 12: Invitation/Report							
Date: 03.07.2007			Client	x	x		SD
			Architect	x	x		FD
Location: Building site, site management container			Site manager BS	x	x	10:00–11:00	KL
			Site manager GC	x	x		OL
Begins: 9 a.m.			SC building shell	x	x		WS
			SC interior finishing	x	x		AS
Ends: midday			SC sanitary facilities	x	x		VE
			SC ventilation				
Distribution list: as per participant list			SC electrical	x	x	10:30–11:00	TH
Additional: ☒							

Invitation			Report	Execution	
Agenda item	Prepared by	Goal	Assessment Result Agreement	Who	Date
Check correspondence since 18.06.07	GC	Identical documents	Assessment Result Agreement	GC and all SC	until 05.07.07
Effect of flood damage on schedule	GC SC Interior finishing	Assessment delay/speedup	Architect receives copy of encroachment complaint of 14.06.07	Client and GC	until 07.07.07
Inspect interior finishing quality	GC SC interior finishing SC sanitary facilities	Assessment execution	Client inspects (together with architect)	Client and architect	until 10.07.07
etc.					

Fig. 15: Example of an invitation also functioning as a meeting report

Tab. 1: Principles for organizing project and site meetings

Basic questions	Is this meeting needed or are there better ways of solving the problem? (What would happen without this consultation session?) Does the achievable effect justify the effort involved (lost working time for all parties)?
Goal of the meeting	Meetings should only be called when they have a concrete goal(s). Is the meeting only of value for the site manager or is it important for all participants? What results can be expected?
Preparation for the meeting	Fix agenda, identify key points Set out goals in writing Decide on procedure Determine who is responsible for the preparation of individual points Who is required to participate? Must every participant be present for the discussion of each point? Distribute agenda with invitation
Organization of the meeting	Limit participation to the necessary parties If required, organize individual discussions Provide agenda in advance and keep to it
Meeting management	Timed is saved by well chaired meetings Maintain focus on the goal Keep an eye on the time allotment Avoid peripheral issues – maintain the central focus Do not allow one-on-one discussions to develop in larger meetings Aim for consensus
Results/meeting report	Select a suitable form of meeting reports (should reports record results or the course of discussion?) Write up report soon after the meeting Clearly identify responsible parties in the meeting report Ensure clear agreement on deadlines is included in report

inspection of the building site. Detailed questions on implementation or coordination between different trades can often only be dealt with in situ. ∎

The form of the meeting invitations and reports should provide a clear Invitation/ Report overview of all relevant points. A form should be chosen that allows for systematic and rapid reporting of results. Each participant should receive a tabularized overview of all agenda items. > Fig. 14 The example below illustrates how the results of the meeting can be entered directly into the table. > Fig. 15 In the simplest case, each participant receives a copy of this report at the end of the meeting. Only where more complex issues are involved will supplementary material be added to the report later. Such material should include explanatory sketches, photos, and data sheets.

In all cases, the invitation and the report should include the following details:

— Construction project concerned
— Work specifications/trades
— Meeting location (for on-site meetings, indicate whether the site will be inspected or discussions will be confined to the site office)
— Beginning, end
— Participants (if required, functions and scope of authority)
— Report distribution list (e.g. including third parties not present at the meeting and definition of internal distribution)
— Record of topics discussed (participants may select which topics they wish to make a note of)
— Type of agenda items (e.g. information, agreement, approval, preparation for a decision)
— Basis of meeting (plans, reports, etc.)

∎ **Tip:** When taking part in site inspections, site managers should carry a folder containing the relevant plans (if necessary, reduced in size). Taking pictures with a digital camera can also be useful for supplementing reports and documentation. Other useful tools include a cellular phone, a folding rule, a Dictaphone if applicable and of course all requisite protective equipment such as safety shoes and helmets.

Reports on meeting results must include the relevant goal, deadline, and responsible parties. Particularly important reports have to be signed by the participants. Such reports (e.g. concerning negotiations and final inspections) should clearly indicate the number of pages involved.

Tab. 2: Communication problems

said	does not mean	→	heard
heard	does not mean	→	understood
understood	does not mean	→	agreed
agreed	does not mean	→	applied
applied	does not mean	→	maintained

○ **Hint:** Even if the a generally friendly atmosphere predominates on a building site, ambiguity must be strictly avoided in meeting and final inspection reports, as it must be in all agreements relating to costs and schedules. If disagreements arise, the previously friendly atmosphere will be of little help. Written agreements are then all that can be relied on.

Scheduling and implementation planning

Scheduling and implementation planning are two of the site manager's most important tasks. It entails identifying all deadlines relevant to the construction process and coordinating all implementation procedures in terms of technology, space and time. This requires a degree of experience in the building field. However, due to the many factors influencing the actual process of construction, there will always be deviations from the original plans.

In order to be able to meet planned deadlines, it is particularly important that one receives information on possible schedule deviations in time to adapt building procedures accordingly. The earlier deviations are recognized, the more possibilities there are to offset them. Scheduling and implementation planning as well as their management constitute one of the three main tasks of site management. The ability to complete a project within the designated time frame is a key factor in assessing the site manager's performance.

TERMS RELATING TO SCHEDULING AND IMPLEMENTATION PLANNING

All scheduling consists of processes and events as well as their relationship to one another.

A process is understood as an occurrence that is defined by a beginning, duration and an end. A typical process within a schedule would be, for example, painting.

Process

An event is an element of implementation that is not assigned a duration. Particularly important events are characterized as milestones and integrated into the schedule. Examples of milestones are the commencement and completion of building and, within the course of construction, the completion of the building shell.

Event/milestone

In the course of almost every building project, milestones are reached that are particularly significant for the client.

Important events for the client

The symbolic breaking of the ground on a site marks the beginning of the construction phase. In the case of large building projects that are important for the public, the owner invites the later users or tenants of the building and official representatives of the political and business spheres to the ground-breaking ceremony.

Ground-breaking ceremony

The laying of the foundation stone usually takes place following the completion of the excavation pit and prior to the initial cement work. In some cases a capsule containing markers of the time at which the building was constructed, such as newspapers, photos of the site or a few coins, is deposited inside the stone, which will later lie under the completed building.

The topping-out ceremony is held when the shell and roof truss of the new building have been completed. Different ceremonies are held in different regions to wish the building and its owner luck. The topping-out ceremony is arranged by the owner in order to thank all participants for the work that has been completed.

Once the building is finally completed, an inauguration or opening ceremony is held. In contrast to the topping out ceremony, the opening is not linked with any fixed rituals. The owner usually thanks everyone who has contributed to the completion of the building and presents it to the public.

EXECUTION OF THE SCHEDULE AND IMPLEMENTATION PLAN

It is the task of the site manager to coordinate all firms working on the building site on the basis of the schedule and implementation plan. It must be clear to all participants which work they must complete at which point so that the following work phase can then begin. The way in which specific jobs are carried out is the responsibility of the firms concerned.

To be able to organize the overall building schedule, the site manager needs to be cognizant of all processes and procedures involved in the project and their interrelationships with one another. Building this knowledge base involves three types of planning:

> ● **Example:** The duration of a process is defined by multiplying the quantity required (e.g. m^2 or m^3) by a performance factor. This indicates how much time is required on average to perform a certain task. The construction of a square meter of masonry, for example, is typically accorded a performance value of 1.4–2.0 h/m^2. A range of standard performance values can be found in the relevant literature, and many site managers establish their own standards on the basis of experience.

The first step involves identifying and organizing all processes and events that are relevant to the construction phase. The goal is to pinpoint the interrelationships between all the relevant processes. This entails arranging all processes in a way that gives the course of construction a clear logic. Scheduling is of course an important factor here. If one wants to determine when and which firms are to be engaged on the building site, then it follows that the individual processes carried out by firms have to be arranged in a logical order.

Implementation planning

Once the relevant processes and interrelationships have been identified, the second step involves determining the possible duration of individual and combined processes on the basis of the overall time available for construction.

Time planning

●

Scheduling essentially entails integrating the time frames defined in the time planning into the implementation planning to create a series of concrete deadlines. The beginning and ending of each process is thus clearly identified.

Schedule planning

Representing schedule plans

Different ways of representing schedule plans can be used depending on the aim, user and/or project involved. A basic distinction is made between four types of representation: bar charts, line diagrams, network plans, and deadline lists. > Fig. 16 The bar chart is now the usual method employed for building projects.

In bar charts, processes and events are listed along the vertical axis. The horizontal axis is used as a timeline. Each process is represented by a bar, the length of which corresponds to the duration of the process. Accordingly, events and milestones are represented as processes without duration. Interdependent processes are linked by arrows. The advantages of the bar chart are that it is easy to read (even by laypersons) and its clarity. Moreover, it is a very effective means of providing an overview of an entire project. > Fig. 17

Bar charts

Bar charts have now become the most common method for representing schedules in the building construction field. There are numerous computer programs on the market that can be used to design schedule plans, particularly in the form of bar charts.

The simplest way of representing a schedule plan is in the form of a deadline list. Depending on the intended use and the user, different ways of representing events and processes can also be employed. When drawing up a deadline list, processes need to be characterized in such a way

Deadline lists

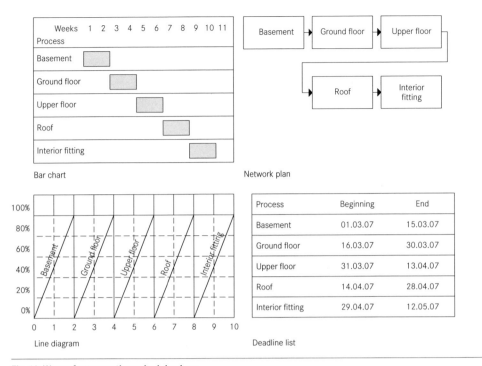

Fig. 16: Ways of representing schedule plans

that they can be sorted according to different criteria, e.g. in terms of trades or construction sections. Representing interdependencies between the processes is problematic in deadline lists and requires additional annotations.

Network plans and line diagrams

Examples of network plans and line diagrams, or volume-time diagrams, are shown in Figure 16 and will not be discussed further here since in normal building construction projects they only play a subordinate role.

Types of schedule plan

Schedule plans are distinguished in terms of their level of detail. Different levels of detail can be used in the dividing up time into months, weeks, days and even hours or in the degree to which processes are differentiated.

Framework time schedule

The framework time schedule is drawn up at the beginning of the project by the client or the planner. This schedule presents the time frame

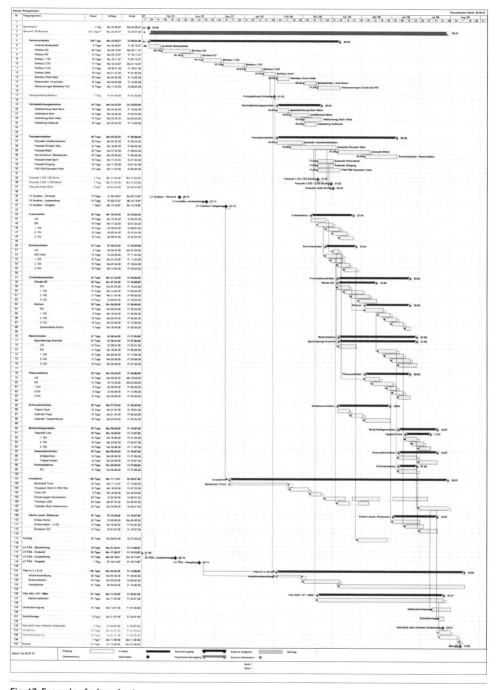

Fig. 17: Example of a bar chart

321

for the entire project and, as a rule, is based on the deadlines specified by the client. These can be divided into the following very general categories:

— Project preparation
— Planning
— Implementation
— Occupation
— Use

Master schedule   In the course of drawing up the tender specifications, the architect usually also develops a master schedule. The deadlines contained in this schedule are included in the tender specifications since these must be agreed contractually with the firms working on the building project. The master schedule is the foundation of the site manager's deadline planning. It is kept general, listing only the most important milestones and process or trade groups. Examples of trade groups are:

— Preparatory measures
— Building shell
— Building envelope
— Interior finishing
— Building services
— Final/subsequent measures

Each group comprises the trades required for that area of work. For example, the building shell group includes concrete and reinforced concrete construction, masonry work, steel construction, etc. > Tab. 3

Refined schedule   The different trade tasks are used to structure the refined schedule. If the project is divided into construction sections, the different processes are arranged in the schedule accordingly. > Chapter Scheduling and implementation planning, Schedule management The processes indicated in the refined schedule must be linked with reference to their spatial and technological inter-
● connections. > Fig. 18

● **Example:** There is a technological interconnection, for example, between screed work and parquet laying. Before the parquet can be laid, the screed must have dried enough to prevent any remaining dampness from damaging the parquet. A spatial interconnection exists, for example, between painting and floor covering work, since these tasks cannot be carried out simultaneously in the same space.

Tab. 3: Trades and assignment to trade groups

Trade	P	S	BE	IF	BS
Excavations	x	x			
Site preparation	x	x			
Water control work	x	x			
Waterproofing work	x				
Drainage work	x	x			
Masonry work		x			
Concrete construction work		x			
Natural stone work				x	
Concrete block work				x	
Carpentry and timber work			x		
Steel construction work		x	x		
Sealing work		x	x		
Roofing and roof-sealing work			x		
Plumbing work			x		
Dry construction work				x	
Heat insulation work			x		
Concrete conservation work	x	x			
Plastering and stucco work			x	x	
Facade work			x		
Tiling work				x	
Screed work				x	
Melted asphalt work				x	
Joinery				x	
Parquet laying				x	
Fitting work			x	x	
Roller blind work			x		
Metal construction work			x	x	
Glazing work			x	x	

Tab. 3: Trades and assignment to trade groups

Trade	Trade group				
	P	S	BE	IF	BS
Painting and varnishing work				x	
Corrosion prevention work on steel and aluminum		x	x		
Floor covering work				x	
Wallpapering				x	
Air-conditioning installations					x
Heating and water-heating installations					x
Gas, water and drainage installations					x
Low and medium voltage electrical installations					x
Lightning protection installations					x
Conveyor systems, elevators, moving staircases/walkways					x
Building automation					x
Insulation for technical installations					x
Scaffolding		x	x		x

Abbreviations: P = preparatory work, S = shell, BE = building envelope,
IF = interior finishing, BS = building services

Planning processes into the refined schedule can, for example, be based on the trades and titles listed in the tender specifications. This ensures that no important processes are forgotten. A possible structure is shown in Table 3. In the additional columns the trades are assigned to the different trade groups.

Detail schedule   A detail schedule can be required to coordinate work involving many workers in confined spaces or when deadlines are very tight. In a detail schedule, the time scale can be divided into units as small as hours. > Fig. 19

○ **Hint:** Depending on the kind of schedule plan, related individual processes can be combined into a collective process in order to provide a clearer overview of overall procedures. Dry construction, for example, is included as a process in the refined schedule. In the detail schedule, the collective process dry construction includes the processes of framework installation, sheeting 1st side, electrical work and planking 2nd side, etc.

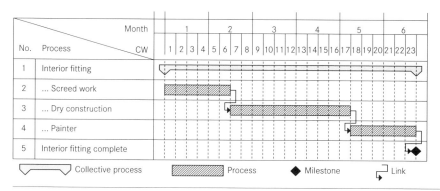

Fig. 18: Collective process/individual process representation in an example of a refined schedule for interior finishing

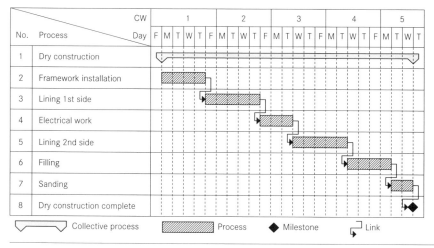

Fig. 19: Collective process/individual process representation in an example of a detail schedule for dry construction

CHECKING SCHEDULES

The date of a building's completion can be determined by a whole range of requirements. Several examples are shown in Table 4. The site manager must be aware of the reasons for the client naming a particular deadline for completion. If the deadline is linked with other fixed arrangements, it is of course not negotiable.

Tab. 4: Examples of reasons for deadlines

Building	Possible reasons for the specified deadline
Stadium	Championships
Shop/department store	Christmas shopping period
School	Beginning of school year
Highway	Beginning of holiday period
Power station	Beginning of heating period
City hall	Cost-effective building time
Factory workshop	Commencement of production (profitability analysis)

Plausibility check of schedule specifications

The possibility of meeting contractual schedules should be checked by all contractual parties before signing by way of a simple plausibility check. This applies both to the site manager, who has to check the entire construction period, and to the contractors, who are responsible for determining the viability of the tasks they have been commissioned to do.

At the beginning of this checking process, the following questions should be considered:

— Can the project be built within the time available?
— Can all required components and materials be delivered within the building period?
— What external factors (e.g. confined space, heavy street traffic) can influence the progress of building?

There are different ways of conducting a plausibility check. The simplest for the site manager entails comparing the current project with projects that have already been completed. The literature provides lists and overviews of finished projects. These lists include not only plans, photos and costs, but usually also time frames. Reference to comparable buildings provides a quick and simple aid for plausibility checks. If such a check shows that the requested deadline is not achievable, the client must be clearly informed.

Schedule connections between individual building elements or trades

In some cases, non-negotiable contractual deadlines are required not only for the final date of completion but also for individual building sections or a certain stage of construction.

In order to be able to coordinate the large number of individual trades, the site manager must also set clear deadlines for the individual contractors. Planning the individual processes within a trade is only of interest for the site manager if work by other trades is affected. This is particularly important in the case of interior finishing, since a large number of firms are working on the building site.

Obstructions

Experience shows that a whole range of changes can take place during the actual building phase. These changes can affect the quality, schedules and/or building costs. Depending on who has caused these changes, contracted firms may have the right to demand an extension of building time and associated additional costs. These claims are checked by the site manager.

Construction can be obstructed by

— Circumstances instigated or caused by the client
— Circumstances for which the contractor is responsible
— Circumstances for which neither the client nor the contractor is responsible

Circumstances for which the client is responsible include:

— Failure to secure permits
— Failure to mark out the main axes and benchmark elevation
— Failure by the client to make decisions e.g. on the implementation of alternative positions
— Insufficient coordination of the contractors commissioned by the client
— Incomplete or defective work by the architect or other planners
— Agreed or required security not provided by client

● **Example:** In industrial construction, machinery and larger plant are moved into the building before the outside walls or roofs are constructed. Otherwise such equipment would be too large to fit through the doors or windows of the completed building.

■ **Tip:** It is of no interest to the site manager when the building shell contractor erects the shuttering for the ground floor and builds in and cements the armoring since these processes are only carried out by the shell contractor. What is important for the site manager is that the completion deadline for the ground floor is met if, for example, plastering work is due to begin at this time.

- Not paying as contractually specified (too late, too little)
- Intervention by the client or architect in the planned program of building
- Quantity increases
- Changes in work requirements
- Safety defects that cause building work to stop.

These circumstances can be the basis for claims by contractors against the client for deadline extensions, compensation and damages.

Apart from the reasons already listed for delays in the construction process, there are also circumstances that are the responsibility of neither the client nor the contractor. Examples include

- A strike or lockout ordered by the employer's trade union in the contractor's or a subcontractor's field
- Force majeure or other circumstances that the contractor cannot avoid.

Should these circumstances occur, the building contractor has a claim to an extension of building time but not to higher compensation for his or her services.

It is self-evident that the contractor cannot base claims on obstruction to work for which he or she is responsible. On the contrary, in such a situation the client may be entitled to claim damages. Several examples of possible causes for delays are summarized in Table 5.

Obstructions by other trades

If prior work done by other trades is insufficient or faulty, this needs to be brought to the attention of the client and the site manager immediately. The site manager must make clear decisions as to how these

○ obstacles are to be eliminated.

○ **Hint:** Where one type of job follows on directly from another, e.g. a dry construction wall is painted, there is usually an inspection during which the second trade confirms that the prior work is of a standard that allows subsequent work to continue without obstruction. The site manager should make a report of this inspection and those involved should witness it with their signatures (see Chapter Final inspection and acceptance).

Tab. 5: Possible causes of deviations and obstructions to the progress of work

	Client's responsibility/ sphere of risk	Contractor's responsibility
Wrong planning and assumptions	Soil class incorrectly estimated	Productivity incorrectly estimated
	Tender-invitation for service incomplete	Incorrect machinery planned for
	Tendered quantities too small	Necessary material quantities incorrectly calculated
	Mistake in schedule	Mistake in own schedule
Interruptions to building process	Missing plans	Materials do not arrive punctually
	Lack of decisions on part of client	Machinery breaks down
	Faulty advance work by other trades	Shuttering/sheeting insufficient Building site closed due to inadequate safety measures
	Schedule overruns by authorities, architects and planners	Staff fall ill
	Unexpected archeological find	Defective quality (demolition and rebuilding)

However, the contractor is also obliged to limit the damage caused by an obstruction as far as possible. It can therefore be expected that if obstructions occur workers will move on to other necessary work rather than waiting for the obstruction to be removed.

SCHEDULE MANAGEMENT

The schedule and implementation plan allows compliance with the planned course of building to be monitored. In this context, it is important to focus in particular on processes that directly follow one another and if delayed can have a direct effect on the completion schedule. The chain formed by these processes in the schedule is referred to as the "critical path." > Fig. 20

Effective and well-targeted schedule management requires clear identification of obstructions and consequent delays. This in turn requires a regular target-performance comparison to be carried out on

Tools of schedule management

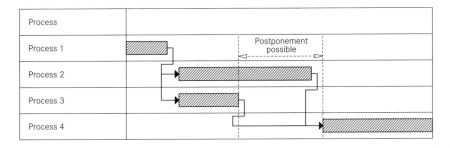

Fig. 20: "Critical path" diagram

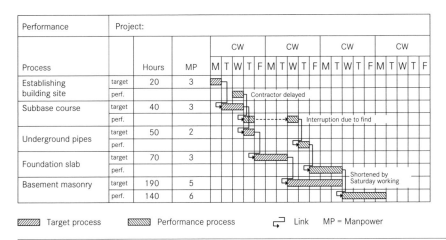

Performance	Project:				CW					CW					CW					CW			
Process		Hours	MP	M	T	W	T	F	M	T	W	T	F	M	T	W	T	F	M	T	W	T	F
Establishing building site	target	20	3																				
	perf.					Contractor delayed																		
Subbase course	target	40	3																				
	perf.							Interruption due to find																
Underground pipes	target	50	2																				
	perf.																							
Foundation slab	target	70	3																				
	perf.														Shortened by Saturday working								
Basement masonry	target	190	5																				
	perf.	140	6																				

▨▨▨ Target process   ▩▩▩ Performance process   ⌐ Link   MP = Manpower

Fig. 21: Bar chart with target-performance comparison

the building site. > Fig. 21 Schedule deviations can be offset by the following measures:

— Increase in capacity (increased workforce/increased machinery deployment)
— Increased working time
— Changes to building and production procedures

— Adaptation of construction sections
— Changes in quality

However, these measures can only offset schedule deviations to a certain degree. The costs they give rise to must be paid by the party responsible for the delay.

It is important to bear in mind that increasing capacity does not necessarily follow the rule that "What one can achieve in ten days can be achieved by ten in one day." Increasing capacity

Often a lack of space makes it impossible to significantly increase the number of people working on a task. Workers will end up getting in each other's way, with the result that work is delayed even further.

Prolonging the working time each day or adding working days is often the simplest means of offsetting delays. Since measures for speeding up the work process normally generate additional costs, it must be clear who is to carry these costs (overtime bonuses or bonuses for work on weekends and public holidays). Increasing working hours

Changing building procedures during construction is often only possible to a limited degree. Changes to procedures are possible, for example, in the case of: Changing building procedures

— Screed work: cement screed to dry screed or dry screed to melted asphalt screed
— Plastering: wet plaster to dry plaster or thick plaster to smoothing plaster

Changes in quality can also allow building procedures to be sped up or the order of procedures to be changed so that other processes are brought forward or accelerated. For one thing, such changes can result Changes in quality

■ **Tip:** If building procedures are changed, it is important to consider the possible effects on other work sections. Using smoothing plaster or dry plaster, for example, can mean that different door frame dimensions will be required. The subsequent work sections thus have to be coordinated with the planned changes.

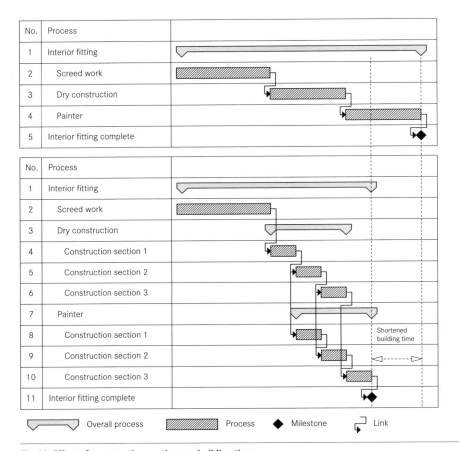

No.	Process		
1	Interior fitting		
2	Screed work		
3	Dry construction		
4	Painter		
5	Interior fitting complete		

No.	Process		
1	Interior fitting		
2	Screed work		
3	Dry construction		
4	Construction section 1		
5	Construction section 2		
6	Construction section 3		
7	Painter		
8	Construction section 1		Shortened building time
9	Construction section 2		
10	Construction section 3		
11	Interior fitting complete		

▽‾‾‾▽ Overall process   ▨ Process   ◆ Milestone   ⌐ Link

Fig. 22: Effect of construction sections on building time

in shorter implementation times on the building site, such as when carpet is used instead of parquet. For another, using more rapidly available build-ing materials can shorten supply times.

Reducing construction sections   The division of the overall project into construction sections allows the time between interdependent processes to be shortened. This is illustrated diagrammatically in Figure 22. Instead of first completing all dry construction work before commencing painting, the latter is begun as soon as the first section of dry construction work is completed. The

Fig. 23: Building using construction sections

smaller the sections, the more processes can be carried out in parallel. However, this makes planning more susceptible to disruptions because if there is a disruption in one section, the work cannot be transferred to other areas.

An example of the division of a building project into construction sections can be seen in Figure 23. Shell construction, facade work and interior finishing take place in parallel. The entire building is divided into construction sections covering different floors.

Quality management

In building projects, quality refers to the contractually agreed condition of a building element after completion or installation. Along with schedule and implementation planning and monitoring costs, quality management is one of the three central tasks of site management. There are regularly disputes over whether building work is of the agreed quality and can thus be defined as free of defects. A fundamental cause of such disagreements has to do with the different ways in which the quality that has been agreed on is understood.

DEFINING QUALITY

The quality required of a building and thus the required standard of work can be defined by the descriptions in tender specifications and plans or, once contracts have been signed, with reference to samples. In this context, it is important that descriptions are unambiguous and are understood in the same way by both the client and the contractor. The following points should be considered:

General descriptions General descriptions such as "sound implementation," "correct work," and "top quality" cannot constitute the basis for an agreement because terms like "sound," "correct" and "top" are not clearly defined.

Special descriptions Special descriptions such as those used in prospectuses or advertising can be defined as an agreed quality in so far as they offer unambiguous statements, e.g. fuel oil use 3 l/m^2 per year.

Hybrid descriptions Hybrid descriptions require a concretization. For example, the term "durable covering" needs to be explained in terms of how long the surface can be expected to remain free of marks from wear.

● **Example:** If a client, an architect and a contractor are all asked what constitutes an acceptable "exposed concrete surface," they will give quite different answers. The client and the architect will expect a perfectly even surface free of color deviations and pores. The contractor, on the other hand, will insist that experience has shown that color deviations, pores, formwork joints, etc. cannot be avoided in even the most careful work and will therefore always be visible.

Individual agreements based on concretely defined aspects of the required results are always preferable to general descriptions. Individual agreements

A sample presents an agreed level of quality and can be used as a guide in the implementation process.

The definition of the desired quality of a building element can take different forms. As already mentioned, descriptions of quality can be found, for example, in tender specifications, plans, sample reports, or photos. Table 6 shows how, for what purpose and with whom quality can be defined. Sample

Tab. 6: Selected tools for reaching agreement on quality

Description of quality through:	Examples	Area of application, details of use	Problems and open questions
Production of samples	Textured plaster Facade coatings	Suitable wherever optical quality relies on craft skill.	Samples are often "too well" made and the same quality is not achieved on the actual surface.
	Hand-worked wooden surfaces Color transitions in natural stone floors and facades	Produce under building site conditions Carry out and document sampling Safeguard samples until final inspection of entire project.	Possible later deviations are often only vaguely described and cover a wide range
"Industrial samples" and their precise names	Paints e.g. RAL colors Sample stones Parquet blocks	Use among specialists possible. Very efficient in this context. Samples must correspond to the subsequent in situ use.	Small samples do not replicate the effect created in the finished space, which is difficult for laypersons to imagine.
Prospectus information and manufacturer supply catalogs	Switches and power sockets Heaters Toilet fixtures		

Tab. 6: Selected tools for reaching agreement on quality

Description of quality through:	Examples	Area of application, details of use	Problems and open questions
Texts of functinal tender specifications	All construction work	Use among planners and implementing and planning contractors. Only partially comprehensible for client.	Specifications are described such that required functions are fulfilled. Implementation qualities are largely left to the contractor.
Texts of detailed tender specifications	All construction work	Use among planners and implementing contractors. Only partially comprehensible for the client.	Specifications must be described in detail since the description is also the basis for the contractor's cost calculations.
Comparable projects	e.g. as illustration of quality of exposed concrete	Very suitable when easily accessible. Shows already achieved quality	Accessibility and time needed for inspection
Sample spaces		Well suited to enabling laypersons to envisage elements in their spatial context.	Quality of sample spaces is usually "too good." Producing a sample space may be very costly.

- Everyone on the building site is responsible for pointing out when a requested specification is objectively impossible.

Tenders/service specifications

All the qualities or characteristics desired by the client should be described in the service specifications is such a way that contractors are made clearly aware of the work they have to perform. Here, a distinction is made between detailed service specifications, which contain precise descriptions of the services required, and functional tenders, which contain descriptions of necessary functions or required features. The description of qualities and required services in service specifications includes:

— Building specifications with general information on the building project
— Contractual conditions
— Planning documents (ground plans, sections, views)
— Textual description of services with quantity information
— Details of reference projects, samples and/or implementation examples

This information should be checked for completeness and validity by the site manager before work begins. In order to clarify the desired quality, the tasks described in the service specifications should be discussed with contractors before work commences in order to ensure that they have understood all requirements and are able to fulfill them.

Sampling inspection

In a sampling inspection the client is shown examples of building elements or implementation quality. Precise agreement on the quality of individual pieces of work is necessary above all in the case of visible surfaces and building elements. The surfaces and elements are subject to highly subjective assessment. The distinction between good and bad quality is dependent on and influenced by ideas, wishes and the observer's own craft experience and tastes.

■

If a particular quality is specified or changed after a contract has been awarded, price changes will usually be made. Potential changes in cost and possible effects on the progress of building (different delivery times for alternatives) should be identified by the time of the sampling inspection so that these factors can be taken into consideration when making decisions.

Effects of the sampling inspection on costs and schedule

It is easy to lose track of the agreements that are made, particularly in the case of large-scale inspections. For this reason, the results must be recorded in a report. It is advisable to draw up an inspection list of all objects to be inspected and the above-mentioned effects that may ensue from changes. > Fig. 24

Inspection list

Fundamental sampling inspections should be undertaken before the contracts are agreed. Sampling inspections that do not affect costs (e.g. colors selected from a fixed palette of standard colors) can also take place during construction. > Chapter Cost management

● **Example:** An objective impossibility would be the construction of a 10 m long external plaster wall with a tolerance of 0 mm. Objective impossibility is understood as indicating that no one is able to build better.

■ **Tip:** If samples are produced, this should be done at the same pace and in the same way as on the building site. It is absolutely essential that the sample closely resemble what will later be featured on the building. If the finished work does not correspond to the sample (the latter is better) the client can demand implementation in accordance with the sample.

| Administrative building for Müller AG | | Sampling inspection result | | | | | | | | | | XY architects |
| | | Kamp-Lintfort | Herne | Dortmund | Haus Witten | Operational samples | Photos | Drawing | Status | Further sampling inspections | Cost increases/reductions | |
Item	Work section											Notes
1	Facade											
1.1	Metal facade – aluminum	x							X			like KL
1.1.1	Lintel /window sill								X			RAL 7016
1.1.2	Panels – ceiling connector							x	X			as per agreement 12.03.03
1.2	Metal facade – steel			x	x			x	X			Sample 9006/9007 – 7016
1.2.1	Facade – canteen							x	X			as per agreement 12.03.03
1.3	Window system – office	x							X			like KL
1.4	Window system – foyer	x							X			like KL
1.5	Exterior sunshading – louver	x	x						X			like KL
1.6	Exterior sunshading - screen			x					–			No
1.7	Cylinder doors								–			No
	Vestibule / entrance								o			Decision by CW 15
2	Interior works											
2.1	Doors	x										
2.1.1	Doors – office areas	x										
	Architraves	x							X			like KL
	Door leaves	x							X			Wooden door leaves
2.1.2	Doors – conference rooms / canteen	x	x									
	Architraves	x	x						X			Metal architrave plates as wall connection
	Door leaves	x	x						X			Wooden door leaves depending on fittings
2.1.3	Doors – lobby / entrance	x										
	Architraves	x	x						X			OK like doors stairwell-office KL
	Door leaves	x	x						X			Steel-glass doors
2.2	Fittings	x	x						X			like KL
2.3	Glass panes	x	x						X			like KL
3	Metalwork											
3.1	Metalwork – interior finishing											
3.1.1	Stairs – foyer/canteen			x	x				X			System as in Witten
3.1.2	Handrails – stairs/gallery	x	x		x				X			As in KL, horizontal rods
3.2	Metalwork – shell											
3.2.1	Formwork – canteen			x					X			RAL 9006
3.2.2	F30 coating				x				X			Application as in paint shop
3.2.3	Enclosure BS/ventilation grills	x							X			"Waste room" KL OK similar
4	Floor											
4.1	Double-floor system	x							X			like KL
4.2	Floor covering											
4.2.1	Floor tiles/washrooms	x	x						X			like KL
4.2.2	Building stone – foyer	x							–			not applicable
4.2.3	Natural stone – foyer			x					X			as per agreement 12.03.03
4.2.4	Building stone – stairs	x	x						–			not applicable
4.2.4.1	Natural stone – stairs								X			aas per agreement 12.03.03
4.2.5	Parquet – canteen			x	x				–			not applicable
4.2.6	Floor tiles – food service					x			X			Sample as per costing
4.2.7	Floor tiles – kitchen					x			X			after agreement with StAfA
4.2.8	Carpet tiles - offices/conference room	x							X			like sample room
4.2.9	Linoleum BS rooms	x							X			like KL

x Sample as per costing
+ Sample more expensive than in costing

Status: Completed X
To be done o
Not applicable -

Fig. 24: Sampling inspection report

MONITORING AND SAFEGUARDING QUALITY

When monitoring the quality of the building work, the site manager must pay particular attention to the following points:

— Type and method of construction (particularly in the case of "damage-prone" types of work
— Geometric quality (maintenance of dimensions, angles and levelness)
— Optical quality (color, surface, uniformity)
— Functional quality (functional efficiency of built-in elements)
— Compliance with plans
— Compliance with public regulations (building approval, ordinances and laws)
— Compliance with manufacturer guidelines and standards

The site manager is especially required to directly monitor particularly complicated or damage-prone aspects of construction. These are aspects that experience has shown to involve a high risk of defects or cost increases.

Examples include:

— Production of job-mixed concrete and semi-finished concrete elements (including armoring)
— Sealing and insulation work
— Relocation of drainage
— Installation of ground pipes (integrity check)
— Installation of building elements relevant to fire protection.

The site manager is responsible for the overall coordination of the building site but is not obliged to be constantly present on the building site and to supervise all work in detail. This applies particularly to the more simple and common building tasks. Examples include: plastering, laying flagstones, dry-construction of walls and ceilings and normal painting work. However, if any of this work proves defective, the site manager must engage more intensively in fulfilling his or her supervisory duties. A site manager must ascertain precisely whether the tradespeople on site have the skills to carry out the commissioned work and meet the agreed standards.

Supervisory duties

Work on the building site should be supervised in a way that ensures that implementation corresponds to requirements. If the demands of this supervision exceed the expertise of the site manager, he or she must encourage the client to appoint technical specialists and specialist engineers. For some aspects of construction, the use of such expertise may even be prescribed:

— Scaffolding
— Building elements relevant to fire protection
— Smoke and heat venting systems
— Fire and smoke alarm systems
— Building elements relevant to structural integrity
— Elevator systems and escalators

The construction and installation of building services are usually supervised by a specialist site manager appointed by the firm responsible for the project's building services planning. This specialist is responsible for supervising the work of the firms commissioned with carrying out all building services work and ensuring this work meets the required standards. In the case of structural engineering elements, it is important that the responsible structural safety engineer is kept well informed about the progress of work so that he or she can monitor and document relevant stages of the work. When this work has been completed he or she must certify that it has been carried out according to regulations. These technical specialists must also be involved in the final acceptance and approval of these construction aspects. > Chapter Final inspection and acceptance

The checking of geometric quality particularly concerns the dimensions of the ground plan and the heights as well as angles and evenness of building elements. If there are no specific agreements in the contract, established standards are taken as a guideline for implementation. Examples of permissible dimension deviations in the ground plan and ceiling heights are shown in Table 7. These examples refer to the German DIN Standard 18202 for tolerances in buildings.

The aim of establishing dimensional accuracy is to facilitate the functional assembly of elements of the shell and interior works without the need for adjustment and refinishing, despite the fact that inaccuracies are unavoidable in the production and fitting processes. It is important that the different work sections are relatively easy to integrate with one another. When limit values are exceeded, the work that follows has to be supplemented with measures to offset these mistakes.

Tab. 7: Examples of permissible dimensional deviations in the ground plan and ceiling heights in the building (based on DIN 18 202)

Dimension to be checked	Admissible tolerances (mm) for a nominal size of ...		
	up to 3 m	3 m to 6 m	6 m to 15 m
Lengths and widths in the ground plan	+12	16	20
Height between floors	16	16	20
Clear dimensions in the ground plan	16	20	24
Clear dimensions in the elevation	20	20	30
Openings (reveals without surface finishing)	12	16	–

LAWS/REGULATIONS/STANDARDS

There is a large body of laws and regulations governing the implementation and characteristics of building projects. Standards are established as a means of standardizing applications, characteristics and procedures and are formulated and published by organizations for standardization. In addition, professional associations and manufacturers provide instructions and guidelines for the use and handling of building products.

Recognized codes of practice

In the present context, recognized codes of practice are to be understood as rules applying to the construction of buildings and building elements. These rules are regarded both by scholars and practitioners as correct and have proved their worth over time.

Complying with the recognized codes of practice is assumed to be self-evident and not to require separate agreement in the contract. Building firms are responsible for keeping themselves informed of the currently recognized codes of practice. If these rules are not complied with then a defect is the result. > Chapter Quality management, Defects and defect correction A contractor can exclude liability for non-compliance if he or she agrees with the client not to comply with these rules and is properly informed about the possible consequences.

State of the art

State of the art refers to a higher stage of technological development than the recognized codes of practice but a stage that has not yet become established in practice in the longer term. Since particular value is placed on durability in the building field, only compliance with the recognized codes of practice is assumed in the construction field.

State of scientific and technical knowledge

The state of scientific knowledge represents the current state of research. This means that in the practical sphere there is very little or no experience of products and implementation forms based on the state of scientific knowledge. Applications of such knowledge in actual building practices are rare. An overview of these terms is given in Figure 25.

Standards

The roles of standards are manifold. They include acting as measures for rationalization, understanding, serviceability, quality assurance, compatibility, convertibility, health, safety, and environmental protection. Standards belong to the general technical specifications with which construction work has to comply. It should be noted that standards can become obsolete and may no longer necessarily accord with recognized codes of practice. For this reason recognized codes of practice take precedence over standards.

Guidelines/information/instructions

Apart from the technical principles already discussed that govern the way in which construction work is carried out, there are a range of guidelines and information that need to be taken into account when building:

— Guidelines drawn up by professional associations
— Manufacturers' instructions
— Handling information
— Mounting/installation instructions
— Directions for use

Guidelines
In formal terms, a guideline is a prescription that is binding but not in a legal sense. Guidelines are issued by organizations such as trade associations (painters, roofers, wreckers, etc.) They are formulated on the basis of the relevant recognized codes of practice, standards, and practical experience. The respective guidelines are usually taken into account in agreements on how construction work is to be carried out.

Terms	Features			
	Scientific knowledge/ confirmation	Practical experience at hand	Generally known in professional circles	Established in practice
Recognized codes of practice	yes	yes	yes	yes
State of the art	yes	partly/ limited	partly	no
State of scientific and technical knowledge	yes	no	no	no

Fig. 25: Terminological structure of development levels of products and processes (based on Rybicki)

Manufacturer's instructions, handling information, installation instructions and directions for use apply to individual building products and building elements and provide precise information, for example, on storage, use or installation. Information is also usually supplied regarding what other products can be used with the product in question. Site managers should inform themselves about the products used on their building sites to be able to check that their use is correct and free of defects.

Handling information and installation instructions

○

○ **Hint:** Instructions are attached to many building products such as paints and glues, stipulating the minimum and maximum temperatures at which these products should be used. If they are used outside this temperature range, their effectiveness and durability is reduced.

Not all paints and glues can be used on all surfaces. Disregarding instructions in this respect can result in material failing to bond or one material damaging the other.

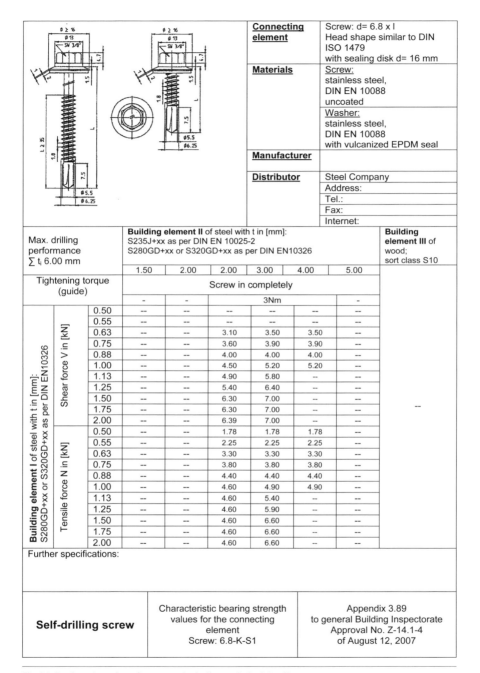

		Connecting element	Screw: d= 6.8 x l Head shape similar to DIN ISO 1479 with sealing disk d= 16 mm

Materials	Screw: stainless steel, DIN EN 10088 uncoated
	Washer: stainless steel, DIN EN 10088 with vulcanized EPDM seal

Manufacturer	

Distributor	Steel Company
	Address:
	Tel.:
	Fax:
	Internet:

Max. drilling performance $\sum t_i$ 6.00 mm	**Building element II** of steel with t in [mm]: S235J+xx as per DIN EN 10025-2 S280GD+xx or S320GD+xx as per DIN EN10326						**Building element III** of wood; sort class S10
	1.50	2.00	2.00	3.00	4.00	5.00	
Tightening torque (guide)	Screw in completely						
	-	-		3Nm		-	

			1.50	2.00	2.00	3.00	4.00	5.00	
Building element I of steel with t in [mm]: S280GD+xx or S320GD+xx as per DIN EN10326	Shear force V in [kN]	0.50	--	--	--	--	--	--	
		0.55	--	--	--	--	--	--	
		0.63	--	--	3.10	3.50	3.50	--	
		0.75	--	--	3.60	3.90	3.90	--	
		0.88	--	--	4.00	4.00	4.00	--	
		1.00	--	--	4.50	5.20	5.20	--	
		1.13	--	--	4.90	5.80	--	--	
		1.25	--	--	5.40	6.40	--	--	
		1.50	--	--	6.30	7.00	--	--	
		1.75	--	--	6.30	7.00	--	--	
		2.00	--	--	6.39	7.00	--	--	--
	Tensile force N in [kN]	0.50	--	--	1.78	1.78	1.78	--	
		0.55	--	--	2.25	2.25	2.25	--	
		0.63	--	--	3.30	3.30	3.30	--	
		0.75	--	--	3.80	3.80	3.80	--	
		0.88	--	--	4.40	4.40	4.40	--	
		1.00	--	--	4.60	4.90	4.90	--	
		1.13	--	--	4.60	5.40	--	--	
		1.25	--	--	4.60	5.90	--	--	
		1.50	--	--	4.60	6.60	--	--	
		1.75	--	--	4.60	6.60	--	--	
		2.00	--	--	4.60	6.60	--	--	

Further specifications:

Self-drilling screw	Characteristic bearing strength values for the connecting element Screw: 6.8-K-S1	Appendix 3.89 to general Building Inspectorate Approval No. Z-14.1-4 of August 12, 2007

Fig. 26: Product data sheet for screws including technical details

Fig. 27: Label on glazing with technical
information and quality information

Delivery notes/labels/certification/data sheets

In order to find out whether the materials being used on the construction site meet the necessary requirements, site managers need
to check delivered materials. The easiest way of doing this is to compare delivery notes and labels with the information in the building contract. The glazing material label shown in Figure 27 includes all required
information:

— Manufacturer
— Firm/purchaser
— Project
— Glazing type and pane composition
— Pane size
— Quality certification

Site managers should collect all labels of important building materials and include them in the project documentation. If no precise specifications are available for material such as glazing, the required quality, or
the quality deemed necessary by the recognized codes of practice, can
be identified from quality certification or comparable information. It is
also possible to request product information from the supplier. > Fig. 26 and
Chapter Handover, Project documentation

DEFECTS AND DEFECT CORRECTION

Reworking, repairs, additional cleaning, and defect correction cost
a lot of time and money and should be avoided where possible. Experience shows that the processes of identifying and documenting defects
and monitoring their correction amount to approx. 10–15% of the site
manager's work.

Defects   Defective work refers to work that does not meet set requirements or that deviates from the defined quality. Defects are divided into two categories:

Optical defects   Optical defects:

— Dirt/stains
— Minor damage
— Color deviations
— Unevenness
— Minor cracking
— ...

Constructional defects   and constructional defects:

— Cracking
— Mechanical damage
— Malfunctions
— Spalling
— ...

Conditions of normal use   When assessing optical defects, the function and significance of surfaces must always be taken into account. The assessment must take place under conditions of normal use. This means, for example, that optical defects should be assessed from the same distance and under the same lighting as would apply when the object concerned was under normal use.

Defects are also distinguished in terms of the following categories:

Apparent defects   An apparent defect is already present and discernable during construction or at the final inspection.

● **Example:**
- Irregularities in the external appearance of a house (plaster, cladding) should be assessed from the street rather than from the scaffolding or lift trucks.
- Irregularities on a front door should be assessed at the distance from which the door is normally seen.
- Irregularities in the surfaces of a basement garage should be assessed under lighting conditions that will apply when the area is in normal use.
- Focused light should be used for assessment only if such light is used regularly under normal conditions of use.

● **Example:** Cladding in a basement or in a prestigious entrance area, color deviations in the flooring of a storage facility or in a reception area, and unevenness in the interior plastering of a stable or a living room have to be assessed in different ways.

A hidden defect is present but not discernable at the final inspection. Hidden defects

Intentionally concealed defects are hidden defects that the contractor is aware of but deliberately does not mention at the final inspection in order to gain advantage. Intentionally concealed defects

To assess whether a defect is present, the following questions should be asked when assessing the work concerned:

— Does the work exhibit the agreed quality?
— Is the work adequate to the contractually assumed use of the product?
— Is the work adequate to the normal use of the product?
— Does the work comply with the recognized codes of practice?

In addition, the concept of a defect can also be applied to situations where

— Fitting/installation has been incorrectly carried out
— A product or delivery item is different to that which was agreed upon
— Too little material has been delivered

Once defects have been identified, their significance needs to be assessed and a decision must be made as to what measures are appropriate.

Correction of a defect is required when the work in question does not comply with the recognized codes of practice, it is clear that further damage will result from the defect, or the required function is only partially fulfilled or not at all. Repairs/defect corrections

The distinctions drawn here make clear that not every defect must necessarily be corrected, since in some circumstances the effort and expense involved are not justified. In this case the defective work is "penalized" with a reduction in remuneration, i.e. a lower payment. Reductions

If the defect is within the range of agreed deviations, is located in peripheral spaces or is not visually significant, it is described as minor and does not have to be corrected. Figures 28 and 29 provide an overview of different consequences of defects. The point of departure is the degree to which the defect adversely affects the object or function concerned. Minor defects

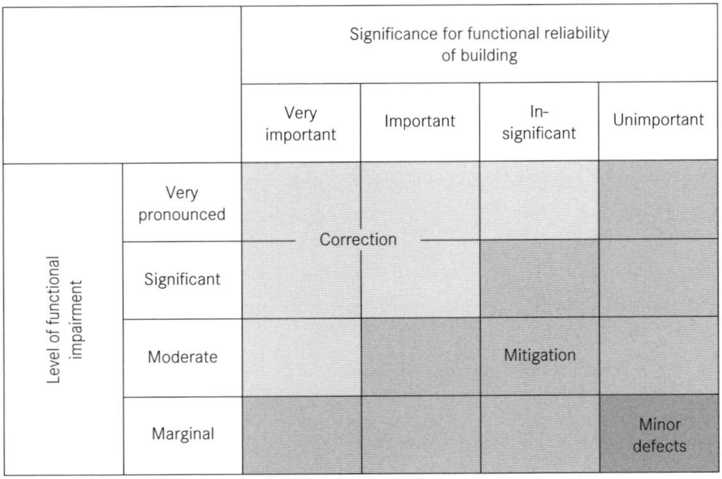

		Significance for functional reliability of building			
		Very important	Important	In-significant	Unimportant
Level of functional impairment	Very pronounced	Correction			
	Significant				
	Moderate			Mitigation	
	Marginal				Minor defects

Fig. 28: Possible consequences of functional defects

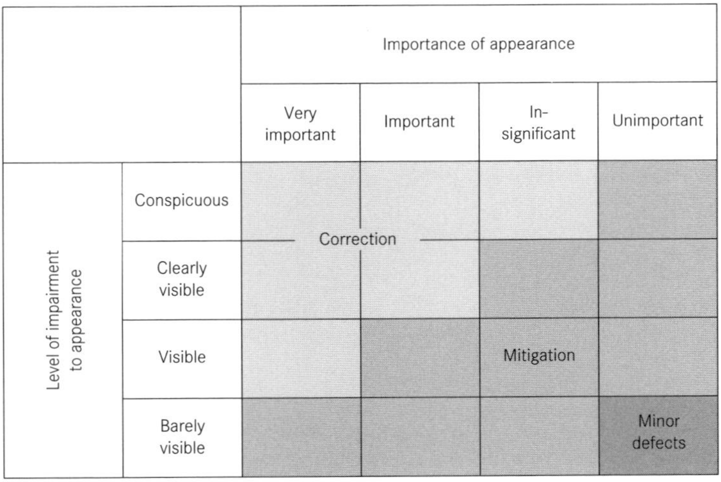

		Importance of appearance			
		Very important	Important	In-significant	Unimportant
Level of impairment to appearance	Conspicuous	Correction			
	Clearly visible				
	Visible			Mitigation	
	Barely visible				Minor defects

Fig. 29: Possible consequences of optical defects

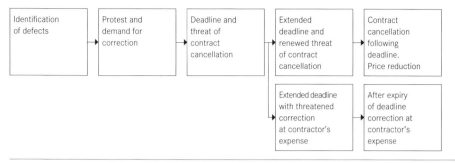

Fig. 30: Procedure for demanding the correction of defects

Work that is already recognized to be defective or contrary to contract during construction must be corrected by the contractor. Since the work involved in correcting defects is not paid for by the client, it can often produce considerable additional costs for the building firm. Defects must be corrected within an appropriate time period, which is defined by the client. The appropriateness of the time allowed is measured in relation to concrete conditions on the building site.

The contractor must be asked in writing to correct the defect. This is particularly important when only a limited amount of time is available for the correction (the project is nearing completion). Figure 30 shows a suitable procedure for demanding correction of defects.

● **Example:** If the firm that has carried out defective work is still on the building site, the client can demand that the defect be corrected within a few days. If staff must be called back to the site, more time should be allowed. If subsequent work is directly dependent on the correction of the defective work, then speedy attention to the problem is expected on principle. If the contractor delays in correcting the defect, he or she can be made liable for additional costs relating to building delays.

Cost management

At the beginning of a building project, the client specifies the budget available. This budget forms the foundation of the planning phases and must be adhered to by the site manager during the building phase.

However, experience shows that building projects are very seldom completed for the price envisaged in the planning phase. Requested changes during the building phase, imprecisely calculated quantities and building elements that were overlooked during tendering can all lead to cost increases. The overview in the first chapter of cost developments during construction indicates which costs the site manager must maintain a focus on and, if necessary, manage. > Fig. 31

BUDGET

Planning includes determining the budgets that are to be allocated to the different service packages. Tenders are then called for and bids are compared with one another and with the budget. This initial tender vetting is important for the client since it shows whether the assumptions made during the planning phase actually correspond with the actual prices.

Tender vetting

Since tender vetting does not actually fall within the site manager's remit, it is only briefly discussed here. Tender vetting entails checking all bids for completeness and correctness and comparing them with one another. A range of computer programs designed for this purpose are available, although these comparisons can also be made using simple spreadsheets.

Once tenders have been vetted, public clients must award the contract to the lowest bidder. Private clients, on the other hand, are entitled to choose which bid they will accept.

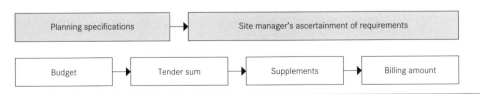

Fig. 31: Budget/tender sum/prognosis/billing amount

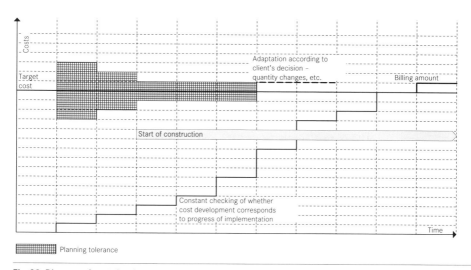

Fig. 32: Diagram of cost development

At this point within the course of the project it is possible to influence costs. If the tendered sum exceeds or is below the estimated budget, then alternatives that have been put up for tender, i.e. simpler or higher quality variants, can be commissioned. > Fig. 32

TENDER SUM/CONTRACT SUM

Once a contract has been awarded to a building firm, the tender sum is fixed. Since private clients are free to negotiate bids with building firms, the contract sum is in some cases lower than the sum that was tendered and vetted. The negotiated reduction in such cases is referred to as an abatement. Usually it is agreed that the abatement will also apply to all subsequent contracts. Abatements for building contracts tend to range between 2% and 8%. In most countries, public clients are not permitted to negotiate bid prices.

Abatement

PROGNOSIS, SUPPLEMENTS

Supplements, i.e. bids for altered or additional work that exceeds the originally commissioned services, are submitted by the contractor. As a rule, supplements are formulated as bids on the basis of the agreed building contract. The additional work and related costs can be the result of:

Supplements

— Quantity variances
— Changes to required services

- Construction delays
- Measures to speed up construction

In this context a distinction is made between:

- Changes to building content (what is built differs from what was originally agreed)
- Changes to building circumstances (the building complies with the original agreement but the construction circumstances change, e.g. the possibilities for access to the site are altered).

The effects of these changes can lead to an increase but also to a decrease in costs.

Supplement assessment   Before the services offered in the supplements are commissioned by the client, the site manager must assess whether the claims are justified. It must first be established whether the services offered as a supplement are not already included in the original building contract. If this is the case, the supplement will be rejected.

Original calculation   In addition, it is important to check whether the prices for the services being offered correspond to the price level of the building contract. To determine this, the site manager can compare and assess the prices on the basis of the contractor's original calculation. The original calculation shows the level of the original costing elements comprising the tender prices.

Supplements can be commissioned by the client alone. As already mentioned, the site manager is not permitted to make decisions for the client that may affect the client financially. For this reason, a supplement must be carefully examined and the client informed whether it is justified and whether the costs are appropriate.

Commissioning supplements   The examination and commissioning of a supplement should take place before the offered services are carried out. However, in practice it unfortunately often becomes clear only when construction is already underway that required services are not contained in the contract. At this point it is too late to wait for the supplement bid, the assessment and the client's approval in writing. However, in order to avoid interruptions to work, the client must be informed that additional costs are being incurred. Furthermore, the approximate costs should be submitted and discussed with the client. Given the client's approval, a preliminary commission can then be issued by way of a written report. In Figure 33 the relevant procedures are represented diagrammatically.

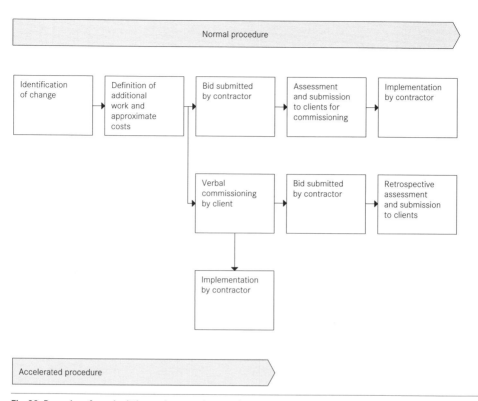

Fig. 33: Procedure for submitting and processing supplements

○ **Hint:** Although a site manager for the client only seldom handles the costing of contract works, he or she should be familiar with the structures involved.

The prices tendered by building firms usually comprise the following costing elements:
– Costs for wages, building materials, tools and, if required, external services
– Costs incurred on the building site that are not included in the individual items of the tender
– Costs for the contractor related to running and administering his or her firm
– Costs for risks that are not precisely known but are shown by experience to be incurred due to construction delays, guarantees or unforeseen events.
– The profit represents the estimate of the appropriate return on the capital invested by the contractor.

COST CONTROL

Cost control refers to the comparison of currently known costs with planned costs. At the time of construction, the site manager must compare the planned budget with the tender sums, including known supplements, and possible further costs (prognosis costs). If variances are noted, cost management measures must be taken. The first step in cost management in this context should be to look for potential savings in the affected work section in order to prevent other sections being affect. If possibilities for cost management here are insufficient, other budgets must be checked for means to cover the increased costs, or the client must increase the relevant budget.

COST MANAGEMENT

The further a project has progressed, the more difficult it is to exercise effective influence over costs. Even with careful planning and cost calculation, it can still be necessary to intervene in the development of costs. The site manager and the planner are then required to develop proposals for possible savings and calculate their feasibility and effects. As in schedule management, there are different possibilities here:

— Changes in quality
— Changes in quantities
— Changes to the implementation schedule

In the case of all measures, it is important to consider that once a contract has been concluded the contractors may also be entitled to compensation for the services that have been dispensed with, since the calculation of tender prices is based on the quantities listed in the tender specifications. The savings that are actually made can only be identified in collaboration with the contractor.

Changes in quality   Changes in quality mean that the standards actually realized differ from those originally planned. This can mean that implementation is either of a lower or higher quality. Such changes are easiest to organize when the tender specifications already include alternative items.

However, it must always be kept in mind that the proposed changes can lead to additional costs in other areas.

Changes in quantities   Changes in quantities are often considered in association with changes in quality. Quantities can simply be reduced, or expensive variants can be limited to important areas and a simple standard applied to the rest.

There is also the possibility of postponing work, as long as the aims of the client permit this. This option is often used by private clients who are having single-family homes built. The attic or basement is fitted out or the garage is built several years after completion of the house.

Postponing work

The suggestions already made on how to manage schedule and implementation planning also apply to cost management. The desired effects on costs always exert effects on other aspects of the project. The site manager must always keep the following points in mind and provide adequate consultation for the client, who will often be unable to maintain the overview required to assess all effects.

Effect of cost management

— What possible effects will changes have on schedules? Can the other materials be just as quickly delivered as the originally planned materials? Delaying completion can have a significant effect on costs.
— Does the changed quality still meet the original requirements or does the more rapid deterioration of a cheap product mean that new costs will soon be generated?
— What new costs are generated by later implementation?
— What additional costs are generated by changing the existing building contract?

SETTLEMENT OF ACCOUNTS

The settlement of accounts for services performed, like the work itself, takes place in stages. Depending on the duration and scope of the work, settlement is made on the basis of an invoice, or made in stages over the period of work on the basis of part-payment invoices and the final account. Settlement of accounts for work thus usually takes place parallel to the progress of construction.

Invoices for construction services can only be submitted for work that has actually been carried out or for building material and elements that the contractor has demonstrably produced for the building site or already delivered but not yet installed.

In this case it is better to make an advance payment against a bank surety bond presented by the contractor.

Payment against surety

Since the construction process generally lasts for a relatively long time, the contractor is entitled to demand payments on account, i.e. part payments, for services rendered on the building site.

Payment on account

○

Settlement documents   Like the final account, each part-payment invoice must be verifiable. The invoice must therefore be accompanied by a list of the quantities relating to the services being invoiced, invoicing plans (listing what is to be invoiced) or a quantity survey.

Invoice verification   Invoice verification entails establishing whether the invoiced work has actually been carried out and is largely defect-free. It must be carefully conducted because if the contractor becomes insolvent before the project is completed, the site manager will be liable to the client for possible overpayment for services rendered.

Quantity survey   In order to determine the scope of services, a quantity survey is produced on the building site. This is particularly important for work that will later be concealed. This applies, for example, to sealing work that will later be concealed under flooring, demolition work, and repair work on walls that will be resurfaced later. Contractors have a particular interest in this work being surveyed since it may later be necessary to prove that the work has actually been carried out. > Final inspection Like invoices, quantity surveys must be clearly laid out and accord with the structure of the service specifications.

Accounting   Accounting in this context refers to the form in which invoices are drawn up. The structure of the invoice should correspond to the structure of the service specifications. This makes it possible to maintain an overview of the costs of individual jobs and work sections in the course of cost control. If invoices are not structured in this way and are not clearly laid out, the site manager may reject them as being unverifiable.

Cumulative accounting   Cumulative accounting has proved advantageous in the building industry. In a cumulative invoice, all services are invoiced that have been carried out up until the point of invoice submission. Services that have
● already been paid for are deducted.

○ **Hint:** This procedure is common, for example, in larger facade projects because the contractor must purchase materials such as profiles, glass, fittings and sealing material for the manufacture of the facade elements and pay suppliers. Otherwise the contractor would be burdened with financing the period between installation and final inspection.

● **Example:** In the third part-payment invoice, the contractor includes all services rendered up until this point (including services from the first two invoices, which have already been paid) and refers them to the relevant items in the service directory. Any agreed abatement and a security deposit are deducted from the calculated amount. Payments relating to the first two part-payment invoices are also then deducted and the unpaid sum is calculated.

Submission of these invoices must also include the relevant quantity survey sheets and invoicing plans. This type of accounting provides the site manager with an immediate overview of the work that has been done, the inclusion of quantity surveys means that a laborious examination of the overall quantity survey is not required when the final account is submitted. > Fig. 34

The final account includes all work carried out and includes agreed and commissioned supplements and quantity changes. Like part-payment invoices, the final account must be clearly laid out and easy to examine. The final account must be accompanied by the final quantity survey. This quantity survey is in principle based on the planning documents that also provide the foundation for the service specifications. In some cases a separate quantity survey on the building site can be required for altered services or services to which planning documents do not refer.

Final account

Site managers have a particular time frame for assessing invoices. In Germany this time frame is regulated by the terms of German construction contract procedures (VOB/B). These stipulate that final accounts must be paid within two months of submission. This only applies, of course, if the account is correct and verifiable. If this is not the case, the contractor must be informed within the two-month period. The same conditions apply to payments on account but the deadline is only 18 working days.

Assessment deadlines

Invoice verification
(Cumulative accounting)

3. Müller AG ref.

Client:	**Vermögensanlagen West AG**	Building element:		
Building project:	**Demolition work**			
Job no.:	**450072820**	Project no.:	**D-06-0996**	Cost center: **Meier**
Title:		No.:		Contractor: **Müller AG**
Date of receipt:	**29.5.2007**	Date of invoice:	**24.5.2007**	Invoice no.: **VF-07-0252**

Verifiable? [X] Yes [ ] No   Reason:

[ ] Verifiable from date/reason:

	Not including VAT €	VAT 19% €	Incl. VAT €
1. Unverified amount	150'000.00		
2. Amount verified prior to deducting abatements	150'000.00		
3. Abatements 3.00 % (-)	4'500.00		
4. Value of work	145'500.00		
5. Security deposit 5% x 10% (-)	14'550.00		
6. Amount	130'950.00		
7. Value of prior payment(s) (-)	90'000.00		
8. Amount	40'950.00		
9. Deductions (Charges as per appendix) (-)			
10. Amount (value of payment)	40'950.00		
11. Discount 0.00 % (-)	0.00		
12. Amount due	**40'950.00**	**7'780.50**	**48'730.50**

Notes:

The invoiced sum corresponds to work performed.

Content	checked:
Calculation	checked:
Approved for payment:	

Fig. 34: Sample form for a cumulative invoice assessment

Final inspection and acceptance

ACCEPTANCE OF CONSTRUCTION WORK/TRANSFER OF RISK

The final inspection and acceptance of construction work or a building is carried out by the client and his or her representatives, i.e. the architect or site manager and the contractor. Final inspection can only take place once all work has been completely finished, with the exception of a few insignificant details. Final inspection can only be refused if particularly serious defects are evident that restrict the usability of the building or building element. ■

By undertaking a final inspection, the client formally recognizes that contracted work has been completed. In most countries inspection and acceptance are legally regulated. Contractors can demand inspection and acceptance of their work when it has been substantially completed. Final inspection involves checking that the services rendered correspond to contractual agreements. If the client confirms this to the contractor, the contract is regarded as fulfilled. If at this time works are known to be incomplete or defective and the client does not register any protest, the client has no subsequent claim to the correction of the defect or completion of work free of charge.

Every contractor is obligated to safeguard completed work up until final inspection and acceptance. If works are damaged prior to inspection, the party causing the damage is responsible for repairing it. If the responsible party cannot be identified, the contractor must repair the damage at his or her own cost.

■ **Tip:** If the site manager realizes that certain work has not been correctly carried out, he or she must inform the relevant contractors immediately and not wait until a partial or final inspection is being carried out. If the responsible parties are not informed immediately, potential damage caused by defective work may increase in the interim. Allowing a wall to be built while knowing that it is in the wrong position or that other work must first be completed ultimately only wastes time and money and causes stress. Having to demolish work that has just been completed has a very negative effect on worker motivation.

Depending on the type of building element, protection must be provided against, in particular:

— Frost, rain and sun
— Dirt
— Premature or improper use
— Mechanical damage
— Theft

Hidden defects

Intentionally concealed or hidden defects must be corrected by the contractor. Up until final inspection and acceptance, the contractor is responsible for protecting his or her work from damage, repairing any damage that does occur and submitting work according to contract.

Partial acceptance/
final acceptance

A distinction is made between partial acceptance and final acceptance. As pointed out in the discussion of part-payment invoicing and quantity surveys, partial acceptance can be carried out for individual services.

Inspection
report
■

If a defect is identified during the final inspection, this must be recorded in writing in the inspection report. > Fig. 35 The type and location of the defect must be described precisely.

Where there are differences of opinion, the contractor's objections must also be recorded in the report. The question of who should correct the disputed defect and who should pay for the work must be decided at a later date.

The legal consequences of acceptance can be summarized as follows:

— Prior to acceptance, the burden of proving that construction work has been completed according to contract lies with the contractor. Following acceptance the client must prove that the defect has been caused by the contractor in question.

■ **Tip:** Defects identified during the final inspection should be described in a report and marked on the ground plan drawings so that the relevant locations can be easily found when work done to correct defects is being inspected. The report and ground plan drawings must be attached to the overall inspection report and submitted to all parties involved.

REPORT   – PARTIAL ACCEPTANCE ☐
                – FINAL ACCEPTANCE   ☐

Project   :
Client   :
Date   :
Work section   :
Scope of inspection   :
Contractor   :
Contractor's representative :
Architect's representative   :
BS representative   :
Client's representative   :
Defects   :

Separate defect list included as appendix ☐ ___pages/no separate defect list included ☐
No (visual) inspection approval given for listed defects.

Contractor will correct the defects in accordance with the contract _____ at the latest.

Inspection papers, instructions for service and maintenance, and documents prescribed by official regulations are

complete ☐/ are incomplete ☐/ are to be submitted subsequently ☐

The contractor will submit the missing documents by _____ at the latest.

Warranty period commences :

Warranty period concludes   :

Notes   :

Contractor objections   :

Signatures   :

_____   _____
Date/Contractor's representative   Date/Architect's representative

_____   _____
Date/BS representative   Date/Client's representative

The report consists of a total of ___ pages.

Fig. 35: Inspection report form

- If defective work is accepted without protest, the client has no right to subsequent correction of the defect free of charge (except if the defect was hidden or deliberately concealed). Once work has been accepted, the warranty period begins.
- The contractor can submit an invoice for the accepted work. Payment falls due.

Due to the significance of the acceptance process, the site manager must be well prepared for it. The following documents should be available at the time of inspection and acceptance:

- Building contract with planning documents and service specifications
- Reports of sampling inspections and other specifications
- Lists or reports of defects noted at an earlier date and not yet corrected
- Plans in which the identified defects can be recorded

WARRANTY

As already mentioned, acceptance also signifies the beginning of the warranty period, i.e. the period of time in which the contractor guarantees the contractually defined quality of the building element. Within this period, the contractor must correct, free of charge, defects for which he or she is responsible. This also applies to hidden and, in particular, deliberately concealed defects. Agreement on the duration of the warranty period can coincide with agreement of the building contract.

ACCEPTANCE BY REGULATORY AUTHORITIES

In addition to inspection and acceptance of construction works by the client, these works are also subject to an acceptance inspection by the relevant regulatory authorities. This inspection involves checking whether construction complies with legal and technical requirements and thus corresponds to the approved plans.

Building shell acceptance

Regulatory authorities must be informed when the building shell has been completed. As a rule, a building shell acceptance inspection is then conducted, during which structural integrity is checked as well as relevant sound and heating insulation and fire prevention aspects.

Final acceptance

Final acceptance takes place following completion of all work required for the construction of the building. The authorities must be informed of completion in writing. All documentation listed in the building permit as required for the acceptance inspection must be provided. This includes:

- Certification regarding heating and chimney systems
- Certification of fire prevention measures
- Certification that construction has been carried out by a specialist contractor

During the final acceptance inspection, the entire building is usually viewed and spot checks are made to ensure requirements have been met. Planning changes that have been made during the construction phase are checked by the regulatory authority and approved if they meet the required standards. Changes that do not meet these standards must be brought into line with the requirements stipulated by the building permit. Once the final acceptance procedure has been completed, the building is approved for use.

Handover

HANDOVER TO THE CLIENT

The scope of the handover to the client depends on the size and complexity of the completed building. During the handover the client and parties who will later have responsibility for the building (building superintendent, facility manager) are instructed on the use of technical facilities and given the project documentation. > Chapter Handover, Project documentation

The structure of the handover procedure should be divided into subject areas that reflect the division of work sections during construction. This facilitates proper instruction of the relevant parties. These areas can be defined as follows:

— Building in general
— Constructional fixtures and fittings such as doors, dividing walls and built-in furniture
— Furniture and specific building equipment
— Facades and facade engineering
— Fire prevention features
— Building services in general

Or, if necessary, divided into building services work sections

— Heating engineering
— Ventilation engineering
— Sanitary engineering
— Electrical engineering
— Media engineering
— Computing
— Communications engineering
— Safety engineering

These instructions should be given by the site manager and the planners responsible for the individual sections. All project documentation must be submitted when the handover to the client takes place.

PROJECT DOCUMENTATION

It is important for the client that he or she receives all documentation relevant to the building in an orderly form. Experience shows that this is also in the interests of the site manager since otherwise the client must consult him or her on every question arising after occupation of the building. Structured building documentation should include the following documents:

— Index of all documents
— List of planners involved in the project and contact persons
— Contact persons for warranties
— Building permit with acceptance reports
— Building shell documentation and acceptance reports
— Interior finishing documentation including acceptance reports, log books, records of materials used, instructions for use, maintenance instructions, etc.
— Facade documentation including planning documents, log books, inspection papers, records of glazing, profile and other materials, sun-protection inspection documents, etc.
— Documents relating to building services works including planning documents, acceptance reports, technical descriptions, inspection papers, log books, etc.

Log books are provided by manufacturers for equipment and fittings that require regular inspections, e.g. elevators, automatic doors, automatic fire protection equipment, and air-conditioning and ventilation systems. The site manager should draw the client's particular attention to stipulations on the regularity of inspections. Failure to comply with such stipulations can result in a loss of claim to warranty and premature deterioration. The maintenance and servicing of large and complex buildings is a time-consuming and labor-intensive process, and today specialized facility management firms are commonly engaged to carry out this work.

Appendix

Literature

Bert Bielefeld, Lars-Philip Rusch: *Building projects in China,* Birkhäuser Verlag, Basel 2006

Bert Bielefeld, Falk Würfele: *Building projects in the European Union,* Birkhäuser Verlag, Basel 2005

Chartered Institute of Building (ed.): *Planning and Programming in Construction,* Chartered Institute of Building, London 1991

CIRIA: *The Environmental Handbooks for Building and Civil Engineering: Vol 1. Design and Specification,* Thomas Telford Ltd, 1994

Sandra Christensen Weber: *Scheduling Construction Projects. Principles and Practices,* Pearson Prentice Hall, Upper Saddle River, NJ, 2005

Institution of Civil Engineers, Association of Consulting Engineers and Civil Engineering Contractors Association: *Tendering for Civil Engineering Contracts,* Thomas Telford Ltd, 2000

Richard H. Neale, David E. Neale: *Construction Planning,* Telford, London 1989

Jay S. Newitt: *Construction Scheduling. Principles and Practices,* Pearson Prentice Hall, Upper Saddle River, NJ, 2009

Guidelines and standards (selection)

TENDERING

SAMPLE INTERNATIONAL CONTRACTS

FIDIC	Fédération internationale des ingénieur communauté
NEC	New Engineering contract

ADDITIONAL SOURCES OF INFORMATION

ISO	International Organization for Standardization
	(http://www.iso.org)
CEN	European Commitee for Standardization
	(http://www.cen.eu)

In addition to the above-mentioned sources, there are a number of national and international associations and institutions that offer leaflets, examples of additional technical contractual terms, as well as sample tender texts for certain items of work. Sample tender texts that can be used by all types of contractors can be found on the following Internet sites:

Internet sites

http://publications.europa.eu

http://www.neccontract.co.uk

http://www.fidic.org

Tendering portal

http://ted.europa.eu

Picture credits

PROJECTMANAGEMENT
Figures 10, 17, 20, 29: Bert Bielefeld, Thomas Feuerabend
Figures 22, 24, 26, 28: Tim Brandt, Sebastian Th. Franssen
Figures 23, 25, 30: Udo Blecken, Bert Bielefeld
Figure 33 (Diagram of building site facilities): Lars-Phillip Rusch
All other figures: The author

TENDERING
Figure 6 left: aboutpixel.de
Figure 6 center right: PixelQuelle.de
Figure 7: PixelQuelle.de
Figure 8: PixelQuelle.de
Figure 10 centre left: aboutpixel.de
Figure 10 right: aboutpixel.de
All other figures: The authors

SITE MANAGEMENT
Figures 14, 15 and 32: after Ulrich Nagel
Figures 28 and 29: Rainer Oswald
Table 3: Bert Bielefeld
All other figures: The author

The authors

PROJECTMANAGEMENT

Hartmut Klein, Dipl.-Ing. Architect, is head of the Mullheim/Baden building department and acts as a competition judge.

BUDGETING

Bert Bielefeld, Prof. Dr.-Ing. Architect, architect teaches construction economics and construction management at Siegen University and is managing partner of the bertbielefeld&partner architecture practice in Dortmund.

Roland Schneider, Dipl.-Ing. M.Sc. Architect, is academic assistant in the construction economics and construction management department at Siegen University and managing director of the art-schneider architecture practice in Cologne.

Thanks go to Ann Christin Hecker and Benjamin Voss for their support in creating the graphics.

CONSTRUCTION SCHEDULING

Bert Bielefeld, Prof. Dr.-Ing. Architect, teaches construction economics and construction management at Siegen University and is managing partner of the bertbielefeld&partner architecture practice in Dortmund.

TENDERING

Tim Brandt, Dipl. Ing., is a civil engineer in Dortmund, specializing in contract and change management; he also works in site and project direction.

Sebastian Th. Franssen, Dipl. Ing. Architect, is proprietor of an architectural practice in Dortmund, specializing in managing private and public building projects.

SITE MANAGEMENT

Lars-Phillip Rusch, Dipl.-Ing. Architect, is a freelance architect and research associate with the Department of Construction Management at the Dortmund University of Applied Sciences.

The author would like to particularly thank Professor Ulrich Nagel for making available textual and pictorial material that contributed significantly to this book.

Professional Practice

Basics Construction Scheduling
Bert Bielefeld
978-3-7643-8873-7

Basics Project Planning
Hartmut Klein
978-3-7643-8469-2

Basics Site Management
Lars-Phillip Rusch
978-3-7643-8104-2

Basics Tendering
Tim Brandt,
Sebastian Th. Franssen
978-3-7643-8110-3

Urbanism

Basics Urban Building Blocks
Thorsten Bürklin, Michael Peterek
978-3-7643-8460-9

Basics Urban Building Blocks
Thorsten Bürklin, Michael Peterek
978-3-7643-8460-9

Landscape Architecture

Basics Designing with Plants
Regine Ellen Wöhrle,
Hans-Jörg Wöhrle
978-3-7643-8659-7

Basics Designing with Water
Axel Lohrer
978-3-7643-8662-7

Available at your bookshop or at
www.birkhauser.com

Series editor: Bert Bielefeld
Conception: Bert Bielefeld, Annette Gref
Layout and cover design: Andreas Hidber
Typesetting and production: Amelie Solbrig
Project management: Annette Gref

Translation from German into English:
Foreword: Michael Robinson
Basics Project Planning: Michael Robinson
Basics Budgeting: Michael Robinson
Basics Construction Scheduling: Adam Blauhut,
Joseph O'Donnell
Basics Tendering: Michael Robinson
Basics Site Management: Joseph O'Donnell

English copy editing: Monica Buckland

A CIP catalogue record for this book is available
from the Library of Congress, Washington D.C.,
USA.

Bibliographic information published by the
German National Library
The German National Library lists this
publication in the Deutsche Nationalbibliografie;
detailed bibliographic data are available on the
Internet at http://dnb.dnb.de.

This book is also available in a German language
edition (ISBN 978-3-03821-461-8).

© 2013 Birkhäuser Verlag GmbH, Basel
P.O. Box 44, 4009 Basel, Switzerland
Part of De Gruyter

Printed on acid-free paper produced from
chlorine-free pulp. TCF ∞
Printed in Germany

ISBN 978-3-03821-462-5

9 8 7 6 5 4 3 2 1

www.birkhauser.com